Studia Fennica
Historica 5

THE FINNISH LITERATURE SOCIETY (SKS) was founded in 1831 and has, from the very beginning, engaged in publishing operations. It nowadays publishes literature in the fields of ethnology and folkloristics, linguistics, literary research and cultural history.

The first volume of the Studia Fennica series appeared in 1933. Since 1992, the series has been divided into three thematic subseries: Ethnologica, Folkloristica and Linguistica. Two additional subseries were formed in 2002, Historica and Litteraria. The subseries Anthropologica was formed in 2007.

In addition to its publishing activities, the Finnish Literature Society maintains research activities and infrastructures, an archive containing folklore and literary collections, a research library and promotes Finnish literature abroad.

Anu Koskivirta

The Enemy Within

*Homicide and Control in Eastern Finland
in the Final Years of Swedish Rule 1748–1808*

Finnish Literature Society • Helsinki

Studia Fennica Historica 5

The publication has undergone a peer review.

VERTAISARVIOITU
KOLLEGIALT GRANSKAD
PEER-REVIEWED
www.tsv.fi/tunnus

The open access publication of this volume has received part funding via
a Jane and Aatos Erkko Foundation grant.

A digital edition of a printed book first published in 2003 by the Finnish Literature Society.
Cover Design: Timo Numminen
EPUB: eLibris Media Oy

ISBN 978-951-746-474-1 (Print)
ISBN 978-951-746-613-4 (PDF)
ISBN 978-952-222-817-8 (EPUB)

ISSN 0085-6835 (Studia Fennica)
ISSN 1458-526X (Studia Fennica Historica)

DOI: http://dx.doi.org/10.21435/sfh.5

A free open access version of the book is available at http://dx.doi.
org/10.21435/sfh.5 or by scanning this QR code with your mobile device.

BoD – Books on Demand, Norderstedt, Germany

Acknowledgements

This study was for the most part carried out as part of the *History of Criminality* project, conducted under the direction of Prof. Heikki Ylikangas of the Academy of Finland, which also funded the project. I worked in the project from 1997 to 2002. I therefore first of all wish to express my debt of gratitude for being able to complete my research to the Academy of Finland, and to Heikki Ylikangas for his visionary and inspiring guidance.

The present work is a considerably abbreviated version of my doctoral dissertation *"Sisäinen vihollinen". Henkirikos ja kontrolli Pohjois-Savossa ja Karjalassa Ruotsin vallan ajan viimeisinä vuosikymmeninä* (Helsinki 2001, 396 pp.). I extend my warm thanks for a number of important suggestions for changes to the opponent in my defence of my dissertation, Antero Heikkinen, Professor of History at the University of Joensuu. Prof. Markku Kuisma has also supported the research in many ways, including inviting me to work for a short period on a project, *Elites and Society*, of which he was the director. I further offer my great thanks to the examiners of my dissertation, Docent Seppo Aalto and Docent Antti Kujala, for their expert comments. I am indebted to many other people for their contributions to the content of the book: Docent Panu Pulma, who guided me in producing the first drafts; Docent Kimmo Katajala, who made some extremely valuable comments in his statement on the publication of my Finnish-language dissertation; Docent Petri Karonen, who suggested some crucial additions to both the bibliography and the content of the work. In preparing my study I also received important hints from Dr. Olli Matikainen and Licentiate Kari-Matti Piilahti, with their profound knowledge of criminological and social history.

In preparing the work, I received crucial support from my friends and colleagues in the *History of Criminality* project: Dr. Martti Lehti, Licenciate Mari Rakkolainen, Licenciate Liisa Koskelainen, Licenciate Mona Rautelin, Licenciate Kirsi Warpula and Licenciate Sari Forsström. I thank you all for your cooperation, the value of which I shall never forget, and I am particularly grateful to the last of them for our joint discussions on the mysteries of life and death, which I hope were as important for them as they were for me.

The manuscript of the book has been translated into English by Gerard McAlester of the University of Tampere, and I am extremely grateful for his expert and careful translation. The maps were drawn by Petri Sirén. The publication of the book by the Finnish Literary Society was due to the good offices of Rauno Endén, the Managing Editor of the Society, and to the work of the editor, Johanna Ilmakunnas, to whom I am ultimately indebted for getting the work published. The staff of several archives and libraries also deserve gratitude for their contributions to the research work: the assistants of the National Archives of Finland, the National Archives of Sweden in Stockholm, the Archives of the Provinces of Vaasa and Mikkeli and the Old Literature Reading Room of the University of Helsinki carried metre upon metre of shelf material to my table. A travel grant I received from the Swedish-Finnish Cultural Fund supplemented the funding from the project to enable me to travel to Stockholm to use the archives there.

At the finishing stage of the work, I received a grant from the Academy of Finland for a project called *Finnish Homicide and the Modernizing Penal System*, and this permitted me to prepare the long roll of references for this English-language work into a publishable format. However, because of the disconnected publication process, there are only cursory references to the most recent books and articles (those published in 2002 and 2003).

On occasions it was a taxing task to harness the grim subject matter of the study, homicide and punishment, and the human suffering revealed by the sources to the exigencies of research. And the whole work would have been jeopardized if I had not tried to give it some kind of message or political dimension; I believe that the only way to prevent violence is the internalisation of control, moral standards and the difference between right and wrong, not the imposition of external punishments. The question of the conditions for the civilizing process, the crucial significance of security and safety in the early development of socialization, is equivalent to the care that is familiar to all parents, including me, for their young children. I therefore particularly wish to thank those who have offered the arms of comfort to my beloved daughter Vilja when I have been seated at my desk, her minder Sirpa and the members of my family: my parents Pirkko and Kalle, my parents-in-law Pia and Reijo Vuorinen, and my husband Jan. The completion of this study would have been without significance had it not been for you and your support.

Helsinki, January 2003

Anu Koskivirta

Contents

The Law and Homicide in Eastern Finland 1748–1808

Introduction

The Subject of the Research

Kirsti Hiltunen, the wife of a dependent lodger,[1] was found bleeding and unconscious in an outhouse of her master's farm in Säyneinen in the parish of Liperi on a February day of 1772. In the evening, she died of her wounds. Her husband, with whom she had lived in a disputatious marriage, was suspected of killing her with an iron key to the granary, a blow from which had fractured her forehead.

Antti Partanen strenuously denied the charge of killing his wife that was laid against him on the basis of Ch. XIV Sec 1 of the Criminal Code (*Misgärnings balk* = MB). He suggested that his wife had either fallen from a ladder, or that she had been butted by a cow. The autopsy revealed that the wounds could not have been caused in this way.

The couple had also quarrelled on the day of the wife's death. The marriage had been over in practice ever since the preceding All Saints Day, since when the partners had slept apart from one another. When the husband had threatened at Christmas that he would be his wife's executioner, she had begun to complain to her acquaintances that she lived in constant fear of her husband carrying out his threats.

Esko Hakkarainen, the farmer of the land on which the couple lived, stated that Antti Partanen had tried to bribe the people who lived on the farm to keep quiet about the circumstances of his wife's death in order that the case should not come to the cognisance of the authorities. The elergy were unable to persuade Partanen to confess to the charge in court. In 1734, the Liperi District Court convicted him without a confession or the testimony of eye-witnesses of the homicide of his wife on the basis of MB XIV:1 and sentenced him to death with mutilation of his body as stipulated by the law. Before the execution, his right hand was to be cut off, and after it his body was to be broken on the wheel and placed on public display.

---

1   Swedish: *inhysesman*. This was a person who was given food and lodging on a farm in return for doing odd jobs. The term "dependent lodger" is used throughout this work to describe such a person.

Despite the incontrovertible circumstantial evidence, the Åbo Court of Appeal was unable to uphold the sentence because a legally valid proof was missing. The case against Antti Partanen for the homicide of his wife was adjourned sine die.[2]

The characteristic features of Kirsti Hiltunen's violent death lead one to consider the connection between homicide and the legal repression of this form of crime. There are several factors that make this crime symptomatic of a typical homicide committed in eastern Finland and specifically in northern Karelia. First, the act was committed within the family, and its main motive stemmed from conjugal problems. Then, the perpetrator tried to conceal the crime, and he managed to avoid the punishment stipulated by the law purely by denying having committed the deed. In the years following Partanen's release, murder and manslaughter were to increase phenomenally in his home parish.

The recurrence of such cases in the eighteenth-century judicial material led me to an investigation of the dialectic obtaining between homicide – murder (excluding infanticide), intentional manslaughter and violent unintentional manslaughter – and the old state penal system in the last years of Swedish rule in Finland. In my dissertation,[3] I made a general study of the relations between homicide and legal certainty (i.e. the predictability and legality of the justice system) by assessing how the penal system that was applied to homicide in the eighteenth century was reflected in the quantity and quality of this type of crime. The problem was addressed in a region constituting the eastern periphery of the state of Sweden at that time: the northern parts of the Savo and Karelia regions in Finland. The main aim of the research was to investigate the extent to which the various factors that curbed crime – the official, unofficial and psychological elements of control – could explain the changes that took place in the quantity and quality of the killings that were committed. Control was seen as a three-level regulatory mechanism, in which each level prevents crime within its own sphere of responsibility: official control in society, unofficial control in the immediate community, and the actor's own self-control in the personal actions of the individual.[4]

The present work is adapted from the last part of my dissertation, which uses the information obtained from an in-depth analysis of official control to explore the psychological and socio-cultural climate of homicide. However, in order to describe the subject of the research, it is also necessary also to provide an account of the geographical and chronological distribution of this form of crime and a cursory outline of the extent of premeditation behind the deeds, the *modi operandi*, and the social status of the parties involved. The aim of the present work is to estimate the

---

2   VMA: VHOA, Alistettujen asiain päätöstaltiot, Kymenkartanon ja Savon lääni, v. 1773, Di 9, no 74.

3   Koskivirta 2001.

4   Norbert Elias introduced the idea of an increase in self-control (self-constraint, self-restraint) as an historical fact. Elias (1939) 1994, pp. 7, 45–57, 115–123, 210–211, 443–447, 514–509, 521–523.

extent to which the dimensions which define homicide – quantity, gravity and motivation – are connected to the legal protection of people at the local level and to the ability of the courts to function effectively.

This research examines the connection between the trinity of official, unofficial and psychological control and the features of homicide in eastern Finland. Is it perhaps the case that the killings were more brutal and more premeditated in those areas of eastern Finland where the ability of the authorities to intervene in homicide was weakest? By means of case studies, it is possible to arrive at a detailed analysis of various structural vacuums in the control which shaped the motivation for the crimes in a way that was unique to this particular time and historical situation. What were the deficiencies in control that caused individuals themselves to become the agents of punitive social control? To what extent did people resort to homicide to defend their lives or their property or other benefits that the law failed to protect?[5] Was the internalization of personal control altogether a favourable development? The motives for the killings are examined case by case because in practice the motivation for a crime was determined by how strong a deterrent the killer considered the risk of being punished for his or her crime to be. The factors that led to acts of homicide are traced not only through the direct motives for the deeds but also through the previous court records of the parties involved. This analysis also made it necessary to assess individually the mechanisms by which social control in its various forms actually gave rise to deviant behaviour as a result of a person being labelled a criminal.[6]

Definition of Concepts and Delimitation of the Subject

In modern criminology, with its historical and sociological emphasis, the homicide process is usually reduced to a dynamics created by social *structures* on the one hand and official or unofficial social preventive *control* on the other.[7] In this study, social and economic structural elements are regarded as contributory factors to the mechanism that leads to homicidal crime only in so far as I consider them to have created pressures leading to the implementation of social control, which was manifested in its most extreme form in homicide. The approach of this study, which emphasizes the elements of situation and *control* rather than cultural, demographic or social structures (*pressures* leading to crime), is justified if the process leading to crime is viewed as a temporal continuum in which social control is a preventive factor – and, correspondingly, the lack of social control a factor that generates crime.[8]

5   Black 1984a, pp. 17–18; Kivivuori 1999, pp. 113–115.
6   Gatrell 1980, p. 246.
7   For the pre-industrial period in the Nordic countries see e.g. Ylikangas 1998a; Lindström 1988, p. 71 ff; Sandnes 1990, p. 74 ff; Österberg 1996, pp. 40–41.
8   Laine 1991, p. 89; Laitinen & Aromaa 1993, p. 33.

The area studied here was certainly in a state of socio-economic ferment during the last decades of the eighteenth century, and this undoubtedly affected the motives for the crimes in one way or another. The major element of this upheaval was a growth in the population, which was first manifested in the settlement of the backwoods areas and the cultivation of the outlying plots of land, and which foreshadowed at a later stage a disturbance of the ecological balance of the region: the slow smouldering of a crisis in burn-beating cultivation.[9] As the relative proportion of the landless grew vigorously, this section of the population became the object of ever-increasing surveillance.[10] Certainly, the socio-historical development of the area investigated here and the features of the homicides committed in it lead one to consider whether the control approach is appropriate in view of some elements that were central to the social history of the region: the sore spots of marriage and the extended family and the particular significance of the proximity of the national frontier in the chain of causes that gave rise to homicide. The last mentioned factor also impinges on the problem of shortage that the incipient depletion of the forests created in the society of eastern Finland, the economy of which was largely dependent on burn-beating cultivation.

The concept of *social control* has been linked by many scholars to the normative dimension of social life. In its earliest use, it referred to all human practices and arrangements the goal of which was to maintain and reinforce social order. In its modern sense, the term is used to indicate the reaction that deviant behaviour encounters. Social control is a mechanism by which an individual or a group reacts to a grievance. It may take on the form of a legal process, personal recrimination or gossip, public protest or violence. Its means are sanctions, both official and unofficial, private revenge, material restitution offered to the victim or arbitration by a third party (mediation).[11]

Unofficial (or unofficial) social control refers to a wide variety of private and communal reactions to crime and other undesirable deviant behaviour. In extreme cases, unofficial social control dons the garb of crime, even homicidal crime; in its more moderate forms it consists of such acts as branding a person a criminal, silencing witnesses or spying on one's neighbours.[12] The subject of this research brings one up against the problems attached to unofficial social control – for example when one tries to estimate the preventive effect on crime of the immediate

---

9   This form of cultivation predominated in eastern Finland. It involved felling and burning tracts of forest and planting crops in the ashes. After the crop was reaped, the forest was allowed to grow again, and a new tract was burn-beaten.

10   Pulma 1985, pp. 206–208; Aronsson 1992, pp. 183–206.

11   Black 1984b, pp. 4–7 and references. On the first formulation and development of the concept of social control *ibid*; for its application to the Swedish justice system of the eighteenth century, see Furuhagen 1996, pp. 10–12. Numerous scholars, e.g. Aalto 1996, pp. 131–177, have elucidated the concept of control as an explanatory factor for the developmental trends of various forms of crime in the Agrarian Age.

12   On the problemization of the concept of local community, see Aronsson 1992, pp. 15–19.

social network. The down side of weak unofficial social control is also reflected in official (or formal) control by a rise in the threshold level for reporting acts of homicide.

In this work, official social control will be used to refer primarily to administrative and legal procedures connected with the apprehension of criminals, the implementation of the law, and with sentencing and the implementation of sentences. In addition to its penal goals, control also answered the therapeutic, conciliatory and compensatory needs and aspects of normative life.[13] Thus the functions of state arbitration and conflict management also fell within the preserves of official control. The judicial system performed these functions in the area under study by settling land disputes and marital disagreements, for example. The official control is described as weak if it patently fails to accomplish its punitive or conciliatory aims.

One way in which official control is implemented is by the legal repression of crime. Legal repression means the methods used by groups in power in order to keep the populace in order. The real effectiveness of these methods varies. In addition to the implementation of punishments, the concept of repression can be used in a *wider* sense to include the policy of prosecution, the judicial process and the anti-crime activities of semi-official institutions of control like the church.[14] The concept of legal repression is used in this work to refer to punishments that were implemented in order to eradicate crime. Unlike the concepts of sanction or social control, the idea of repression also covers the direct *prevention* of crime. Sanction refers to normative control, the consequences both favourable and unfavourable of a deed.[15]

The term "legal culture" is used to mean the attitudes and values that uphold the system of justice and define its position within the culture as a whole.[16] Legal protection is defined as the safeguarding of life, physical inviolability and property.[17] The concept entails the possibility to successfully defend the infringement of a legal good in a peaceful way in a public forum of arbitration. In the present study, the concept does not embrace the idea of equality before the law. This is because the subject is chronologically limited to a period when the society of the estates with all its privileges still existed.[18]

In my dissertation, two concepts were used to assess the official control of homicide. I studied the *legal certainty* of the juridical practice, in other words the legality of the judgments and the extent and principles

---

13   Black 1984b, pp. 4–9.
14   The definition has been formulated in this way by Pieter Spierenburg. Spierenburg 1984, p. viii. On the control implemented by priests and teachers, see also Österberg 1991b, p. 21.
15   Cf. Laine 1991, p. 16; Laitinen & Aromaa 1993, p. 186 ff.
16   Hans Andersson has used this concept, which was thus formulated by Lawrence Friedeman. Andersson 1998, p. 2.
17   Cf. e.g. Laitinen & Aromaa 1993, pp. 13–14.
18   Cf. Andersson 1998, p. 63; for a contrary view, Karonen 1998a, pp. 584–590.

of the superior courts' arbitration, i.e. how far they deviated from statutory justice. On the other hand, I made a parish-by-parish analysis of the punishments that were meted out for homicide in order to estimate the extent of *penal certainty*, that is the actual dimensions of the implementation and range of the judicial consequences of homicide. I explored the symbiotic interrelationship between homicide and the control of this form of crime by locating the problems in the legal repression of homicide and estimating how the quality of the repression determined local differences in homicidal crime. These concepts will not be analysed any further in the present study, although, for example, the concept of penal certainty is to some extent problematic because it is a later construction. The use of the term is justified, however, because the debate initiated by Cesare Beccaria in the 1760s concerning the risk of being punished had spread during the period studied here to the circles of jurisprudential scholars in Sweden.[19] In the same way, the idea of the predictability of justice has to be understood in a pre-modern sense; otherwise the use of the concept would involve the danger of being unhistorical. Predictable justice in the sense of the concept as used by Max Weber refers to the pure universality of modern, i.e. formal and rational, justice, irrespective of the object of that justice.[20] There is no point in trying to assess the consistency and the extent of justice in the society of the estates,[21] because the implementation of reliability and predictability in western Europe would have required among other things a clear, public, written code of laws and the abandonment of the existing requirements of the statutory presentation of proof. Nor, according to Michel Foucault, can justice be predictable in the modern sense as long as the king has any significant power to pardon. It is also difficult to realize legal certainty without an organ subordinated to the justice system, such as a police force.[22] Some of these elements were still in their infancy in the system of justice that existed in Sweden in the eighteenth century.

It was necessary to assess the predictability of the justice meted out for homicide in eastern Finland purely on the basis of the conditions that prevailed there and of the objects of that justice. In my dissertation this entailed a consideration of the following questions: How far were judgments based on statutory law, and to what extent was the content of positive law available to the public? What kind of factors undermined the predictability of justice in the eyes of the people, and what role did the long unbroken historical traditions of the dispensation of justice take on in this respect? In the present work, however, I have excluded these questions.

19   Calonius 1800, 1801, 1802, pp. 43–34.
20   Nousiainen 1993, pp. 28, 38 and notes, also pp. 4, 11–17. Nousiainen is referring here to Weber 1956, p. 128.
21   On the question of the extent and the consistency of justice in the Law of 1734 see e.g. Nousiainen 1993, p. 348.
22   Foucault 1977.

In my dissertation I attempted to penetrate the concept of control by means of three different interpretative approaches: those of historical and sociological criminology and qualitative analysis. The first of these approaches has been condensed in the present work, while the second has been omitted altogether, as have a critique of the sources and a discussion of methodology.

This study covers the period 1747—1808. The starting point was dictated by an historical factor, the establishment of the Province of Kymenkartano and Savo in 1748. The most natural end point for the research was Sweden's Finnish War in 1808. Within this chronological span, there is a watershed in Swedish legal history: the 1779 law reform of Gustav III, the basic principles of which, however, did not undermine the foundations of the prevailing penal policy.[23] The criminal policy that had been typical of the early centuries of the modern age, with its emphasis on the deterrent effect of brutal public punishments, continued to predominate until half-way through the nineteenth century.[24] Thus the chronological limits of the study provide an excellent framework for an assessment of the effectiveness of the old system in a rapidly changing society.

There was a population explosion in northern Savo and northern Karelia in the second half of the eighteenth century that in its own day was unparalleled anywhere else in the world.[25] A populace of about fifty thousand had more than doubled by the time Finland became an autonomous grand duchy of the Russian Empire after the Finnish War.[26] Indeed, in northern Karelia, the total growth of the population between 1749 and 1805 was 170 per cent; in other words, it almost trebled, and in some localities it quadrupled.[27] The population increase was a reflection of improved living conditions and a surplus rise in the birth rate over mortality.[28] The form of settlement remained predominantly agrarian throughout the period of this research, and burn-beating cultivation was the main source of livelihood for the majority of the people, especially in the early years of the period. The cultivation of arable land gradually spread when the Land Distribution Act, which changed the conditions of land ownership, began to take effect in the 1780s. There was only one city in the region: Kuopio, which was made the centre of local government in 1775, but it had a population of under a thousand.

---

23 Modée 1781, pp. 587–593, *Den 20 januarii. Kongl. Maj:ts Förordning, angående ändring uti Allmänna Lagens stadgande i åtskilliga rum.* On the reform of the Criminal Code see Anners 1965, pp. 9–12 and *passim.*

24 The penal system of the early modern age is dealt with in depth by e.g. Spierenburg 1984; Foucault 1977; Kekkonen & Ylikangas 1982; Sharpe 1990.

25 Jutikkala 1934, pp. 118–120.

26 KA: VÄ.

27 Saloheimo 1980, p. 62.

28 Jutikkala 1997, pp. 7–15; Wirilander 1989, pp. 48–55; Saloheimo 1980, pp. 60–66; Soininen 1974, pp. 322–325; Sirén 1999, pp. 28, 34.

The greatest increase in the size of the population in eastern Finland took place in the sparsely populated parishes of the north, where there was still room for burn-beating cultivation to expand. Settlement in these parts spread out mainly through the establishment of crofts on the outlying lands of the farms proper.[29] Local government units in these areas were extensively divided up into smaller entities at the end of the eighteenth century.[30] However, the rise in population was only relative; the growth in pre-industrial times was never even, and the high mortality rates caused by wars and by crop failures and the epidemics that followed them caused deep dips in the upward curves. In fact, all over the province the population fell as a result of epidemics in the years of famine of the 1790s and early 1800s.[31]

From 1748 onwards, northern Savo and the bailiwick of Karelia had belonged to the Province of Kymenkartano and Savo. In 1775 the northern part of this area was made into the Province of Savo and Karelia. The region was under the jurisdiction of the Åbo Court of Appeal up to 1776, but in the following year it was transferred to that of the recently founded Vasa Court of Appeal. See Map 1.[32]

Map 1.

The parishes of northern Savo and northern Karelia in 1748

29   KA: VÄ. Also Wirilander 1989, pp. 70, 138–139.
30   Wirilander 1989, pp. 344–351; Saloheimo 1980, pp. 372–375; Sopanen 1975, p. 26. The divisions are listed in Koskivirta 2001, p. 17.
31   Jutikkala 1997, pp. 8–15; Wirilander 1989, pp. 49–56; Björn 1993, p. 22
32   Source for Map 1: Teerijoki 1993, p. 120.

The main source of material for the present research is the judgement registers (*designaatioluettelot / designationsförteckningar*) of the Vaasa Court of Appeal (= VHOA), the judgment records (*päätöstaltiot / utslag*) of referred cases for the years 1754—1813 and the enquiry records (*alistusaktit / handlingar på underställda mål*), pertaining to the Province of Savo and Karelia (until 1775 the northern part of the Province of Kymenkartano and Savo), insofar as they have survived. The trial records for the years before 1776 were mainly destroyed by a fire in the archives of the Åbo Court of Appeal. The judgment records of the Åbo Court of Appeal sent to the Governor of the Province of Kymenkartano and Savo from the beginning of the 1740s to 1775, which are preserved in the Provincial Archives of Mikkeli (= MMA), have also been examined. These sources used in parallel with the lists of prisoners make it possible to regard the source material as sufficient if not completely satisfactory in all respects with regard to quality.[33] The most important sources of the extensive material offered by the Swedish State Archives (*Riksarkivet* = RA) in Stockholm are the Register of Appeals (*Justitierevisionens registratur* = JRR), records of homicide cases referred to the King (= KM), who was represented by the Council of Justice (*Justitierevisionen*) until 1789 and subsequently by the Supreme Court (*Högsta domstolen*), and the relevant minutes (= *högsta domstolens protokoll*, HDP). In addition, decisions regarding appeals and pleas for clemency are preserved in the series *Justitierevisionens utslagshandlingar* (= JRU).

Proportional homicide rates have been adjusted to the average populations of the parishes, which have been calculated on the basis of the parochial population tables.[34] I also gathered information about persons murdered and executed from the cause of death statistics in the population tables, but the material turned out to be unusable for estimating the amount of homicide in eastern Finland. Naturally, in view of the original purpose of these records, one could not expect them to provide such information.

The Traditions of Criminal Research

The historical trends of crime, in particular violence and crimes against property, in the western world have been connected with macro-level social processes such as modernization (and urbanization) and the civilizing process. In his socio-historical study of crime, the American historian of criminality, Eric A. Johnson, outlines three principal, chronologically separate, trends in this field,[35] of which only the last actually represents historical research proper.

---

33 On the nature, advantages and defects of the various sources, see Koskivirta 2001, pp. 19–21.

34 On the source value of the populations table and problems in establishing population figures, see Sirén 1993; Sirén 1999; Pitkänen 1976; Wirilander 1964.

35 Durkheim 1985; Tönnies 1963; for another view of the origins and development of criminology and its connections at different stages with other disciplines, see Laine 1991, pp. 39–47.

The first trend in the history of crime and its control is represented by the classical sociological arguments, which are still frequently referred to. Max Weber's interpretations of the modern state's assumption of a monopoly of the legitimate use of power and violence have inspired many scholars, particularly through Norbert Elias' theory of the civilizing process.[36] In addition, there still lives on, especially in interpretations of the history of urban crime, a dichotomy between the traditions inspired by Ferdinand Tönnies and Émile Durkheim respectively. Briefly put, the dividing line between them depends on how, on one hand, agrarian communal life and, on the other, the consequences of industrialization are seen: either, as with Tönnies, the *Gemeinschaft* – the united *community* of the past – is idealized, and the social problems of its contrary, the *Gesellschaft* (the urban *society*) are emphasized, or conversely, in the fashion of Durkheim, stress is laid on the repressive criminal justice system and the coercion to conform of the olden days.[37] The latter's most important contributions to sociological criminology also involve an analysis of both the pressures that lead to crime and the control of crime. Durkheim introduced the idea of official and unofficial social control and formulated the theory of anomy, both of which are indispensable references in any study that aims to problemize violent crime.[38] The major argument of the theory of anomy is that the economic factors, like poverty or lack of opportunity, proposed in many studies do not in themselves produce crime as a by-product of frustration; rather, the frustration erupts from a loss of values or a conflict between the system of values and people's real opportunities for succeeding in life.[39]

The second phase in the history of crime is seen by Johnson as being manifested in the works of American sociology, particularly the Chicago school, in the 1920s and 1930s, which subjected the theories of classical sociology to American empiricism; it found that the city downtown was more criminal that the suburbs and rural areas, and that criminals were mainly recruited from among the ranks of those who had migrated to the cities from the countryside and were generally from the lower classes. In their own theory of anomy in the 1950s, Robert Merton and his students developed the "frustration-aggression model", the theory of which had been formulated by John Dollard and his colleagues in the classic work *Frustration and Aggression* (1939). Merton sees the mechanism that creates deviant behaviour, including crime, as being a situation in which people lack the institutional means to achieve their culturally determined goals. When people are prevented in one way or another from achieving their aims, the traditional system of social norms loses it authority, and a situation of anomy reigns. The idea of a connection between aggression

36 Elias 1994, pp. 447–451 and *passim*.
37 Johnson 1996, pp. 8–9; Tönnies 1963; Durkheim 1985 (1899).
38 Durkheim 1990; Durkheim 1985. The concept was formulated into a term of social control by Edward Ross in 1901.
39 Laine 1991, p. 60. Cf. also Ylikangas 1973, pp. 292–310; Ylikangas 1976, pp. 322–326.

and the prevention of goal-directed behaviour, that is behaviour directed to the production of pleasure or the avoidance of pain, originally comes from Freud.[40]

From the 1960s on, the American findings have been tested on historical material concerning the pre-industrial age and the period of industrialization.[41] For example, a classic Finnish work in the history of violence, *Puukkojunkkareitten esiinmarssi* (1976, trans. *The Knife Fighters*, 1998), is situated within the tradition of frustration-aggression models. In this study, Heikki Ylikangas connects a wave of mass violence that took place in Southern Ostrobothnia in western Finland at the turn of the eighteenth and nineteenth centuries with weak control and social structures that created pressures leading to crime, such as a downward spiral in social position and in the prevailing system of values.[42]

The Belgian scholar, Xavier Rousseaux, considers that there are two main approaches in the European tradition of research into the history of crime in the pre-industrial age: a view that emphasizes a Marxist class struggle, and conversely, arguments that stress consensus. By the latter, Rousseaux is referring to interpretations that regard the authorities and the public as having coinciding views about harmful behaviour and the control of crime.[43] The former perspective was accorded a strong position in some classic large-scale studies of property crime, hanging sentences and executions. These studies, which were made in the 1960s and 1970s, were inspired by a movement called "History from Below", a Marxist view of society that made the proletariat into an active agent in history, and by the radical criminology of the 1960s and 1970s.[44] The main thread running through the pioneering works of such scholars as Douglas Hay, E.P. Thompson, Eric Hobsbawn and Michael Weisser is the idea of the law as a tool used by the ruling elite to further its own class interests in both feudal and industrializing societies.[45]

This kind of approach, which was called the "class struggle perspective" by Rousseaux, is described in the Nordic countries as the "conflict perspective" because research into the history of the judicial system has not generally been explicitly Marxist in this part of the world. The view of the imposition of a harsh law as a tool to promote the power interests of the ruling classes particularly in the seventeenth century has, nevertheless, been shared by numerous scholars in the Nordic countries, too. They have described the legal and social development that took place during the time that Sweden was a great power in terms that emphasize the conflictual

---

40   Berkowitz 1962, pp. 26 ff, 310; on the Chicagon school, see e.g. Vold & Bernard & Snipes 1998.
41   Johnson 1996, pp. 9-10.
42   Ylikangas 1976; 1985; 1998a, pp. 288–293, 323.
43   Rousseaux 1997, pp. 1–3; Österberg 1987, pp. 321–340; Österberg 1989, pp. 73–95; Aronsson 1992, pp. 17–36; Furuhagen 1996, pp. 15–20.
44   For descriptions of these approaches, see e.g. Aalto 1996, pp. 14, 16; Rakkolainen 1996, pp. 12–21, also Laine 1991, p. 79 and notes.
45   Linebaugh 1992, pp. xix–xv.

aspect; they regard the increase in the severity of criminal law that took place in the seventeenth century as a consequence of an attempt on the part of the state to intervene in the life of the local community. The main – if not the only task – of the law was to focus the control of the groups who held power on those who were bereft of power. They interpreted the real aim of the harsh criminal code – and of pardons – as a means of reinforcing the position of the rulers and the hegemony of the power elite.[46] However, views like these that emphasize the conflict of interests between the supervisors and the supervised have become less clear-cut in recent years.[47]

The other flank of research into the history of crime in Scandinavia, one which emphasizes a kind of consensus and interaction between groups in society, is represented by Eva Österberg. Österberg uses the concept of interaction to refer to a situation in which the law was to a great extent the ideological cement that held society together. The function of the system of justice was not just to advance the interests of the state or those of a particular class by imposing coercion or disciplinary control.[48] The change in the function of the district court from a social arena oriented towards the settlement of conflict into a stage for the execution of the state's campaign to impose discipline has been one of the major arguments in Nordic research on the history of crime and control ever since the 1980s.[49] The differences in interpretation between those scholars who emphasize consensus and the adherents of a conflict perspective are partly the result of differing conceptions of the general state of social relations.

Swedish criminal law, even at its harshest, has been regarded as lenient by general European standards. The fact that it lacked the cruellest forms of punishment has been explained by various factors: for example, the relatively egalitarian nature of Swedish society, the country's remote location, the limited extent of feudalism in Sweden, the peaceable nature of domestic affairs and the low population density. For example, the Old Testament commandments that were imposed along with orthodox Protestant dogma were for the most part observed literally only in the lower courts, the sentences of which anyway generally lacked legal authority. In the superior courts, the application of these commandments was considerably limited.[50]

In contradistinction to Xavier Rousseaux, Eric A Johnson considers the European historical-cultural debate that has been going on since the 1960s and 70s to be the main trend in the history of crime at the moment. Sim-

---

46   Aronsson 1992, pp. 23–24, 167; Sundin 1992, pp. 10–11. Aalto 1996, pp. 188–190; Ylikangas 1983; Kekkonen & Ylikangas 1982; Lappi-Seppälä 1982, pp. 39–50; Pajuoja 1991, p. 16.; Ylikangas 1991; Sharpe 1990, pp. 30, 39. For a partly opposing view, see e.g. Österberg 1982, p. 32 ff; Österberg 1989, p. 73 ff; Karonen 1999a; Thunander 1993, p. 54 ff.
47   Ylikangas 1999, pp. 101–119.
48   Österberg 1996, p. 36.
49   E.g. Österberg 1991b, p. 8 ff; Taussi Sjöberg 1991, p. 25 ff.
50   Thunander 1993, p. 5 ff. Karonen 1998, pp. 139–140; 1999a, pp. 217–218., 224–225. Aalto 1996, pp. 215–217; Karonen 1998, pp. 139–140.

plified dichotomies, such as conflict – consensus, arbitration – discipline or city – countryside, or a theory of anomy, cannot, in his opinion, alone explain general trends in the history of crime; rather, explanations for fluctuations in these trends must be sought in society's reactions to criminal acts.[51] In articles written by Central European scholars, the panorama of local crime has been variously studied from the perspective of the history of the law and legal institutions, deviance and marginal groups.[52] The anthropologically and culturally oriented mentality-historical approach, which stems from the Annales school, continues to be a vigorous line of research. The most recent Finnish research in the field is represented in Olli Matikainen's work *Verenperijät*, which studies the cultural history of violence in eastern Finland at the inception of the modern age.[53] For example, Nordic historians at the turn of the 1970s and 80s attempted to reconstruct long-term fluctuations in crime with special reference to the most common forms of crime in the pre-modern period: witchcraft, violence, theft, disobedience and sexual crimes.[54] In the early 1990s there was still a big demand for quantitative global analyses of the work of the law courts, but since then there has been a paradigm shift in research from quantity to quality. The field of the history of norms and the control of deviance from them has fragmented in numerous directions; in the Nordic countries, for instance, there have been works dealing with micro-history,[55] gender history, types of peasant resistance and the culture of folk justice.[56] In Norway, the departure of approaches to the study of violent crime in the direction of normative and social history on one hand and constructivism on the other has led to a heated debate on the justification of the different orientations.[57]

Like most scholars who attempt to make a synopsis of the field, Eric A Johnson emphasizes Norbert Elias' theses regarding the modernization of society. In describing trends in the history of crime and control, the birth of the modern state (sociogenesis) has been regarded as the most important element of Elias' civilization theory. It is thought that this changed people's collective mentality and views about what was acceptable behaviour (psychogenesis).[58] As a consequence of the sociogenetic and psychogenetic processes, violence between individuals is considered

---

51   Johnson 1995, pp. 10-12.
52   Rousseaux 1997, pp. 5-6.
53   On the mentality-historical tradition in research on crime and control see Gaskill 2000, pp. 3–29. See also Matikainen 2000, p. 9 ff; Matikainen 2002.s
54   Österberg 1996, pp. 37–38.
55   Heikkinen 1988; 1997 ; 2000.
56   On the first of these see e.g. Österberg 1987, pp. 321–340; Sundin 1992; Aronsson 1992; Taussi Sjöberg 1991; Ågren, M 1988; on gender history see e.g. Lindstedt Cronberg 1997; Aalto, J. 1997; Andersson G. 1998; Rautelin 1993; Rautelin 1996; Taussi Sjöberg 1996; on peasant resistance see e.g. Reinholdsson 1999; Katajala 1992; 1994; Ylikangas 1977; 1996; on the culture of folk justice see e.g. Andersson 1998; Aalto & Johansson & Sandmo 2000.
57   Imsen 1998; Sandmo 1999.
58   Elias (1939) 1994, pp. xiii-xvii.

to have decreased at the same time as property crimes increased. [59] It can be claimed that, in his idea of the civilizing process, Elias took issue with the relationship between the state's and the individual's control of affects. The subject of the civilization model, which examines control in depth, is the process of change in manners, as a result of which western man began to exert an ever stronger control over his instincts, including his aggressions. Elias considers that the extensive suppression of aggressions was based on the coming into existence of the superego, a development that launched an interaction between three factors. The gradual assumption by the state of a monopoly on the use of violence and on taxation was a manifestation of the strengthening in state control. In addition, members of society became ever more dependent upon one another. According to Elias, the enlargement of the network of dependencies was a consequence of society becoming more complicated and faceless in character. Two sources of external control, the growth of the power state and the specialization of labour in society, led to a psychological development that was both collective and individual, as a result of which a fear of external punishment was replaced by internal self-restraint as the source of people's control of their actions and impulses among increasingly large sections of the population. It has been thought that the process began among the higher ranks of society and spread from them to the lower social strata.[60]

***

The quantitative analysis of personal violence has – like the study of the repression of property crime – been one of the major subjects of research into the history of criminality. The attraction of criminological research is partly a result of the fact that the source material is relatively unproblematic and an empirical examination of it reveals considerable fluctuations over time. The linking quantitative changes in personal violence with periods of social upheaval has made the study of homicide into a classic method in the pluralizing field of history, enabling one to examine the interrelationship between the structural macro-level and individual or collective and cultural behavioural models. Of all types of crime, homicide offers the material best suited to this kind of study because the amount of undiscovered crime is purely marginal, and at the same time a source of errors resulting from changes in the effectiveness of official social control is eliminated.

59   Gurr 1981, pp. 295–353; Stone 1983, p 22 ff.
60   The first pillar of Elias' thinking, the state monopoly of violence, goes back to Weber; the second, the specialization of labour in society, originates with Durkheim. Elias (1939) 1994, pp. 156–167; 335–524. See also e.g. Spierenburg 1994, pp. 702–703.

Violence, often measured by the number of homicides prosecuted in court, has been considered to be a pervasive characteristic of mediaeval and early modern age societies. Over wide areas of Europe during the Middle Ages, deaths arising from personal violence amounted to dozens per 100,000 inhabitants per year. However, in a period dating from approximately the 1660s to the beginning of the nineteenth century it is known that the relatives figures for homicide in western Europe plunged to a fraction of their previous levels.[61] The decrease in homicide, which had actually begun in the thirteenth century, to its present level in Europe took place in a series of jumps. [62] Killings became momentarily more common in England and in some places in the Nordic countries in the early seventeenth century, and again in conjunction with a wave of violence and crimes against property in the nineteenth century, but in the longer term perspective, from the coming into being of the state, lethal violence definitely decreased. The central areas of Sweden, which by European standards were originally extremely violent, as indeed were some regions of Norway and Finland, were *in this respect* in the vanguard of the civilizing process from the 1620s on.[63] And as killing decreased, the social status of the killers also became marginalized.[64]

Not all Nordic scholars believe that violence monolithically enveloped the whole of Scandinavia in the Middle Ages and the beginning of the modern age. Among others, Ylikangas, Sundin and Liliequist have observed in a number of studies that in some outlying areas such as Savo and Ostrobothnia in Finland and the provinces of northern Sweden the numbers of homicides prosecuted in the courts was small in comparison with the more central regions,[65] albeit with the reservation that in the sprawling parishes of the periphery it was perhaps possible to conceal some of the killings from the legal authorities and to come to illegal arrangements outside the courts.[66] The propensity of the Finns for lethal

---

61 Stone 1983, p. 30; Beattie 1986, pp. 107–112. Cf. also Lindström 1988, p. 67 and notes; Söderberg 1990, p. 244; Sharpe 1984, pp. 183–185; Spierenburg 1994, pp. 707, 712; Ylikangas 1999, pp. 88–119.

62 There is information available about homicide in the pre-industrial age mainly in Britain, Holland, France and the Nordic countries. See e.g Stone 1983, p. 22 ff; Gurr 1992; Johnson 1996, p. 9; Spierenburg 1996, p. 702 ff; Beattie 1986, pp. 107–13; Sharpe 1996, pp. 22–23. For a summary see also e.g. Ylikangas 1999, pp. 15–29. For differing views, see e.g. Cockburn 1991, pp. 75–78.

63 Jansson 1998; Liliequist 1999, pp. 180–181; Emsley 1999, p. 148; Österberg 1983, p. 28; Österberg 1991b, pp. 12–18; Söderberg 1990, pp. 242–243. Sundin 1992, p. 684. Cf. also Thunander 1993, p. 151; Jansson 1998, p. 16 for the Göta Court of Appeal.

64 This decrease was not, however, completely uniform. See e.g. Ylikangas 1974; Österberg 1991b, p. 12 ff; Österberg 1996, pp. 42–46; Söderberg 1992; Karonen 1998, pp. 160–171; Spierenburg 1996, pp. 71, 89; Ylikangas 1999, pp. 83–101.

65 Ylikangas 1976b, pp. 88–140; Ylikangas 1988, pp. 130–134; Liliequist 1999, pp. 174–175.

66 Liliequist 1999, pp. 175–177.

violence does not seem to have been any greater than that of the Swedes before the eighteenth century, but from half-way through that century up till the present day Finns have committed more homicides than their western neighbours.[67]

Trends in violence have generally been connected with two other forms of crime: slander and property crimes.[68] Violence between individuals and families was sustained by an element characteristic of feudal and collective societies: a strong dependence on the respect of people living in one's immediate environment, which made a person highly sensitive his own personal honour and that of his kin.[69] In fact, just at the inception of the modern age, the social distribution of people who committed homicide was weighted towards the higher classes of society. The following decrease in the proportion of the gentry among the killers has been considered an indication that an easily wounded sense of honour gradually began to disappear from the spectrum of motives for crimes of violence.[70] The pre-eminent criminologist of the Age of Enlightenment, Cesare Beccaria, thought that duels fought in defence of a person's honour were indispensable because he did not believe that society could protect its members from the consequences of slander.[71] According to Ylikangas, the protection of property by means of violence and terror was another factor that created a high level of aggression among the upper classes in society.[72]

One basic explanation for violence has been sought in the tension that existed between the rulers and the ruled.[73] According to Arne Jansson, the history of Sweden does not lend itself to such interpretations in their most simplistic forms, because relations between the social classes were most strained in the very decades of the seventeenth century when the numbers of homicides prosecuted in court demonstrably decreased most sharply. Moreover, the position of the peasants[74] has been seen as having become so weak that this class was incapable of violent protest.[75] The

---

67   Lehti 2001, pp. 7–8, 11–12; 24–31.

68   The interrelation between these forms of crime was first examined in the Nordic countries in Ylikangas 1971.

69   In this context, the word "feudal" refers generally to societies where the machinery of the state was not centralized and in which the implementation of the law was partly in the hands of private persons. On feudalism in the Nordic countries, see e.g. Jutikkala 1978, pp. 41–59; Winberg 1985, pp. 212–212; on feudalism in European historiography, see Nurmiainen 1998.

70   Johnson 1966, p. 12; Stone 1983, p. 22 ff.; Gurr 1981, p. 295 ff. The argument "from violence to theft" in its various forms has been widely criticized, e.g. by Jansson 1998, p. 4 and notes; Johnson 1996, p. 9; Österberg 1996, pp. 48–53; Spierenburg 1996, pp. 67—69; Sharpe 1996, pp. 20—29.

71   Beccaria (1763) 1995.

72   Ylikangas 2000, pp. 44–47, 55–60.

73   Originally Rusche & Kirchheimer 1939, p. 139 ff.

74   Jansson 1998, p. 86; Ylikangas 1976a, pp. 81–103.

75   The word "peasant" is used in this book to translate the Swedish "*bonde*", which refers to an independent farmer who either owned his own land or held permanent tenure of it, and not just to any person living off the land. In Swedish society, the "Peasants" formed the fourth estate after the Nobles, the Clergy and the Burghers.

constant state of war has also been regarded as a factor that upheld violence between civilians, particularly in the early seventeenth century. [76]

Classical European studies of pre-capitalist society surmised that that the emphasis in values gradually began to shift away from the maintenance of personal and family honour towards the accruing of material property. The same phenomenon was used to explain the permanent increase in theft and other crimes against property in the 1970s, but this view has since been strongly rejected.[77] The shift in the emphasis of crime from violence towards property crime has been regarded as part of a complex mechanism which includes among other things the development of production and ownership relations, their increased legal significance and the increasing effectiveness of means of surveillance. In the spiralling process of change in the power mechanisms that framed the life of the individual, the threshold of violent crime also rose. At the same time, the public's attitudes towards crimes against property hardened.[78]

As in Central Europe, the number of property crimes in the Nordic countries rose abruptly in the eighteenth century. However, theft, and the punishments that it incurred, never assumed as important a role in the Nordic countries in the eighteenth and nineteenth centuries in the theatre of crime and repression as they did in the central areas of Europe.[79]

Throughout western Europe, the civilizing process, accompanied as it was by a considerable fall in the number of homicides, indisputably reflected some profound social changes.[80] The causes of this far-reaching phenomenon have been traced to broad cultural, demographic, economic, social and disciplinary dimensions, and above all to the institutional upheaval that the building of the modern state together with all its concomitant effects constituted.[81] Like Elias, many scholars have found a central connection between the decrease in private violence and the creation of the modern state.[82] Elias' own model of the formation of the state was to a great extent founded on the birth of French absolutism, on which Michel Foucault also based his partly opposing theoretical model

---

76　E.g. Österberg 1996, pp. 41-42.
77　Johnson 1996, p. 12. On the modernization of crime and the advent of the "new crime", see e.g. Zehr 1976; Weisser 1979; Sharpe 1996, pp. 19–29.
78　Foucault 1977.
79　Österberg 1996, pp. 38–41; Jansson 1998, p. 85. For a more general discussion of the commonly noted influence of economic conditions on fluctuations in homicidal crime, however, see Gillis 1996 p. 1275 and notes.
80　On the decrease in violent crime generally, see e.g. Stone 1983, pp. 22–33; Spierenburg 1994, p. 702; Gurr 1992; Ylikangas 1999, pp. 15–34; Österberg 1996, pp. 40–46; Sundin 1992; Naess 1994; also Lehti 2001, pp. 3–31; Matikainen 1996, pp. 32–34; Karonen 1996, pp. 79–81. On the social environment of crime in the pre-industrial age as a determining factor in the crime rate, see Sharpe 1996, p. 31.
81　Gillis 1996, p. 1275; Österberg 1991b; Jansson 1998, p. 72, Johnson 1996, p. 141.
82　Elias (1939) 1994, p. 335 ff; Sharpe 1984; Spierenburg 1984 *passim*; Österberg 1996, pp. 30–59; Ylikangas 1999, pp. 23–28, 88–119; Johnson 1996; Tilly 1990, pp. 67–68. See also Lane 1997, p. 30; Karonen 1999a; Giddens 1985, pp. 172–197; Zemon Davis 1987; Lehti 2001, pp. 3–20; Spierenburg 2001.

of the shift from physical, public juridical repression into psychological and private suppression. [83] Neither of these authorities actually regards cruel, harsh punishment as an effective means of external control but rather as a tool for the inculcation of control in order to obviate the need for repressive criminal law.

The connection between the formation of the state and the decrease in private violence has been interpreted as a consequence of the transfer of the institutions of control, which were previously based on compensation and revenge, from the kin to the state.[84] When public authority and the law grew strong enough to be able to offer disputant parties the means to settle their disagreements peacefully, members of society began increasingly to turn to the representatives of the state to settle their disagreements. [85] Judicial methods thus displaced the violent settlement of accounts.[86]

All over Europe, the initial stage in the process involved an increase in the harshness of criminal law and penal practice in order to reassert the state's monopoly of the use of violence,[87] but when the authority of the modern state became sufficiently strong, the strictest ordinances of criminal law were replaced by more lenient sanctions. Some scholars consider that, although brutal punishments that legitimated the state's use of violence served to augment general violence in the Middle Ages and the early modern age,[88] they nevertheless did provide some legal security against the local abuse of power by the strongest members of the community.[89] During the 1980s and 1990s, Heikki Ylikangas has discussed the building of the modern state and the effects of the legislative reforms that it entailed on homicidal crime. Through his theses of a society based on kinship relations and state terrorism, Ylikangas arrived at a Lockian interpretation of the reasons for the extensive spread of violence: it was, he suggests, to a great extent a consequence of the state's inability to offer its subjects protection, above all for their property.[90]

Intimately connected with the formation of the state is also the concept of a *judicial revolution*, i.e. the creation of a centralized state machinery for the settlement of disputes. The judicial revolution has been described in two ways: it has been seen as either a series of individual reforms that

83   In addition to the afore-mentioned, see also Spierenburg 1984, p. x. See also Lane 1979, p. 60; Horgby 1986, p. 234 ff; Jansson 1998, pp. 97–98
84   E.g. Lane 1997, p. 10.
85   Johnson 1996, p. 12.
86   Lane 1997, p. 30, Johnson 1996, p. 13. This argument has been justified by the claim that as grievous homicidal crime decreased, an increasing number of cases concerning slight disputes and misdemeanours were dealt with in the courts. However, empirical evidence also suggests the opposite: in England, at the same time as homicide waned, the numbers of cases involving other kinds of crime and civil actions also decreased. See e.g. Stone 1983, pp. 220–222; Monkkonen 2001; Thome 2001; Roth 2001.
87   Ylikangas 1998, pp. 53–95; 1999, pp. 53–96.
88   Thunander 1993, pp. 82–83; Spierenburg 1984; Jansson 1998.
89   Ylikangas 1998, pp. 80–111; Ylikangas 1999, pp. 50–111.
90   Kekkonen & Ylikangas 1982, pp. 52–54; Ylikangas 1994, pp. 3–25; Ylikangas 1999, pp. 348–350.

took place within a short period of time in the early seventeenth century or as a long-term process lasting from the beginning of the seventeenth century to the mid-nineteenth century.[91] With the judicial revolution, the state's juridical control and competence displaced the previous implementation of justice, which had been conducted by the kin and the local community.[92] In Sweden this process led to the adoption of a multi-tiered court system. Thus, in accordance with European principles of justice and views about the jurisdiction of the courts, all capital offences had to be submitted to a legal organ of the state; in Sweden this organ was the courts of appeal, the first of which, the Svea Court of Appeal, was established in 1614.[93]

According to Björn Furuhagen, even in its initial stage the judicial revolution did not involve an increase in the harshness of punishments at the practical level as much as making their application more professional, explicit and precise. It was not until half-way through the nineteenth century that the final reorganization of criminal and procedural law and the penal system took place. Among other things, this reorganization resulted in the final disappearance of the feature of public display from punishments.[94]

While there are few who would any longer dispute the fact that the civilizing process was manifested in a decrease in personal violence, there is still debate about the origins of the process. Some scholars trace the roots of the process to politics, i.e. the formation of the state, while others find them in the economic sphere. Elias' theory serves as the starting point for both interpretations. In the vertical political sense, the decrease in violence is seen above all as the result of a disciplinary campaign imposed from above by the church and the state.[95] A representative of the opposite, horizontal, perspective, which emphasizes the importance of the economic aspect, is Arne Jansson, who considers that in the seventeenth century the Swedish state did not in fact wage a campaign primarily against violent crime; rather, he believes that one of the main targets of the disciplinary measures was the supervision of monogamous sexual relations.[96] Critics of the so-called "control perspective" regard control purely as discipline imposed by the authorities and only rarely as an element of legal security.[97]

---

91 Cf. e.g. Furuhagen 1996, p. 23 ff.
92 On the dimensions of the assumption of responsibility for justice by the state, see e.g. Ylikangas 1983, pp. 125–159, 164–173. Modeér 1997, pp. 80–81; Letto-Vanamo 1992, p. 31; Aalto 1996, pp. 62–63; Furuhagen 1996 *passim*; Ylikangas 1999, pp. 51–53. The term "judicial revolution" was introduced in Lenman & Parker 1980a, p. 42, 68, 156–157, 245, 278.
93 E.g. Anners 1965, p. 34. For Europe, see Diestelkamp 1990, pp. 19–45; Inger 1994, p. 119.
94 E.g. Furuhagen 1996; Foucault 1977.
95 Bergfeldt 1997, p. 6.
96 Jansson 1998, pp. 93–94, 96. Nor do Söderberg and Jarrick conside the actions of the state to be in any way significant for the civilizing process.
97 Exceptions to this, however, are Jansson and Andersson, who in their studies redefine the conceptual formulation of the old control perspective.

Among others, Jan Sundin expresses doubts about the capacity of the Swedish state to undertake purposeful measures against violence in the seventeenth century.[98] In practice, however, I believe that the efforts of the legislators and the authorities to reinforce the penal monopoly of the state is apparent in the extensive laws against blood vengeance, duels and other private forms of revenge.[99]

The economic historians, Arne Jarrick and Johan Söderberg, examine the civilizing process from an economic perspective. Like Hans Peter Duerr, a well-known critic of Elias, they see the process as a horizontal, spontaneous one that rose up through society from below. The motive force of this development is considered by Jarrick and Söderberg to be a rise in the general standard of living and an expansion of the economy.[100] This affluence also created a culture which enabled a general increase in people's capacity for empathy. Jarrick and Söderberg conclude that violence decreased for the same reasons as sensitivity to wounded honour: the economic and social sphere fragmented, thus making relations between people more distant and less personal;[101] the collective culture, which was based on face-to-face relations, began to crumble. Söderberg believes that the civilizing process got under way spontaneously in the seventeenth century, when the number and importance of the civil actions brought to court and of written contracts grew at the same time as the vital significance of upholding one's honour or social respect in everyday life decreased. Non-violent court actions replaced physical fights.[102] Söderberg considers that the civilizing process proceeded during the eighteenth and nineteenth centuries in areas of Sweden where the earlier tight network of contacts based on personal relationships broke down, and economic life expanded.[103] Jonas Liliequist, for his part, has sought an explanation for the decrease in lawlessness in the demise of the code of honour and other social mechanisms that encouraged violence.[104]

Among the characteristics peculiar to the history of crime and control in the Nordic countries in the sixteenth century, scholars have identified the continuing strict control of even the most trivial of sexual offences, an increase in the numbers of cases of infanticide and bestiality, which both became serious problems for criminal policy, and the need of the authorities to guard and maintain the class boundaries of the society of the estates by means of various statutes concerning opulence and hired labour. The authorities' surveillance of people's private lives was further increased by criminalizing drunkenness and regulating the production of strong spirits. At the end of the century the activities of the early revivalist religious movements, which caused concern among the authorities at

---

98   Sundin 1992, p. 456; Sundin 1996, p. 182.
99   Ylikangas 1999, pp. 101–110.
100 Bergfeldt 1997, p. 7.
101 Jarrick & Söderberg 1994a, p. 15.
102 Söderberg 1990, pp. 229–258.
103 Söderberg 1993, pp. 224–227.
104 Liliequist 1999, p. 204.

the very hub of the realm, Stockholm itself, were also made criminal. On the other hand, it is believed that in the eighteenth century the opposition between the local communities and the central power decreased in intensity, and that there was no longer a need for the struggle that the state had waged with the help of the church against disobedience and religious and sexual crimes, at least in its most intense form, because the central power had succeeded in consolidating its legal, fiscal and political structures. The need for deterrence had decreased as broad ranks of society had associated themselves with the aspirations of the Crown. By the eighteenth century, the process towards greater egalitarianism in the justice system may have had a part in increasing the public's confidence in it. Instead of trials concerning matters of discipline and the supervision of law and order, the courts came increasingly to deal with economic disputes and property cases.[105] The fact that the civilizing process took place in Sweden slightly earlier that elsewhere in Europe may even indicate that the legal protection offered to the people by an advanced administrative machinery and a strictly tiered system of legal instances was not just an illusion.[106]

***

These questions, which have been the subject of considerable speculation in the field of the history of crime and control in the Agrarian Age, also present various challenges for this study. As the work proceeds, it will be necessary to address the question of how applicable to an explication of the subject of this research as outlined above are many themes that are of central relevance internationally. This entails above all answering the following questions: What does the control of homicide in eastern Finland tell us about the preconditions of the civilizing process, the quality of legal security offered by the state to its citizens, or conflict and consensus as defining categories in relations between the state and its subjects? What does it tell us about the division of functions between the courts and their success as organs of control?

---

105 Furuhagen 1996, p. 220 and *passim*; Inger 1972, p. 21; Liliequist 1992, pp. 1–5; Andersson 1998, p. x; Österberg 1996, p. 51; Ågren, M 1988; Ylikangas 2000 *passim*; Sundin 1996, pp. 166–195.

106 Cf. Andersson 1998; on the feudal and fragmented dispensation of justice in central Europe at the end of the eighteenth century, see e.g. Foucault 1977.

Homicide and Legal Certainty

*Forms of Homicide and Penal Ordinances at
the Time of the Law of 1734*

The Law of Sweden of 1734 came into force in September 1736, thus
supplanting the obsolete Law of the Land of King Christopher of 1442.
Because of the long period of time over which it was drafted, the Law of
1734 continued to exhibit principles of criminal law that were characteristic of the previous century. The Criminal Code, *Missgärnings Balk*
(= MB), was still in its entirety casuistic, that is, based on the definition
of individual types of crime and on the stipulations separately prescribed
for them. The principles of Old Testament Mosaic Law were also incorporated into the Criminal Code practically *in toto*. The Criminal Code
continued to stipulate the death penalty for altogether 68 different types
of crime.[107]

The penal prescriptions for homicide (with the exception of those
relating to infanticide) in the Law of 1734 remained in force throughout
the period of this study; the law stipulated the death penalty for various
types of homicide: for example, *intentional manslaughter*, i.e. committed
with intent to injure (MB XIV:1, XXIV:1, 5, 6, 8, 9, XXXIX:2), poisoning
(MB XVII:1), manslaughter in conjunction with a breach of the peace
(MB XX:1, XXIII:1) or insurrection (MB VI:3) and for various kinds of
murder (MB XII:1—2), including infanticide (MB XVI:1).[108]

The ideological foundation of the sanctions for intentional manslaughter and more serious forms of homicide lay in several injunctions
of the Old Testament, above all in the verse which says: *"Whosoever
smiteth a man, so that he die, shall be surely put to death."* (Exodus 21:
12). The conservative elements of the harsh old penal system continued
to prevail with regard to homicide during the early years of the modern

---

107 Seth 1984, p. 15.
108 The casuistry of the law also listed numerous other forms of manslaughter, see
Koskivirta 2001, p. 48–59 and notes.

age much longer than they did for other types of grievous crime. Two principles were emphasized above all others in the repression of intentional manslaughter from the early seventeenth century to the nineteenth century: the principles of requital (*talio*) and general prevention, which was manifested in an attempt to create a powerful deterrent by means of harsh public punishments.[109] In the stipulations of the Criminal Code of the Law of 1734 on manslaughter, the principle of *talio* is embodied in the words "render a life for a life" (*gifve lif för lif*: MB:XV:5, XXIV:1, 7, 9, XXXIX:2).[110] The principle of requital is thought to have satisfied[111] any emotional need for vengeance that the killing might have aroused in the public. The *talio* principle was reinforced by the doctrine of blood vengeance and the theocratic doctrine of propitiation – that is, the view that the people shared the guilt for a homicidal crime that was not punished with death by the court. An unpunished crime was thought to incur divine retribution.[112] The idea of execution as an act of propitiation to God only disappeared finally in Sweden in the Criminal Code of 1864, and in Finland even later, in the Criminal Code of 1889.[113]

The essential elements of intentional manslaughter (*1734 års lag*, MB XXIV) were defined in a royal circular sent to the courts of appeal in 1740. The definition of a crime as intentional manslaughter required first of all that it be committed with intent to *injure* (but not necessarily with intent to *kill*), second a weapon which the perpetrator knew to be lethal, and third an indisputable causal relationship between cause of death of the victim and the violence he had suffered. If one of these elements was missing, the case remained unproven, and the category of the crime was reduced to unintentional manslaughter (MB XXVIII), for which the law prescribed a blood money fine, a wergild, to be divided three ways between the Crown, the local court and the relatives of the victim. If more than one essential element was missing, the case was usually considered one of accidental manslaughter, for which a recompense of twenty silver *dalers* to be paid directly to the interested parties was stipulated (*dråp af wåda*, MB XXIX cap).[114] Certain circumstances concerning the perpetrator and the victim, the *modus operandi* or the site of the crime and the motive were considered to be aggravating, in which case the death by beheading stipulated for this particular crime was augmented by having the body of the executed person mutilated by breaking it on the wheel and in some cases by cutting off the condemned person's right hand before the execution. Aggravating circumstances could change the category of the crime. The most grievous *methods* included killing by sorcery, poi-

109 Seth 1984, p. 15.
110 Anners 1965, p. 125.
111 Anners 1965, p. 17, on the philosophy of the Enlightenment, see ibid. p. 173.
112 E.g. Bergman 1996, pp. 18–21.
113 Bergman 1996, p. 75.
114 Nehrman 1756, V cap.

soning or arson, while the *site* of the crime was an aggravating factor if it was committed in a place that was protected by the King's Peace, i.e. a local court, a church, the highway or the victim's home (MB XVII; MB XX). A relationship between the perpetrator and the victim might also aggravate the crime. In the Law of 1734 (as indeed already in King Christopher's Law of the Land) the killing of a close relative was made a separate criminal act (MB XIV:1). Particularly the simultaneous breaking of the Fourth and Fifth Commandments,[115] in other words patricide and matricide, was considered an extremely grievous act by the Criminal Code, for it violated "the love that one should feel for one's nearest and dearest". The requirement of loyalty and obedience imposed on subjects of the realm also meant that the killing of one's master or mistress or a servant of the Crown was considered aggravated manslaughter. [116]

Intentional homicide was commonly committed in a fit of temper (*brådskilnad*), in other words, without premeditation. In contrast, a murderer might lie in wait for a long time for an opportunity to carry out his deed against his unwary victim. In order that there should be no witnesses, the site of a murder was typically deserted, and the deed was committed clandestinely. Premeditation was not included in the essential elements of *murder* before the Law of 1734, which contained the following requirement: "if a man, or a woman, kill another furtively and clandestinely" (*Dräper man, eller qwinna, annan försåtliga och i löndom*, MB XII:1). Thereafter, murder was also distinguished from intentional homicide on the basis of malice aforethought, which could be proved by the murder weapon and other circumstances attendant upon the crime.[117] Both King Christopher's Law of the Land and the Law of 1734 also defined as murder any homicide committed against a victim who was helpless, in which case the killing was considered particularly reprehensible (MB XII:2). [118] Another especially grievous form of homicide was considered to be one that was committed in order to conceal a less serious crime. For example, infanticide committed in order to hide an illegitimate birth came under this category. [119]

Homicides (murders) that were inspired by motives of revenge, profit or greed were also considered to be exceptionally reprehensible. Therefore, killings committed for reward (contract murders) or in conjunction with robbery were classed among the most grievous types of

---

115 The numbering of the commandments throughout this work follows the Lutheran (and Roman Catholic) system. Thus the Fourth and Fifth Commandments correspond to the Fifth and Sixth Commandments respectively in Orthodox and most Protestant faiths.

116 Nehrman 1756, V:II:33, p. 230; V:II:42–48, 60 p. 240 ff; V:II: 63–64, p. 238 ff; V: III:30, p. 229; V:II:35–40, 66–67, p. 231 ff.

117 Nehrman 1756, V:II,56, p. 237. 1734 års lag, MB XII:1.

118 Nehrman 1756, V:I:30–46, pp. 209–213.

119 Nehrman 1756, V:II:77–79, p. 243. Matthias Calonii commenter öfver Landslagen. Högmåla balk, I–II cap.

homicide,[120] only surpassed in gravity by murder committed in order to allow a prisoner to escape or the killing of a shipwrecked person. The former was already aggravated by the fact that the mere wounding of a prison guard was a capital offence, the latter by the element of profit from another's misfortune.[121]

The Jurisdiction of the Courts in Homicide Trials[122]

Penal practice in the lower courts (the district courts: *häradsrätter*) was traditionally much more severe than in the higher instances; the courts of appeal (*hovrätter*) and the Council of Justice (*justitierevisionen*). The latter was created in the 1660s and replaced in 1789 by the Supreme Court (*Högsta domstolen*) – see Tables 5 and 6 on page XXX). All cases of homicide had to be submitted at least to the court of appeal, and depending on the circumstances the courts of appeal referred many cases to the King (represented by the Council of Justice and later the Supreme Court) for review. There were three simple factors that explain the differences in penal practice in the different instances: the limited jurisdiction of the district courts, the liberal interpretation of procedural law in the courts of appeal and the statutory criterion of the essential elements of a crime. The definition of crimes was strictly applied only in the higher instances, and, unlike the superior courts, the district courts had no power to take mitigating circumstances into consideration in making their judgments. The harsh penal practice adopted by the lower courts was completely in line with the criminal policy of deterrence promoted by the Crown. Therefore, the superior courts allowed them to deviate quite freely from the statutory rules of legal proof, the so-called legal theory of proof, which required two competent eyewitnesses or a confession by the perpetrator as a precondition of a conviction, and to convict defendants on the basis of weaker evidence that the law required. The court of appeal or the highest instance would then anyway commute the sentence to conform with the law. The judgments meted out by the superior courts were from the point

---

120 Nehrman 1756, V:II:65–70, p. 239 ff.
121 Cf. 1734 års lag, XIX:2; Nehrman 1756, V:II:75–76, p. 242.
122 This section is based on Koskivirta 2001, pp. 95–221. This section is based on Koskivirta 2001, pp. 95–221. E.g. Pihlajamäki 1997; Bergman 1996; Anners 1965; Modéer 1997; Liliequist 1991; Jägerskiöld 1964; Foucault 1977; Hood 1996; Bowers & Pierce 1980; Hay 1975; Wolfgang 1967b; Taussi Sjöberg 1996; Thunander 1993; Liliequist 1992; Kekkonen & Ylikangas 1982; Schmidt 1951; Phillpotts 1913; Antell 1892; Spierenburg 1984; van Dülmen 1985; Christie 1983; Olivectona 1891; Karonen 199b; Koskelainen 1995; Forsström 1997; Hirvonen 1997; Lappalainen 1998; 2000; Koskelainen 2001; Sharpe 1990; Ylikangas 1998–2000; Dereborg 1990; Nousiainen 1993; Ylikangas 1982a; Inger 1994; Inger 1976; Nehrman 1751–1759; Calonius 1800, 1801, 1802; Calonius, Commenter öfver Lagboken, I–II; Calonius (Arwidsson) 1833–36; Modée 1751–1803; Flintberg 1796–1803; Jusleen 1751, 1787; Norell 1800; Af Ugglas / Ugla 1780–1798; Schmedeman 1706.

of view of criminal and procedural law completely bound by statutory law: the fate of the accused was determined by the existence of a legally valid proof and the essential elements of the crime.

The jurisdiction of the courts of appeal was considerably limited by the Mitigation Statutes of 1753, 1756, 1762 and 1803 and by the procedural instructions sent to the courts by Gustav III. In practice, the rules concerning court procedure during the period studied in this work placed the final jurisdictional right in cases of homicide in the hands of the King. The courts of appeal were deprived of the right to commute the punishments awarded for *homicide*, that is to make the sanctions stipulated for this form of crime harsher or more lenient on the basis of the attendant circumstances. Similarly, cases in which the proof was in doubt were to be referred to the King. The granting of letters of safe conduct to escaped homicidal criminals had also been made the King's sole prerogative in the Constitution of 1720. The limitations on the jurisdiction of the courts of appeal culminated in 1778, when Gustav III deprived them of the final right to have criminals executed by requiring that all capital sentences be referred to the King, i.e. the Council of Justice.

The mitigation of sentences given to the principle defendants in homicide cases by Finnish courts of appeal was mainly based on either *deficiencies in the essential elements or in the proof, and not on extenuating circumstances*. Thus it was not literally a matter of mitigation, which meant adjusting the punishment stipulated by the law for a crime to fit the circumstances of the deed. The principles of adjustment were no longer applied except in the most exceptional cases.

In practice, the increased strictness in the mitigation process applied only to homicide cases. The sentencing practice for most other capital crimes in Sweden's higher courts, in fact, became more lenient during the Age of Enlightenment: it became ever rarer for the gravest sexual crimes, infanticides and burglaries to be punished with a capital sentence. For *proven* murder and intentional manslaughter, the penal practice based on the law remained just as harsh during the period from the end of the 1740s up to the Finnish War (1808—1809) as it had been before, and indeed it may have become more severe. This tightening-up in strictness is evident in the fact that in northern Savo and northern Karelia not even the Supreme Court pardoned a single principal defendant on the basis of extenuating circumstances from the death sentence in *legally proven* cases in this period. This indicates that not only the courts of appeal but also the Supreme Court adopted a stricter policy on the mitigation of sentences for homicide: the Criminal Code was applied ever more stringently to all such sentences. The Constitution of 1772 had excluded crimes that contravened "God's express commands" (*emot Guds klara ord*) from the royal prerogative of pardon. The mitigation implemented by both the courts of appeal and the King, the letters of safe conduct granted to runaways by the King and the royal prerogative of pardon were all in different ways contrary to the principle of the predictability of justice; they made the justice that was meted out unequal and arbitrary. [123] That is why the restrictions on the mitigating jurisdiction of the courts of appeal that took place during the period of this study, which were part of the continuing development of a system based on a hierarchical structure, centralization and delegation, [124] served to modernize the justice system in the long-term perspective. The circumscription of the possibility of mitigating the punishments prescribed for homicide – just like the limitations on the right of the courts of appeal to pass capital sentences that were legally binding – suggests that the judicial revolution was approaching its culmination at the conceptual level. It was a part of the process of the modernization of the justice system, the triumph of positive law and the predictability of justice, and it was reflected in a more professional, explicit and precise grip on the punishment of homicide.

The Legality and Predictability of Sentencing Practice[125]

What then was the penal system for homicide like? The penal practice for murder and intentional manslaughter (MB XII, XIV and XXIV) retained the Old Testament character of its legal principles throughout the period studied here, from the late 1740s to 1808. The system, which was bound to the *talio* principle of an eye for an eye and the institution of blood vengeance, manifested a long-standing continuity, which went back to a time even before the founding of the courts of appeal in the early decades of the seventeenth century. Without exception, all levels of justice required a life for a life in accordance with the Criminal Code for the above mentioned types of crime, providing that the essential elements were present, the accused person confessed and there were no strong extenuating circumstances attendant upon the crime. The application of criminal law to homicide in the superior courts was predictable throughout the period that has been studied here. In the case of the principal defendant it was based directly on statutory law. Thus the goals of consistency that were attached to the application of justice in conjunction with the establishment of the courts of appeal were undoubtedly achieved.

---

123   Foucault 1977.
124   Thunander 1993, p. 7.
125   This section is based on Koskivirta 2001, pp. 95–221

Table 1.

*Sentences for homicide. The sentences received by the principal defendants in ho-
micide cases in northern Savo and northern Karelia in the period 1748–1807 in
the different legal instances and the requirements for the sentence according to the
category of crime.*

Crime	The requirements for conviction in the highest instance *	The punishment received by the *main defendant* when the requirements for conviction were fulfilled
Murder MB XII	Presence of the essential elements + confession by the accused (if responsible).	– Death with mutilation, unconditionally and without exception in all instances. – No possibility of reprieve. – If the circumstances of the murder were extremely aggravating, or it was committed in conjunction with other crimes (robbery, rape, more than one victim), the King increased the sanctions stipulated by the law with supplementary forms of corporal punishment and infamy.
Intentional manslaughter MB XIV:1, XXIV:1,9	Presence of the essential elements + confession by the accused (if responsible).	– Death in all instances (with mutilation under MB XIV:1). – Mitigation of capital sentences under MB XIV:1 or XXIV, generally to a full *wergild* plus hard labour or maximum corporal punishment purely on the basis of extenuating circumstances, was exceptional. Most mitigation rulings were based the crime being recategorized by the superior courts because of the essential elements. (MB XXXIX:2:2.).
Intentional/unintentional manslaughter MB XXXIX:2	Presence of the essential elements + confession by the accused (if responsible) or two competent eyewitnesses; for capital sentences only confession by the accused.	– Death in all instances. – Death in the district court or, the court of appeal, mitigation to a full *wergild* by the King on the basis of either circumstances or the cause of death. – Death in the lower court, mitigation to a full *wergild* in the court of appeal. – A full *wergild* in both the district court and the court of appeal. – The variation in sentences was due to either the cause of death, the conditions of the crime or matters of proof, and it was based on the law.
Manslaughter in breach of the peace MB XX:1, XVII:7.	Presence of the essential elements + confession by the accused (if responsible).	– Death in all instances.

* *In practice, the evidence of two competent eyewitnesses was never sufficient for
a capital sentence.*

Despite the legality of the penal practice of the superior courts, several of the maxims then employed in restricting the scope of capital punishment are not to be found in written law: no more than one person was ever condemned for one homicide, nor was anyone ever sentenced without a confession on the basis of testimony by witnesses, not were escaped criminals who returned voluntarily even when they did not have a letter of safe conduct from the King. In all these cases, the King (through his royal courts) reprieved the condemned persons from the death penalty although in principle there was no normative justification for mitigation on the basis of these circumstances; in such cases the Criminal Code required the death penalty. The royal courts commuted the sentence to a full wergild or corporal punishment, in some cases supplemented by hard labour. The absence of certain mitigating circumstances from formal statutory law was part of the age's control policy, which was based on deterrence. Since the application of these extenuating circumstances made judicial practice considerably more lenient, the legislators probably thought that the publishing of the norms concerning mitigation would weaken the illusion of the inevitability of capital punishment that they sought to create in the eyes of the people. The covert nature of the justice meted out by the superior courts was reinforced by instructions disseminated to the courts of appeal through royal circulars ordering them to keep secret other kinds of procedural elements that restricted the practical application of the death penalty: for example, they were not to specify any of the extenuating circumstances to the condemned persons, nor were they allowed to inform them of the duration of any period of "confessional remand" to which they might be committed. "Confessional remand" meant incarceration of the accused with hard labour until such time as they confessed. This procedure, which had been employed in Swedish judicial practice since the 1540s, was made official in the Mitigation Statute of 1756.

In Sweden, the courts of appeal applied the procedure of mitigation that had been their traditional prerogative to some grievous forms of crime until the 1820s, and it was this long historical continuity which dated back to their founding in the second and third decades of the seventeenth century that rendered justice predictable to the people rather than the content of law, which was not made completely public. In this respect, the law that was applied can only be described as predictable in a pre-modern sense. For jurists, on the other hand, the law was made predictable in the modern sense as well by the fact that it was fairly firmly based on statutory law.

The popular illusion of the continuity of justice, however, was broken by three factors: the spread of the institution of confessional remand, the increased strictness of the reprieve policy in connection with the circumstances of the crime, and the gradual acceptance of partial confessions as constituting a full proof. Especially in the beginning, the increasing use of confessional remand became a trap for murderers, who thought that this would allow them to go unpunished for their crimes. A partial confession, for its part, meant the palliation of certain facts about the crime; an intentional crime might be claimed to have been an accident, committed while of unsound mind, or the *modus operandi* might have been presented as less brutal than it really was. The courts began increasingly to accept such incomplete confessions as a basis for capital sentences. On the other hand, the Criminal Code's penal system for homicide cannot be properly considered apart from the question of proof, which was inextricably connected with judicial procedure. However, before we turn to an examination of the crisis that developed around the matter of proof and procedure during the period of this study, we must describe the most important fundamental features of the qualitative and quantitative change that took place in homicide in eastern Finland during the last six decades

126 Koskivirta 2001, pp. 95–195 and notes.

Homicide in Eastern Finland and in the Western World in the Early Modern Age

How did the characteristics of homicides committed in eastern Finland compare with the main features of killing elsewhere in the western world at the beginning of the modern age? Several of the structural features of western European homicide have remained the same from the pre-industrial age down to the turn of the new millennium. The most typical type of killing is an act of manslaughter involving two young males. The reasons for the deed may appear trivial to an outsider in relation of the gravity and the consequences of the crime. One regular contributory factor to homicide was the excessive consumption of alcohol. There has also been a statistical connection between the availability of weapons and the homicide rate. This is so despite the fact that firearms were used less during the pre-industrial age than today. [127]

There have also been significant changes in the internal structures of homicide in western Europe over the ages. The most obvious of these is of course a decrease in the amount of this form of crime. However, the quantitative decrease was followed by a qualitative increase in the gravity of homicide. In the early years of the modern age there were very few murders, i.e. premeditated killings, unlike in the period after industrialization. Moreover, at least in towns, the most common scene of lethal violence was then the street or the tavern, whereas homicides today are most commonly committed in the home.[128] At least a quarter, in many cases indeed the majority, of modern homicides take place within the familiy.[129] In the pre-industrial period this proportion was well below a fifth in western countries generally; in most cases, the victim and the per-

---

127 Jansson 1998, pp. 4; 72; Stone 1983, p. 23 ff; Johansson 1997, pp. 221–225; Spierenburg 1996, p. 88; Spierenburg 2001; Thome 2001; Roth 2001; Monkkonen 2001; Thunander 1993, pp. 144–153; For the present-day United States, see Kleck 1993. The terms "pre-industrial" and "pre-modern" are used in this context to refer to the period preceding 1789.

128 Ibid.

129 Morris & Blom-Cooper 1967, pp. 31–32; Daly & Wilson 1988, pp. 18–27. The data relate to Britain, Philadelphia, Canada and Denmark from the1950s to the 1980s.

petrator were not closely related.[130] Even so, there is something common to both the pre-industrial age and modern times: ever since the beginning of the modern age right up to the most recent times, the most likely victim of familial violence has been the spouse of the perpetrator.[131]

Some of the characteristic features of homicide in eastern Finland during the last decades of Swedish rule differ completely from the general picture presented by Scandinavian and British research into the history of crime in the agrarian age: distinguishing features included the high incidence of premeditation in the killings (about one third of the homicides committed in northern Savo and northern Karelia can be regarded as murders), the large proportion of relatives and family members among the victims (also about a third), and the typical site of the crime, which was most commonly (in 44% of the cases) the home of the victim or the principal defendant. These are generally regarded as characteristics of urban homicide in modern times,[132] but, despite this coincidental resemblance, the chain of events that led this state of affairs in Savo and Karelia was certainly fundamentally very different from today's situation.

A Quantitative Survey of Homicide in Eastern Finland

The material for the research consisted of 198 violent deaths in the period 1748—1807.

Of the victims, 81 died in northern Savo and 117 in northern Karelia.[133] Ten of those who were killed in Karelia were Russian citizens. There were only two Swedish citizens killed by Russians, and of these, one case is not dealt with at all in the court of appeal material.

The homicides committed in northern Savo and northern Karelia are distributed unevenly, but from the provincial perspective the relative trend in homicidal cases is fairly clear. In northern Karelia, homicide prosecutions were quite frequent until the end of the 1760s (seven victims per year per 100,000 inhabitants)[134] During the last two decades of Swedish

---

130 Lane 1997, pp. 18–19; Sharpe 1981, p. 34. It is possible that this view of the paucity of lethal family violence is based on a classic misinterpretation in analysing relative crime rates or proportions. Since the level of all violent crime was extremely high in the Middle Ages and the early modern age everywhere in Europe, familial violence constituted merely a drop in the ocean. Nevertheless, its proportion in relation to the size of the population might have been fairly high. Daly & Wilson 1988, pp. 27–28; Lane 1997, p. 17.

131 Daly & Wilson pp. 19–20.

132 Cf. e.g. Keltikangas-Järvinen 1978, pp. 24–25.

133 The homicides have been classified according to the year and the locality in which they happened.

134 In the 1920s, the criminologist Veli Verkko defined the limit for a high homicide rate as four victims per year per 100,000 inhabitants. Although this may not be the most suitable yardstick to measure violence in the early modern age, the frequency of homicide had by the end of sixteenth century dropped to a level where this value can be considered a suitable boundary for "a high homicide rate". Even so, the amount of homicide in Karelia was not exceptionally high compared with some areas of Sweden and Finland in the sixteenth century and the beginning of the seventeenth century, such as Upland, Småland or Western Uusimaa. Cf. Ylikangas 1976b, pp. 88–140; Ylikangas 1988, pp. 130–134; Österberg 1991b, p. 12 ff; Österberg 1983, pp. 5–30; Jarrick & Söderberg 1994; Söderberg 1993.

rule, homicide in the region began to decline, reaching a figure of approx. 4.5 homicide victims per year per 100,000 inhabitants. It was mainly cases of spontaneous manslaughter that decreased, rather than murder. See Tables 2a and 2b and Maps 2 and 3.

Clearly fewer homicides were committed in northern Savo than in the neighbouring region of Karelia in the east. In the central parts of Savo (Pieksämäki, Rantasalmi, and Leppävirta) the homicide rate was approximately the same as in Stockholm in the eighteenth century or modern-day Finland (3.5 victims per year per 100,000 inhabitants).[135] Northern Savo also remained relatively non-violent up to the Finnish War (1808—09), apart from its northern and eastern fringes. In the easternmost parts of northern Karelia, the number of violent manslaughters was many times greater (in some places during the period studied here over ten per year per 100,000 inhabitants) than in the more peaceful areas of northern Savo.

The region of eastern Savo, which lay south of the area investigated in this study, was one of the most violent parts of the whole Swedish realm in the latter half of the eighteenth century.[136] However, the wave of violence did not sweep over the whole of Savo; in both the 1790s and in the period when Finland was an autonomous Grand Duchy of the Russian Empire (1809—1917), northern Savo was one of the least violent parts of Finland in terms of the number of homicides committed.[137]

In the mid-eighteenth century, the focus of violence was in the parishes that lay along the border with Russia, but it shifted after the end of the 1760s.[138] The long period of peace, which in places lasted from the Peace of Åbo (1734) until the War of Gustav III (1778—1790), certainly had some influence in curbing the killing, for the homicide rate in the parishes on the eastern border began to rise slightly once again during and after the War of Gustav III.[139] As violence abated in the frontier parishes in the period up to the 1770s, the front line of homicide became more firmly established in the hitherto more peaceful north of the region: the absolute figure for homicide in the parish of Liperi rose 14- to 15-fold in a period of twenty years. In this increase in homicide, almost every other case was a murder.

Although the city of Kuopio, which was founded in 1775, had a rather modest population during the period of this study,[140] the grip of violence rapidly took hold of the town and its immediate surroundings. Kuopio became a miniature centre of unrest, which was exacerbated by a burgeoning

135 Kaspersson 2000, p. 85. Cf. Kivivuori 1999, att. 6.
136 Sirén 1996, pp. 166–168; Koskivirta 1996.
137 Rautelin 1997, p. 187; Turpeinen in Ylikangas 1976, p. 19. Turpeinen's data are based on the population tables.
138 Koskivirta 1996, p. 50.
139 The development in the easternmost regions was different from that which took place in the kingdom overall, where the number of homicides decreased during the War of Gustav III. Cf. Ylikangas 1976, p. 43 ff.
140 Viitala 1997, p. 4; Sopanen 1975, pp. 26–27; Wirilander 1989, pp. 310–311; Katajala 1997, p. 52.

Map 2.

The number of homicides (murder and manslaughter) per year per 100,000 inhabitants in the period 1748–1807 in northern Savo and northern Karelia.

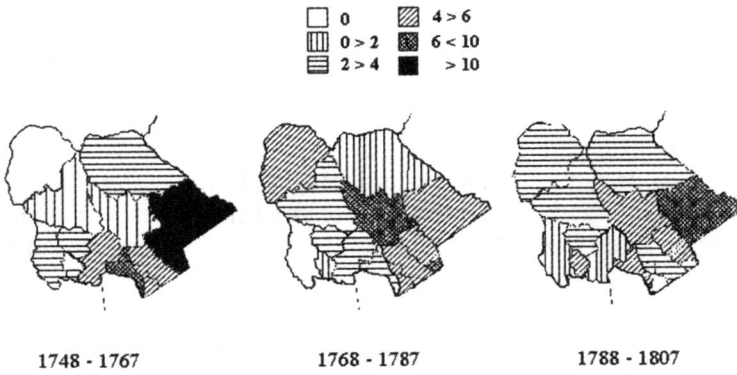

☐ 0	▨ 4 > 6
▦ 0 > 2	▨ 6 < 10
▤ 2 > 4	■ > 10

1748 - 1767   1768 - 1787   1788 - 1807

Map 3.

The number of murders in the period 1748–1807 in northern Savo and northern Karelia.

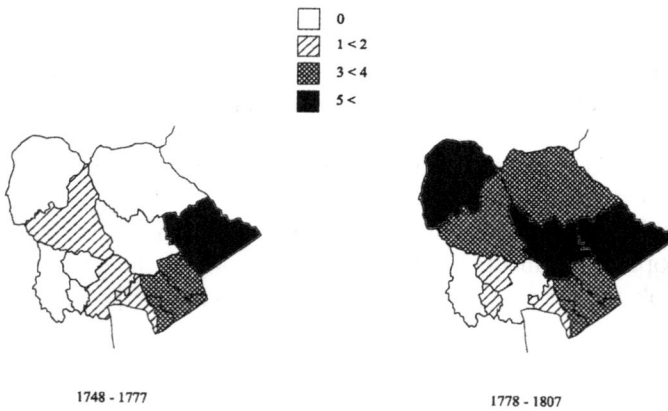

☐ 0	
▨ 1 < 2	
▨ 3 < 4	
■ 5 <	

1748 - 1777   1778 - 1807

Table 2a. Victims of homicide in absolute and proportional terms in northern Karelia in the years 1748–1807

Parish	Number of homicides 1748-67	Number of homicides 1768-87	Number of homicides 1788-1807	Number of homicides 1748-1807	Homicide rate per year per 100,000 inhabitants 1748-67	Homicide rate per year per 100,000 inhabitants 1768-87	Homicide rate per year per 100,000 inhabitants 1748-1807
Pielisjärvi	2	3	8	13	3.3	1.9	3.4	2.6
Ilomantsi	14	6	11	31	18.2	5.0	8.7	12.8
Liperi	1	15	14	30	0.8	7.4	5.3	5.1
Tohmajärvi	9	5	7	21	10.0	4.3	4.8	5.9
Pälkjärvi	3	2	1	6	15	8.1	3.9	9.6
Kitee+Kesäl.	5	7	4	16	4.2	4.5	2.5	4.0
Northern Karelia	34	38	45	117	6.8	4.7	4.5	5.3

Table 2b. Victims of homicide in absolute and proportional terms in northern Savo in the years 1748–1807

Parish	Number of homicides 1748-67	Number of homicides 1768-87	Number of homicides 1788-1807	Number of homicides 1748-1807	Homicide rate per year per 100,000 inhabitants 1748-67	Homicide rate per year per 100,000 inhabitants 1768-87	Homicide rate per year per 100,000 inhabitants 1748-1807
Iisalmi	0	7	9	16	0	4.8	3.8	2.7
Kuopio	3	8	10	21	1.8	3.0	2.8	2.8
Leppävirta	3	3	6	12	3.2	2.4	3.7	2.9
Pieksämäki	4	1	3	8	3.5	0.7	1.6	1.8
Joroinen	2	1	3	6	3.9	1.6	4.1	3.1
Rantasalmi	6	4	3	13	4.3	2.3	1.5	2.9
Kerimäki	2	1	2	5	7.9	3.0	4.4	4.7
Northern Savo	20	25	36	81	3.2	3.0	3.2	3.1

Sources: VMA: VHOA, Alistettujen asiain päätöstaltiot and designaatioluettelot for the years 1754–1813; MMA: KmLKa, Saapuneet kirjeet, Hovioikeus maaherralle for the years 1748–1775; RA: JKÄA: Kungliga remisser (Royal Circulars), Fånglistor (Lists of prisoners), E III cc, 1751–1779.

youth problem combined with a simultaneous increase in drunkenness. The latter problem had got out of hand after the deregulation of alcohol production.[141] The five killings committed in the city of Kuopio in the years 1776–1807 correspond to a rate of over 30 homicide victims per year per 100,000 inhabitants.[142] On the other hand, the southernmost parishes of northern Savo remained non-violent at least up till the Finnish War.

The Parties Involved

Homicides in eastern Finland mainly involved just two parties.[143] Gang violence, which raised its head in Southern Ostrobothnia in western Finland at the end of eighteenth century, is a characteristic of homicide in eastern Finland only in a few exceptional cases. The social status of the principal defendants was polarized particularly in northern Karelia between the "cream" and the "dregs" of this demographically fairly homogenous society: at one end, the independent peasant farmers, at the other, the dependent lodgers, the vagrants and the deserters from the armies of Russia and Sweden. The polarization was clearer the more common homicides, and especially murders happened to be in a particular place. The floating population was responsible for a third of the murders, but in northern Savo, where few murders were committed, the lower ranks of the landless population were indicted for them much less frequently than in Karelia.

Similarly, in northern Savo peasant farmers committed lethal crimes relatively less frequently than in Karelia, although the proportion of peasants involved in all forms of homicide rose at a dizzy speed as lethal crime increased in the northernmost parts of Savo in the 1780s and 1790s. It is possible that the phenomenon was connected with the growing risk of downward social mobility among the peasants and their incipient material impoverishment at a time when the ecological resources of the land were beginning to be strained to their utmost. The numbers of the peasants grew considerably more rapidly than the number of farms – and this process inevitably meant an expansion in the form of the family and an increase in the number of the male members in it.[144] Homicide was most rife in Finland during the 1790s in those areas where the growth in the size of the landless population was most rapid: Savo, Karelia and Ostrobothnia.[145] On the other hand, the number of farms also continued to increase considerably even

---

141 For the country as a whole, see Mäntylä 1995, pp. 187–189.
142 However, the population of the city was extremely small with only 751 inhabitants in 1800. Therefore, the assessment cannot be considered statistically reliable. Kuopio had no town court of its own; instead cases were tried in the District Court of the Parish of Kuopio, the sessions of which were held in the city. Mäntylä 1985, p. 152.
143 Cf. also Rautelin's similar evidence for 1791–95. Rautelin 1997, s. 193.
144 Wirilander 1989, pp. 93–94.
145 Rautelin 1997, pp. 196–197. Ylikangas 1998a.

at the end of the eighteenth century in the most violent parishes of both northern Savo and northern Karelia. [146]

Although soldiers came to constitute an extremely violent group in Sweden in the seventeenth century, [147] they did not yet make for a particularly disruptive element in the northern parts of eastern Finland around the mid-eighteenth century, for they were responsible for under a tenth of the killings there at most. The region obtained its own regular recruited force of light infantrymen during the War of Gustav II, and they took over the task of guarding the eastern frontier. The number of homicides committed by them then increased during the 1790s. [148]

The number of members of the estates (apart from the peasants) who were involved in homicides in eastern Finland was marginal: three members of the lower estates were the principal defendants in homicide cases, two of whom were found guilty of murder. Three members of the estates were victims of homicide in the area of this research: the wife of the curate of Joroinen, Gustav Hielman and two children of Barber-Surgeon Johan Fredrik Geisse.

The proportion of farmers involved in different kinds of killing can be considered high both in northern Savo (31% of the perpetrators, 37% of the victims) and in northern Karelia (46% of the perpetrators, 42% of the victims), and it remained considerable throughout the period of this study despite the rise in the number of the landless. This was partly a result of the eastern Finnish custom of registering all the adult children of a peasant farmer's stem family as "farmers" in the judicial sources. This social homogeneity particularly in southern Savo meant that there was less friction between different groups there than elsewhere. [149] Consequently, the criminal proclivities of the parties involved in homicide there were not necessarily determined by their social rank as clearly as in many other regions. The bipolar character of the social positions of those who were accused of the most grievous killings may nevertheless indicate that there was a reaction among the peasant population to demographic pressures and also a need to respond with violence to possible threats to their property from the lowest social groups. The validity of this conclusion will later be considered in the light of individual cases.

Violence is predominantly committed by men.[150] The major demographic factor describing fluctuations in homicidal crime is the proportion of the population constituted by the group most liable to commit crimes of violence: young males. The motivation of young men to commit lethal acts is considered to stem from a need to show off their prowess in public

146 Saloheimo 1980, p. 261; Wirilander 1989, pp. 98–99, 221–223.
147 Österberg 1983, pp. 5–30; Österberg 1991c, pp. 65–87; Liliequist 1999, pp. 182–183; Jansson 1998, p. 82; Karonen 1998, p. 169.
148 Saloheimo 1980, p. 307, pp. 474–502.
149 Cf. e.g. Wirilander 1989, pp. 81, 95–98; Waris 1999, pp. 61–62.
150 E.g. Spierenburg 1999, p. 141; Kaspersson 2000, p. 200.

as part of a competition for the favours of the opposite sex. [151] The growth in the population of Savo and Karelia caused an increase in the proportion of young males in the populace from the mid-eighteenth century on. [152] The increase in the amount and the brutality of homicide was more pronounced in those areas where the rise in the population was greatest and at a time when the large age groups that were born half-way through the century had grown to adulthood.

By the eighteenth century, this traditionally male type of crime had begun to find favour with women too; during the Great Northern War in the early eighteenth century, the proportion of women among the perpetrators of homicide in Finland rose to nearly ten percent,[153] while in Stockholm their numbers accounted for over a third of all killers. In Stockholm, this phenomenon was a result of an explosive increase in the number of so-called "suicidal murders" in the early eighteenth century, for it was mainly women who committed this form of homicide, which was born out of a combination of a taboo against suicide and a death wish. The motive for the deed was a desire to be executed. In the area of eastern Finland studied here, however, the female populace seems to have been totally unfamiliar with the practice of suicidal murder. It is likely that the rural community of eastern Finland and the kinship network there protected women better than urban life from loneliness, insecurity and exploitation – factors that are regarded as particularly instrumental in creating a fertile soil for suicidal murder. [154] On the other hand, the population tables and the judgment books do indicate that some women committed, or attempted to commit, suicide.

Women are nevertheless fairly well represented among the parties involved in homicide in eastern Finland: approximately one tenth of the perpetrators and over twenty percent of the victims were female, mostly wives of farmers and wives of dependant lodgers in Karelia. The significant involvement of women in homicidal crime is connected with the large number of killings committed within the family and the relatively high proportion of murders. [155] During the first half of the period studied, a third (5 out of 15) and in the second half 16—20% (4—5 out of 25) of the murders in Karelia were either directly committed or commissioned by women. The most ruthless of the killings perpetrated by Karelian women took place after 1780. [156] Women in Savo, on the other hand, were not involved in the wave of murder. Spontaneous acts of manslaughter committed by women were rare in both of these regions of eastern Finland.

---

151 Daly & Wilson 1988, p. 288. Cf. Jansson 1998, p. 77.
152 Wirilander 1989, pp. 72–75.
153 Kujala & Malinen 2001, p. 432.
154 Jansson 1998, p. 62.
155 Cf. Sharpe 1981, pp. 36–37 on the proportion of women involved in homicide inside and outside the family.
156 VMA: VHOA, Alistettujen asiain päätöstaltiot, Savon ja Karjalan lääni, v. 1791, Di 26, no 7; v. 1807, Di 45, no 4, 30; Alistusaktit, Savon ja Karjalan lääni, v. 1798, Ece 96, no 4; v. 1795, Ece 32, no 45.

Murder

The degree of premeditation in homicide in Karelia was extremely high by the standards of the age. The crimes that were ranked as most serious – murder, poisoning, clandestine manslaughter, and manslaughter in breach of the peace – constituted over a third of the homicides. In northern Savo, too, the proportion of murders rose towards the turn of the eighteenth and nineteenth centuries from less than a tenth to over a quarter. In Southern Ostrobothnia in the west of Finland murder was considerably rarer at the turn of the century than in northern and eastern Finland, but there, too, it became more common.[157]

In pre-industrial Europe, murders were extremely rare; most killings were committed in a fit of rage.[158] Where the proportion of murders did grow considerably in the eighteenth century, for example in Stockholm, the increase was due almost entirely to suicidal murders.[159] In eastern Finland at that time suicidal murders were a marginal, almost unknown, phenomenon. In this work, suicidal murder is regarded as a social problem specifically connected with urban life[160] and, as such, a phenomenon that should be kept distinct from other types of murder. Consequently, murder is regarded in the present work as excluding homicidal murder, and thus the claim that murder was a rare type of crime in pre-modern times is justified.

Women in eastern Finland were driven to murder by a wish for revenge and the desire to obtain an advantage particularly in conjugal relationships. Men, too, were induced to commit this most grievous of crimes by financial aspirations, such as the desire to obtain an inheritance or robbery, or by the need to avenge various denunciations that they regarded as bringing shame upon them. The most conspicuous feature of the murders was, however, the high incidence (in over 60% of the cases) of a family relationship between the parties involved.

The actual circumstance of a murder were extremely difficult to prove in court if the accused decided to deny it; after all, the essential elements of the crime required that it be committed clandestinely. Consequently the number of premeditated homicides was certainly much higher than the accompanying table indicates:[161]

---

157 Ylikangas 1976, pp. 15, 129.
158 To some extent the rarity of murder may be a statistical illusion, as Daly, Wilson and Kaspersson have indicated; when killing is rife and there is consequently a high homicide rate, murders tend to "get lost" in the material, although in reality they may have been as common as they are today. Jansson 1998, p. 49; Karonen 2000, p. 55 ff; Kaspersson 2000, p. 96 ff.
159 Kaspersson 2000, p. 96 ff.
160 Heikkinen 1996a, p. 49.
161 For example, it was in practice impossible to prove that a drowning was a violently inflicted death even if the circumstances pointed to homicide. Cf. VMA: VHOA, Alistusaktit, Savon ja Karjalan lääni, Ece 1807, no 85; MMA, KymLKa, Saapuneet kirjeet, v. 1758, Hovioikeus maaherralle, D 20 a1, no 21/3. See also e.g. VMA: VHOA, Alistettujen asiain päätöstaltiot, Kymenkartanon ja Savon lääni, v. 1773, Di 9, no 10.

Table 3a.

Number of victims of murder compared with the number of victims of all homicides in northern Karelia in the periods 1748–1777 and 1778–1807

Parish	Number of murders / number of all homicides, years			Crime rate per year per 100,000 pop. 1748–1807	
	1748–1777	1778–1807	1748–1807	Murders	Intentional manslaughters
Pielisjärvi	0 / 4	3 / 9	3 / 13	0.6	2.0
Ilomantsi	7 / 17	6 / 14	13 / 31	4.3	9.9
Liperi	0 / 7	10 / 23	10 / 30	1.7	4.7
Tohmajärvi	4 / 11	3 / 16	7 / 27	1.7	2.1
Kitee	4 / 10	3 / 6	7 / 16	1.7	2.1
Northern Karelia	15 / 49 (31%)	25 / 68 (37%)	40 /117 (34%)	1.4	3.9

Table 3b.

Number of victims of murder compared with the number of victims of all homicides in northern Savo in the periods 1748–1777 and 1778–1807

Parish	Number of murders / number of all homicides, years			Crime rate per year per 100,000 pop. 1748–1807	
	1748–1777	1778–1807	1748–1807	Murders	Intentional manslaughters
Iisalmi	0 / 3	6 / 13	6 / 16	1.0	1.7
Kuopio	1 / 8	3 / 13	4 / 21	0.5	2.3
Leppävirta	0 / 6	1 / 6	1 / 12	0.2	2.7
Pieksämäki	0 / 4	0 / 4	0 / 8	0.0	1.8
Joroinen	0 / 3	1 / 3	1 / 6	0.5	2.6
Rantasalmi	1 / 9	0 / 4	1 / 13	0.2	2.7
Kerimäki	1 / 3	1 / 2	2 / 5	1.9	2.8
Northern Savo	*3 / 36 (8%)*	*12 / 45 (12%)*	*15 / 81 (19%)*	*0.6*	*2.5*

Source: Provincial archives of Vasa: Archives of the Vasa Court of Appeal, Enquiry indexes (designations förteckningar) and judgment records of referred cases for the years 1754–1813. Provincial archives of St. Michels: Archives in the Office of provincial administration of Kymmenegård and Savolax, The referrals of the judgment records of the Åbo Court of Appeal for the years 1748–1775. The National Archives of Finland: Population tables.

Like the other forms of homicide, murders were concentrated in northern Karelia, where there were forty of them, compared with fifteen in northern Savo. [162] In the border parish of Ilomantsi there were nearly as many murders prosecuted during the period covered by this study as in the whole of northern Savo. In the years 1748—67, almost eight persons per year per 100,000 inhabitants were victims of murder alone. The relative number of victims began to drop in the parish in the 1760s, but relatively more murders were committed there than elsewhere throughout the period studied here.

In Liperi, on the other hand, there was not a single murder trial during the first half of the research period, but in the second half at least ten murders were committed in this parish. Although the number of murders committed by the Karelians did not necessarily increase everywhere towards the end of the century, the nature of premeditated killings became more grievous throughout that region.

In northern Savo, there was only murder case per decade in the thirty-year period beginning in 1784, making a total of three. In the last three decades of Swedish rule, the number quadrupled. In northern Savo, too, there was one particular parish that was responsible for the increase in the number of murders: Iisalmi together with its associated chapelries. In the years 1748—1777, not a single murder was prosecuted there, while between 1778 and 1807 the figure rose to six.

Murder cast its shadow most darkly over the extreme northern and eastern parts of this outlying province, where the population increase was also most rapid. As a result of expanding settlement, several chapelries were split off from the mother parishes of Iisalmi and Liperi during the research period. Because the number of government authorities could not keep up with the growth in the population, their surveillance of the people probably became more superficial, especially in geographically spread-out and sparsely populated administrative units. A murderer might assess the risk of getting caught to be smaller there than in more strictly administered regions. The similar trend that took place in Ilomantsi and Liperi was exacerbated by a religious division within the populace: the area was inhabited by people of both the Greek Orthodox and the Lutheran faiths. Furthermore, it was extremely difficult to recruit decent Finnish-speaking Orthodox priests and other church servants, who could have had a controlling influence on the behaviour of their flocks, to work in the outlying parts of Karelia. [163]

162 During the period covered by this research, the district courts also dealt with thirteen cases of homicide which had actually taken place outside the period.
163 Saloheimo 1980, pp. 420–428.

**

The "laws" describing quantitative fluctuations in homicidal crime that were formulated by the Finnish criminologist Veli Verkko in the 1940s have been extensively modified over recent decades. A growth in homicide is generally assumed to be composed mainly of acts of impulsive manslaughter carried out by young males on victims that were not known to them. Originally, Verkko assumed that the absolute number of women involved in homicide remained relatively stable, in which case the ratio of killings committed by women would decrease as the rate of homicidal crime rose. Since then, a similar claim has been made for murder, the manslaughter of relatives and homicides committed by the higher social classes and by insane persons. Daly and Wilson, who have analysed this phenomenon, state that such regularities are prone to exceptions.[164] For example, an examination of the area in eastern Finland dealt with here reveals that such statistical correspondences do not hold there. When homicide increased, for example in Iisalmi and Liperi, the rise was not typically made up of cases of intentional manslaughter, nor were young men in the vanguard of the trend. As lethal aggression grew, both the absolute and the proportional numbers of murders increased significantly. And, irrespective of the amount of other kinds of homicide, murder mainly took place between members of the same kin or family. However, in northern Karelia homicide within the kin or the family was much more frequent than in northern Savo, where anyway homicides of all kinds were rarer. These individual exceptions to the general global picture naturally do not mean that we should abandon the models based on extensive statistical material. But the exceptions do require some explanation.

---

164 Daly & Wilson 1988, pp. 284–286. On the social groups involved, see also Wolfgang 1967b, p. 6.

Homicide and Penal Certainty

The Increasing Brutality of the Deeds

During the early years of the modern age, many murders were committed in conjunction with robbery, some in the cities – Amsterdam in particular – but above all in the countryside, where the settlement was sparse, the law weak, and deep forests offered hiding places. The victims were usually ordinary people and the booty small. [165] Murder with robbery, which was classified in the jurisprudential literature as particularly reprehensible because of its motive, did not constitute a significant part of the culture of homicide in the years of peace during the eighteenth century in the kingdom of Sweden. Only four murders with robbery were actually prosecuted in Finland during the Great Northern War, [166] but in practice this kind of violence was rife during the years of war and occupation. Moreover, it is known that Russian robbers constantly harassed the remote communities of *Raskolnik*[167] settlers in the late 1740s. [168] There were apparently no prosecutions for any of the murders with robbery in northern Karelia before the mid-1770s. The unwillingness to bring such cases to trial was probably influenced by the people's inurement to such killings in the recent period of occupation during the Lesser Wrath (1742–43), when many partisans on both the Russian and the Swedish side had committed deeds of this kind. Perhaps the trend was also reinforced by folk memories of the violent plundering by the nobles during the Great Wrath (1713–21) and above all in the years of famine in the late seventeenth century. [169]

There were certainly a few persons journeying in the border regions of southern Savo and Kymenlaakso who were robbed and murdered in

---

165 Lane 1997, pp. 16, 20–21; Spierenburg 1994, p. 712.
166 Kujala & Malinen 2001, p. 431.
167 The *Raskolniki*, or Old Believers, were a sect that seceded from the national Russian Orthodox Church over reforms in liturgy and forms of worship in the seventeenth century.
168 Björn 1993, p. 155; Saloheimo 1980, p. 303.
169 Katajala 1994.

the 1750s.[170] The forested tracts of eastern Finland offered excellent opportunities for robbing travellers. Robberies were by no means rare in the period of this study, but there were hardly any killings in connection with them in northern Karelia and northern Savo before the 1770s. This may indicate two things concerning the risk of getting caught: it was not necessary to murder the persons who had been robbed because the risk of being punished for the robbery itself was slight, and not all murders with robbery came to the cognisance of the authorities.

In the area studied here, trials for murder with robbery gradually became more common on the threshold of the last quarter of the century. In Southern Ostrobothnia, this form of crime spread after the Finnish War from the second decade of the nineteenth century on. In the 1820s the number of trials there surpassed the level of Savo and Karelia several decades before.[171]

The sites and dates of murders with robbery in Savo and Karelia 1748–1807:

(Ilomantsi 1748)
Kerimäki 1772
Iisalmi Kiuruvesi 1783
Old Finland:[172] Räisälä 1788 (perpetrator from Leppävirta)
Kuopio 1791
Iisalmi 1795
Kitee Oravisalo 1797

Robbery was also one major motive among others in murders in Ilomantsi 1765, Pälkjärvi 1786, Ilomantsi 1787, Pielisjärvi 1788, Ilomantsi 1805, Liperi 1806

In 1772, Pauli Tiilikainen of Kerimäki together with Iivana Tarnanen of Liperi raped, strangled and robbed Maria Nyberg, a woman who was previously unknown to them, and who was described in the judgment records as a "female person" (*qvinsperson*).[173] She had asked them to row her over a lake. Tiilikainen and Tarnanen had slain her when they discovered that she was carrying a considerable sum of money with her. In the same year, a mother and her four

---

170 VMA: VHOA, Alistettujen asiain päätöstaltiot, Kymenkartanon ja Savon lääni, v. 1754, Di 1, no 12; MMA: KymLKa, Saapuneet kirjeet v. 1754, Hovioikeus maaherralle, D 16 a1, no 47; ibid. v. 1760, D 22 a1, no. 24:1. RA: JRR 3.7.1754.

171 Cf. Ylikangas 1976, pp. 94-95. In that material, which comprises 239 homicides, there are ten cases of murder with robbery, while in this research robbery was the motive behind seven murders.

172 Old Finland (*Gamla Finland*) was the name given to those parts of eastern Finland ceded to Russia by Sweden in the peace treaties of Nystad and Åbo.

173 This appellation was used to designate a woman of dubious morality.

children died as a result of murder with robbery and arson in the newly settled area of Paltamo in the northern part of the region researched here. [174]

In the village of Heinäjärvi in Kiuruvesi, a crofter called Matti Huttunen killed Heikki Tikkanen, a farmer who was travelling home, with an axe in May 1783. The clothes and silver coins the victim was carrying in a bark knapsack were stolen. It is probable that the brothers–in–law of the victim, who hoped to inherit from him, had Huttunen murdered.[175] The body of a soldier called Antti Järppe, who had travelled to Kuopio to sell a horse, was found in Rautalampi at the end of 1791, months after he had disappeared. The victim had been killed and robbed. In Iisalmi, six peasants used logs and axes to slay a deserter called Heikki Grön, who was a stranger in the locality. As a pretext, they said they were trying to capture an outlaw, although their real motive, robbery, was quite apparent according to witnesses.[176]

Travellers like Maria Nyberg and Heikki Grön or deserters from outside the locality could be murdered without their bodies ever being found, or even being missed. Such crimes could easily go undetected even by the people of the times. The criminal's profit-seeking goal and the victim's alienness and unfamiliarity with the local roads is particularly apparent when the latter was a Russian who had strayed over to the Swedish side of the border.

Two brothers-in-law, Olli Pitkänen, a dependent lodger, and Antti Laukainen, a farmer, robbed and murdered Timofei Molldokainen, a Russian bag merchant from Suojärvi, with an axe in January 1797 in the parish of Kitee. The body was hidden in the ice. The victim had asked Pitkänen to show him the way and help carry his load on his journey to Savo. Merchandise belonging to the victim was found in the possession of Pitkänen, who had also sold off some of the goods. With the money he thus obtained, he had moved to his home parish of Nilsiä. [177]

Nuutti Parikka, returning from St Petersburg, where he had been trading, was found dead on his sledge in the hinterland of Räisälä in 1788. The horses of the victim had also been strangled. It turned out that Parikka had been travelling from the city in the company of a one Aatu Kähkönen, a peasant farmer from Leppävirta. Goods stolen from the victim were found in the possession of Kähkönen in Tuppuralanmäki: a barrel of sugar and an ox hide. The web of evidence tightened around Kähkönen, but he denied having murdered Parikka. Despite the lack of a confession, the Russian Land Court of Käkisalmi found him guilty of murder with robbery and sentenced him to

---

174 RA: JRR 30.4. 1777, fol 467. VMA: VHOA, Alistusaktit, Savon ja Karjalan lääni, v. 1779, Ece, no 6; Alistettujen asiain päätöstaltiot, Savon ja Karjalan lääni, v. 1776, Di 11, no 57; v. 1777, Di 12, no 25; v. 1783, Di 18, no 2.RA: JRU, 30.4.1777, no 105; RA: JRR 22.9.1772, f. 751b.

175 VMA: VHOA, Alistettujen asiain päätöstaltiot, Savon ja Karjalan lääni, v. 1784, Di 19, no 40; v 1785, Di 20, no 1; 32.

176 VMA: VHOA, Alistusaktit, Savon ja Karjalan lääni, v. 1794, Ece 28, no 1; v. 1792, Di, no 89; v. 1797, Ece 41, no 4; Alistettujen asiain päätöstaltiot, Savon ja Karjalan lääni, v. 1796, Di 31, no 84; v. 1797, Di 32, no 4

177 VMA: VHOA: Alistusaktit, Savon ja Karjalan lääni Ece 52, no 10. Alistettujen asiain päätöstaltiot, Savon ja Karjalan lääni, v. 1798, Di 33, no 14; v. 1799, Di 34, no 10.

have his right hand cut off and to be beheaded, with his body to be broken on the wheel after execution. Because of the nationality of the accused, the case was referred to the Vasa Court of Appeal on the Swedish side. Kähkönen died in the Crown Prison in Kuopio before the Court of Appeal passed judgment, and the case was dropped. [178]

Murders with robbery were most commonly committed in the backwoods of the sparsely populated hinterland, where the risk of getting caught was clearly smaller than in more densely settled areas. There were no witnesses to such a robbery, since the only person who could have reported it, the victim, had been killed. None of the accused in trials of murder with robbery confessed to the crime without being subjected to strong pressure, and in each case at least one of the main defendants avoided the punishment stipulated by the law. Potential criminals naturally remembered this ineffectiveness of the legal system.

A murder committed in order to allow a prisoner to escape was categorized as an even more grievous type of homicide than murder with robbery in the classification of crimes of the times. [179] During the period of this study, prisoners killed a total of six persons in three escape attempts. One of these occasions claimed four lives.

Murders committed in connection with the escape of prisoners:

Ilomantsi—Pielisjärvi 1766
Liperi 1806 (four victims)
Joroinen (prisoner from Rantasalmi) 1807

In 1766 three prisoners beat to death a peasant called Juho Heikura as he was transporting them from Ilomantsi to Pielisjärvi. Immediately after the murder, two of the men managed to escape from the clutches of the law. The third, a vagrant called Olli Turtinen, however, was caught and brought to justice. He stubbornly denied any participation in the murder. Because two of the accused were absent, the court adjourned the case for a year and a night in accordance with MB XXVI. When, the following year, Turtinen persisted in denying his guilt at the Pielisjärvi District Court, the case against him had to be adjourned *sine die* because there were no witnesses.

Since the other two culprits had escaped and had not applied for a letter of safe conduct within the prescribed limit of a year and a night, they were declared outlaws in the territory of the realm on the basis of MB XVI:2 and XXVII. The court ordered that a wergild (a blood-money fine) be distrained upon the property of each of them. [180]

---

178 VMA: VHOA, Alistettujen asiain päätöstaltiot, Savon ja Karjalan lääni, v. 1788, Di 23, no 42. RA: JR, 8.8.1788, no 13.

179 Nehrman 1756, V:II:75, p. 241.

180 MMA: KymLKa, Saapuneet kirjeet, v. 1767, Hovioikeus maaherralle, D 29 a 1, no 67.1, 12.10.1767. VMA: VHOA, Alistettujen asiain designaatioluettelot and päätöstaltiot, Kymenkartanon ja Savon lääni, v. 1767, Di 6, no 48; v. 1768, Di 7, no 8; v. 1769, Di 7, no 6; v. 1772, Di 9, no 5; v. 1773, Di 9, no 9; v. 1775, Di 10, no 4.

Contract murders constituted another category of homicide that was regarded as one of the gravest by the public's sense of justice of the times. Like murders with robbery, they became more common in the area of this study in the 1780s. They claimed the lives of at least eight or nine Karelians and one victim in northern Savo.

Contract murders in the Province of Savo and Karelia 1748–1808 (some also listed under murders with robbery):

Ilomantsi 1757, 3 victims

Iisalmi, Kiuruvesi 1783 (mentioned above)

Pälkjärvi 1786

Pielisjärvi 1789
(possibly also Pielisjärvi 1794)

Kitee 1795

Ilomantsi 1805

Ilomantsi 1806

The threshold to crime was also made lower for those who commissioned and committed contract murders by the fact that they were convinced that they would escape the legal consequences of their deeds.[181] The chances of proving the guilt especially of a person who commissioned a contract murder were extremely limited if he or she obtained an alibi for the time of the crime. None of those who contracted another to commit a murder on their behalf confessed to their crime, whereas two of those who actually committed contract murders broke down under cross-examination.[182] As a last resort, a contract murderer could avoid the consequences of his crime by fleeing across the border into Russia out of the reach of justice. That is what a triple murderer called Teppo Huurinainen from Ilomantsi did in 1758.

The most serious types of crime all spread over a wide area at the same time. Since it was not a matter of individual local cultures, the roots of the phenomenon must be sought not only in psychological variables but also in some kind of structural impetus, in other words the breakdown of restraints. The main cause was a juridical one: the system of proof with its judicial loopholes that was then applied, i.e. the so-called theory of proof, which required either the concurring testimonies of two competent eyewitnesses against the defendant, or a confession by the latter. The use of torture to extort a confession from the accused was finally prohibited in the 1770s. In addition to the juridical reasons, in eastern Finland there were also social factors that directly paved the way for the increase in the brutality of the homicides committed there. The most significant of

---

181 Cf. Ylikangas 1976, p. 97.
182 VMA: VHOA, Alistettujen asiain päätöstaltiot, Savon ja Karjalan lääni, v. 1788 Di 23, no 2; v. 1787, Di 22, no 5.

these was the formation of village communities by vagrants, the numbers of whom had grown along with the population increase. These rootless, landless persons became estranged from their own families and the unofficial social control that the latter imposed. It was relatively easy and cheap to recruit criminals from this element of the population.[183] After all, a murder could hardly drag such a person any lower down the social scale, but it might make him a great deal richer.[184] Those men who undertook to commit murder for reward were farmhands or dependent lodgers who had already gone down the road of crime. Selling their services to commit murder was just the last step that turned them into professional criminals.

The more reprehensible the crime was, the more certain it was that confession would cost the accused his or her life. This fact led to a contrary end result: the graver the type of homicide, the more likely it was that the *actor moralis* would deny his guilt. In consequence, the legal repression of the most ruthless forms of homicide was particularly ineffective. Murder with robbery and contract murder were concentrated in those areas where the homicide rate was otherwise high. Some kind of centrifugal force cast the most grievous murders committed for personal gain out to the furthest corners of the province, the administrative periphery on and beyond the eastern border as well as into the northern greater parish of Iisalmi, where the expansion in settlement directed itself. With the exceptions of Iisalmi, Kuopio and the eastern border parish of Kerimäki, northern Savo was completely spared any cases of murder with robbery or contract murder; indeed, the nature of homicide there was altogether less brutal than in those regions that were also quantitatively more violent.

Problems in Obtaining a Proof and the Debilitation of Repression[185]

In the rules of judicial procedure (Rättegångs Balk = RB) of the Law of 1734, a conviction required the concurring testimonies of two competent eyewitnesses or a confession by the accused (RB XVII:29—33). For

---

183 Cf. e.g. Berkowitz 1962, pp. 316–317 on alienation as a factor that increases aggression.
184 Cf. Elias (1939) 1994, p. 159. Elias believed that the risk of being excluded from social life was extremely effective in inhibiting the discharging of aggressive instincts. In practice, this amounts to the same thing as unofficial social control.
185 This section is based on Koskivirta 2001, pp. 95–221. E.g. Pihlajamäki 1997; Bergman 1996; Anners 1965; Modéer 1997; Liliequist 1991; Jägerskiöld 1964; Foucault 1977; Hood 1996; Bowers & Pierce 1980; Hay 1975; Wolfgang 1967b; Taussi Sjöberg 1996; Thunander 1993; Liliequist 1992; Kekkonen & Ylikangas 1982; Schmidt 1951; Phillpotts 1913; Antell 1892; Spierenburg 1984; van Dülmen 1985; Christie 1983; Olivectona 1891; Karonen 199b; Koskelainen 2001; Sharpe 1990; Ylikangas 1998–2000; Dereborg 1990; Nousiainen 1993; Ylikangas 1982a; Inger 1994; Inger 1976; Nehrman 1751–1759; Calonius 1800, 1801, 1802; Calonius, Commenter öfver Lagboken, I–II; Calonius (Arwidsson) 1833–36; Modée 1751–1803; Flintberg 1796–1803; Jusleen 1751, 1787; Norell 1800; Af Ugglas / Ugla 1780–1798; Schmedeman 1706.

capital crimes, it was also necessary that the circumstances should support the confession (RB XVII:36), [186] The competence of witnesses was further strictly regulated (RB XVII:7),[187] but in capital cases, incompetent witnesses could also be heard without their taking an oath (RB XVII:9). Strong circumstantial evidence and the testimony of one eyewitness was enough for only a half proof of the guilt of the accused. This meant that for serious crimes the case had to be adjourned *sine die* (*absolutio ab instantia*, RB XVII:32), and in practice the accused could return home a free man. Because of this, it was necessary that the judges should try to get the accused to confess in order that the justice system might function properly. [188]

In his work *The Knife Fighters*, Heikki Ylikangas has shown how this principle of legal testimony constituted a jurisdictional loophole and paralysed legal repression at the turn of the eighteenth and nineteenth centuries in Southern Ostrobothnia. [189] Similar problems of proof connected with denial of guilt and the silencing of witnesses also led to a deep crisis in crime prevention in Savo and Karelia half-way through the eighteenth century: only a third of the indictments for the most grievous crimes of homicide were proved. Based on the number of victims, in northern Savo approximately a quarter, and in northern Karelia, a third of the homicides committed between 1748 and 1807 went unpunished because of the lack of valid proof. In theses cases, it was not possible to assemble a legal proof despite strong circumstantial evidence pointing to the accused's guilt. In northern Karelia six out of ten, and in northern Savo two out of five, of these crimes were categorized as aggravated.

In practice, the majority of murderers in Savo and Karelia avoided the death penalty and indeed any kind of punishment. Only 23 (31%) of the 75 principal defendants in murder trials were sentenced to be executed in the court of appeal. In the years 1748–77 a quarter of the murders, and in 1778–1807 a third, led to a capital sentence in the highest legal instance, although in the lower courts over half (53%) of the principal defendants had been sentenced to death: of the capital sentences given for murder, only a little over a half (58%) were upheld in the highest instance.

---

186 See also Nehrman (Ehrenstråle) 1759, X:60, p. 185
187 Nousiainen 1993, p. 255.
188 Nehrman (Ehrenstråle) 1759, IX:48, p. 149.
189 Ylikangas 1998a.

Sentences given for grievous forms of homicide

Table 4.

The punishments for murder (MB XII:1), poisoning (MB XVII:1), clandestine man-slaughter (MB XXVII:1) and murder in breach of the peace (MB XX:1) given in the district courts and courts of appeal in the years 1748–1807 according to the number of principal defendants.[190] The material is based on homicides committed in the Province of Savo and Karelia in the years 1748–1807.

Period Court Punishment	1748–1777 District court Ct. of appeal [191]		1778–1807 District court Ct. of appeal		Total 1748–1807 District court Ct. of appeal	
Death with mutila-tion, MB XII:1, XX:1	10	6	30	17	40	23
Adjournment sine die + confessional remand, RB XVII:32	–	3	–	8	–	11
Adjournment sine die, RB XVII:32	5	1	11	9	16	10
Acquittal, RB XVII: 29 or 33	3	6	6	8	9	14
Defendant not responsible or prema-turely deceased	3	3	2	4	5	7
Defendant escaped: outlawed, etc., MB XXVI:1	2	4	0	1	2	5
Clandestine man-slaughter. Parish fine, MB XXVII:1	1	1	1	2	2	3
Royal mitigation to corporal punishment and hard labour[192]	–	0	(1)*	2	1	2
Total	24	24	51	51	75	75

*Previously sentenced by the district court to a year's imprisonment for participation in a homicide in breach of the peace.

Sources for Table 4: VMA: VHOA, Alistettujen asiain päätöstaltiot ja designaatio-luettelot 1754–1813; MMA: KymLKa, Saapuneet kirjeet, Hovioikeus maaherralle, 1748–1775.

190 This chart is based on the perpetrators, i.e. the persons directly involved in carrying out the crimes, including in cases of contract murder both the contracting parties. Persons accused of minor involvement or complicity are excluded. Each accused person has been included only once irrespective of the number of his or her victims.

191 The instance in which the sentences were passed.

192 For murder, a capital sentence was mitigated by Royal pardon for the other principal defendants if one of them was sentenced to death in the highest instance. In practice, an accomplice in a murder was always reprieved and had his or her sentence commuted to lifelong hard labour and maximum corporal punishment.

Only a third, altogether 25 out of 75 principal defendants, were sentenced to some kind of punishment for murder in the highest instance. The small number of convictions was purely a result of difficulties in obtaining a legally valid proof. The avoidance of punishment was a result of an acquittal in the superior court, an adjournment sine die or the accused escaping. Assuming only one principal accused for each case of grievous homicide (totalling 55 victims altogether), only 40% of these were punished with the death penalty stipulated by the law.

The legal repression of intentional manslaughter and violent unintentional manslaughter was more effective than in the case of murder. In the period 1748–1777, altogether 21 out of 74 (» 28%) of the principal defendants in cases of intentional or unintentional manslaughter escaped the legal consequences of their actions, while during the years 1778–1807, 29 out of 84 (» 35%) succeeded in this – see Table 5. If we ignore differences in the forms of capital punishment, the penalties implemented for manslaughter were more numerous and harsher than those for murder, for which over half the cases resulted in no conviction. This was because the perpetrator of a spontaneous killing was more likely to confess to the charge brought against him than a calculating murderer.

Table 5.

The legal punishments for manslaughter in the district courts and the courts of appeal in northern Savo and northern Karelia in the period The chart shows the numbers of the perpetrators.

Punishment	1748–1777 District court Ct. of appeal		1778–1807 District court Ct. of appeal		1748–1807 District court Ct. of appeal	
Death with mutilation, MB XIV:1	5	3	9	4	14	7
Death, MB XXIV; MB XXXIX:2	30	10	28	11	58	21
Wergild / corporal punishment, MB XXXIX:2, XXV:2	9	14*	5	12*	14	26*
Wergild / corporal punishment, MB XXVIII: 2–3 and MB XXX (2 cases)	3	3	7	6	10	9
Royal mitigation to hard labour and a wergild and maximum corporal punishment	–	7	–	2	–	9
Royal mitigation to a wergild and corporal punishment	–	7	–	4	–	11
Royal commitment to confessional remand, RB XVII:32	–	0	–	3	–	3
Adjournment *sine die*, RB XVII:32	4	5	13	10	17	15

Acquittal, RB XVII: 29, 30, 33 §§	11	11	12	18	23	29
Defendant escaped / outlawed, MB XXVI:1	4	5	1	1	5	6
Other fine (MB XXXV), self-de-fence, MB XXV:1, XXVI:4	3	4	2	5	5	9
Not known	1	1	1	1	1	2
Total	74	74	84	84	158	158

Sentences passed by the courts of appeal. Those who received a royal reprieve and had their sentences mitigated to a wergild or maximum corporal punishment are listed separately.

Sources for Table 5: VMA: VHOA, Alistettujen asiain päätöstaltiot ja designaatio-luettelot 1754–1813; MMA: KymLKa, Saapuneet kirjeet, Hovioikeus maaherralle, 1748–1775.

Despite its legality, the penal system for homicide was anything but comprehensive; in the courts of appeal, circumstantial evidence alone was not enough for a conviction. The strict application of the legal theory of proof to legal sentences made what had previously been indisputable legal certainty into weak repression in some places. There was a clear connection between penal certainty and the quality and quantity of the homicide in those areas of eastern Finland where there were few homicides, the regions of Pieksämäki and Joroinen, where penalties were implemented much more stringently than in the most violent localities such as Ilomantsi in northern Karelia and Liperi after the 1770s – see Figures 1a–1d. In the latter parishes, the characteristics of the crimes were also patently more grievous than in the Savo parts of the province. The connection between weak official control and an increase in homicide also manifested itself in a serious way at the same time in Southern Ostrobothnia in western Finland. The two manifestations of the phenomenon had common roots in the application of procedural law in the Kingdom of Sweden at the time.

Figure 1a.

Murder rate (per year per 100,000 inhabitants) and the proportion of punished homicide in the parishes of northern Savo and northern Karelia.

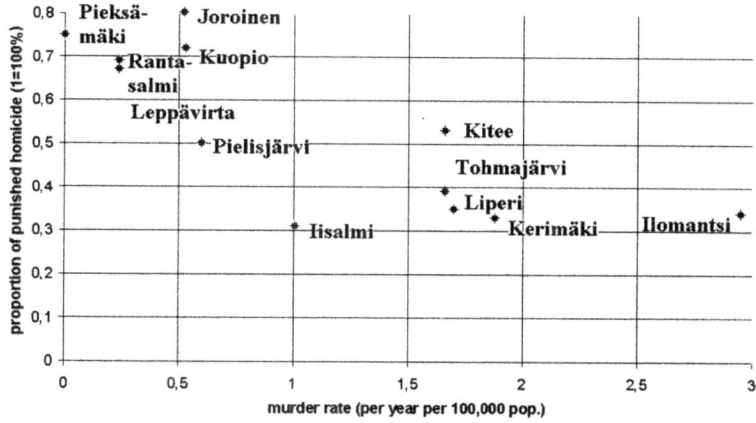

Figure 1b.

Murder rate (per year per 100,000 inhabitants) and the proportion of unpunished homicide in the parishes of northern Savo and northern Karelia.

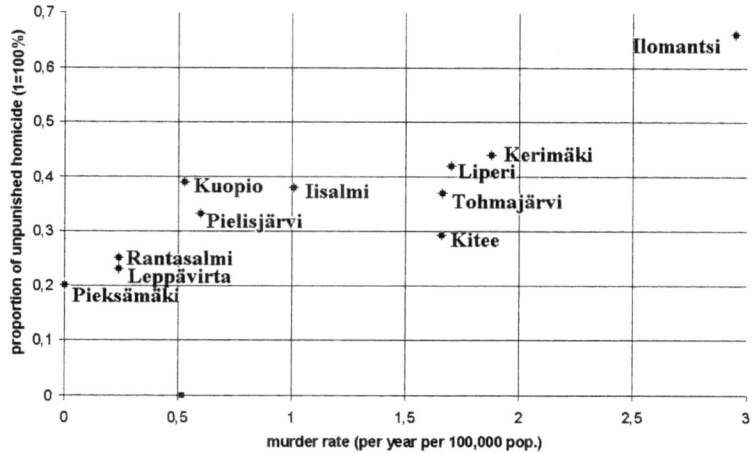

63

Figure 1c.

Rate of intentional manslaughter (per year per 100,000 inhabitants) and the proportion of punished homicide in the parishes of northern Savo and northern Karelia 1748–1807.

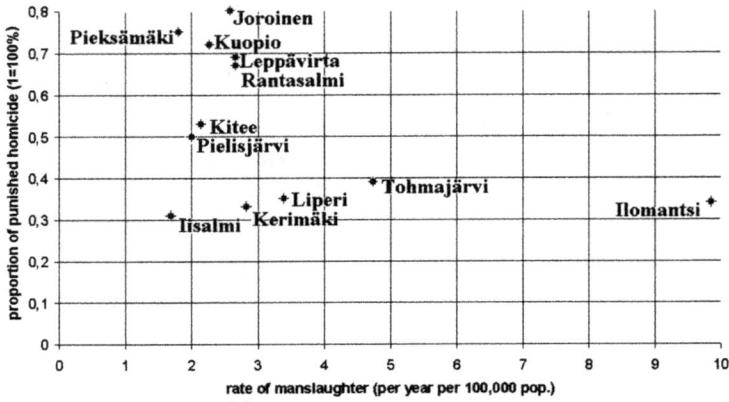

Figure 1d.

Rate of intentional manslaughter (per year per 100,000 inhabitants) and the proportion of unpunished homicide in the parishes of northern Savo and northern Karelia in the period 1748–1807

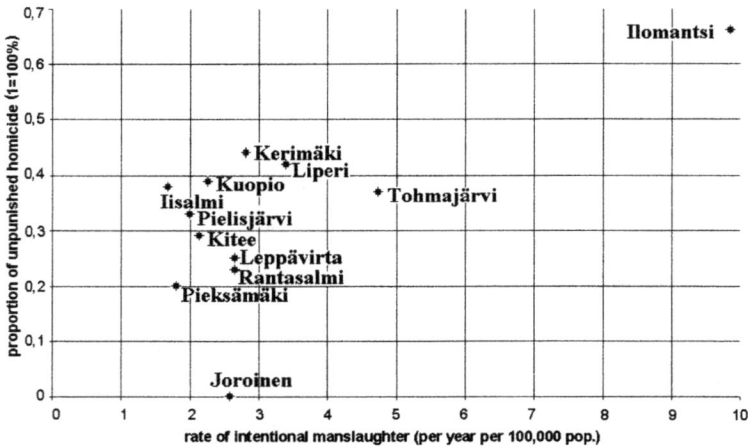

The application of the strict requirements of proof by the superior courts gradually became common knowledge among those who appeared in court; in order to avoid being convicted, the accused began to deny their guilt of charges of homicide with increasing frequency and bribed or pressurized witnesses to keep silent about what they had seen. This was particularly true of cases of murder with robbery and contract murder. When these forms of crime became more prevalent in Karelia from the 1770s on, the local district courts began to apply the requirements of the statutory presentation of proof less stringently in order to be able to obtain a conviction. This was undoubtedly influenced by the pressures on the jurymen and the district court judges not to offend the sense of justice of the local people.

Table 6a.

Death sentences passed by the district courts in contravention of procedural law (without a full proof) and legal sentences in homicide cases in northern Karelia in the period 1748–1807. The death sentences are based purely on strong circumstantial evidence unless otherwise mentioned.

Parish, year, eyewitnesses	Crime	Legal sentence in the courts of appeal or the royal courts (= RC)
Tohmajärvi 1754	intentional manslaughter MB XXIV:6	RC: RB XVII:32 Adjourned *sine die*
Liperi 1772	intentional manslaughter of a wife MB XIV:1	RB XVII:32 Adjourned *sine die*
Liperi 1779 (two competent eye witnesses)	intentional manslaughter MB XXIV:1	RB XVII:32 adjourned *sine die*
Tohmajärvi 1781	intentional manslaughter of a master MB XIV:1	RC: RB XVII:32 confessional remand
Liperi 1787 (two death sentences)	intentional manslaughter of a man and a brother-in-law MB XIV:1 and XXIV:1	RB XVII:32 adjourned *sine die*, RB XVII:29 release on probation
Tohmajärvi 1787 (two death sentences)	intentional manslaughter of a wife MB XIV:1 and XV:1	RB XVII:32 adjourned *sine die*
Ilomantsi 1787	murder MB XII:1	RC: RB XVII:32, later in 1801 confessional remand
Pielisjärvi 1789 (two death sentences)	(contract) murder MB XII:1	RC: RB XVII:32 confessional remand, second accused died before sentence passed
Ilomantsi 1793 (two death sentences)	murder MB XII:1	RC: RB XVII:32 confessional remand
Liperi 1802 (several eye witnesses)	intentional manslaughter MB XXIV:1	RC: RB XVII:32 confessional remand
Tohmajärvi 1802 (one minor eyewitness)	Intentional homicide in breach of the peace MB XX:1	RC: RB XVII:32 adjourned *sine die*
Ilomantsi 1805	Murder MB XII:1	RC: RB XVII:32 confessional remand

Table 6b.

Death sentences passed by the district courts in contravention of procedural law (without a full proof) and legal sentences in homicide cases in northern Savo in the period 1748–1807. The death sentences are based purely on strong circumstantial evidence unless otherwise mentioned.

Parish, year, eyewitnesses	Crime	Legal sentence in the courts of appeal or the royal courts
Kuopio 1748 (one minor witness)	Murder MB XII:1	Confessional remand
Rantasalmi 1770	Murder of a wife MB XII:1	Case adjourned because accused escaped
Kerimäki 1772 (one minor witness and one accomplice as a witness)	Murder with robbery, rape	RB XVII:32, confessional remand
Iisalmi 1783 (one accomplice as a witness)	Contract murder, murder with robbery	Death sentence after confession in solitary confinement
Leppävirta 1788	Murder with robbery	Case dropped on death of the accused
Iisalmi 1800	Fratricide MB XIV:1	RB XVII:32 adjourned sine die
Kuopio 1805	Intentional manslaughter MB XXIV:1	RB XVII:32 confessional remand

Sources for Tables 6a and 6b: VMA: VHOA, Alistettujen asiain päätöstaltiot ja designaatioluettelot v. 1754–1813; MMA: KymLKa, Saapuneet kirjeet, Hovioikeus maaherralle, v. 1748–1775.

The superior courts commuted capital sentences that were in contravention of procedural law by adjourning the cases sine die, and they also reacted to the illegal procedure of the lower courts by extending the institution of confessional remand, which in practice meant committing the accused to incarceration with hard labour if the circumstantial evidence against the accused was particularly incriminating, but he or she refused to confess. Although this measure proved to be ineffective, the increase in the use of confessional remand was unavoidable in order that there might be at least some kind of sanction for the most shocking crimes.

Homicide as Unofficial Social Control

The Frontier Region and
the Grip of Authority

Homicide in the Outlying Parishes

The increase in homicide in the parishes of Savo and Karelia on the Russian border followed a particular logic of its own. Up to the 1760s, killings were patently more frequent in Ilomantsi, Tohmajärvi and Kerimäki than in places further west. Over the following decades, however, the relative number of homicides fell in these parishes, as they did in all the frontier parishes of Savo and Karelia, including Kitee, Pielisjärvi and Rantasalmi. In places further removed from the frontier, there was a diametrically opposite development: from the 1740s to the late 1760s, relatively few homicides were prosecuted there, but then at the end of the latter decade the numbers began to rise slightly. It is, therefore, pertinent to assess the socio-cultural factors that promoted violence up to the 1760s. By this I am referring to factors created by unsuccessful forms of community, to developments in society that were unfavourable to the individual, or to elements that alienated the individual from society.[193] And then, what kind of changes in the social environment can we assume to have been behind the decrease in homicide that began in the 1760s?

The homicides that took place in the frontier parishes exhibit a number of features which distinguish them from those committed in other parts of the area under investigation here:

1. Near the eastern frontier, homicides were more frequently motivated by land disputes than elsewhere.
2. More killers escaped justice in the frontier parishes,.
3. Vagrants, who were totally outside organized society, tended to congregate in this area, particularly in Ilomantsi.

Charges of homicide were more frequently denied in the east than in the west. The loophole in procedural law that made denial an effective defence was complemented by a practical loophole in the administration: until the 1770s, it was easy to avoid the consequences of a crime by

193 Cf. Keltikangas-Järvinen 1978, p. 17.

escaping over the open frontier. In some places in the border region of southern Savo, bands of robbers from both sides of the border terrorized the local people.[194] The Karelian robber bands, on the other hand, apart from one woman in Hattuvaara in 1784, did not kill any of the people of the area during the period of this research, or at least they were not accused of doing so in court, though there are certainly records of acts of robbery and theft and homicidal threats made by them at least in the years 1748, 1749, 1783 and 1793.[195] In Ilomantsi in particular, the other homicides committed locally were mainly the work of deserters who had fled to the area, of unassimilated new settlers from Russia and of Greek Orthodox inhabitants of the parish. The last-mentioned group, who were discriminated against and living in circumstances that offered no alternative way of making a livelihood, were particularly guilty of fratricide and of murders of vagrants who had come from Russia.

The particular nature of homicide in this area is described in the accompanying outline of crime and control. The bipolar relationship between homicide and control is delineated for two localities. The first is the parish of Ilomantsi, where justice was most acutely influenced by the above-mentioned features of the frontier area. Here, the relative number of homicides during the period studied was almost 13 per year per 100,000 inhabitants. To partner it, I selected Pieksämäki, including the chapelry of Suonenjoki, from inner Savo. This major parish witnessed the smallest number of homicides in the area investigated: 1.8 per year per 100,000 inhabitants. Ilomantsi and Pieksämäki contrast completely with each other in terms of the degree of premeditation of the deeds, the effectiveness in bringing the culprits to justice and the disposition of the accused to plead guilty or innocent. In Pieksämäki, the judicial control of homicide was almost complete. In the violent parish of Ilomantsi, on the other hand, the authorities' control over homicidal crime remained lax throughout the period studied here.

1. In Pieksämäki sentences were passed in all trials. Culprits were brought to justice for their crimes. In Ilomantsi eleven of the principal defendants had either fled at some point in the trial or had died before the sentence was passed.

2. In Pieksämäki seven out of eight killers confessed to their crimes. In the eighth case, the court determined that the probable motive for the crime was self-defence. In Ilomantsi only 31 persons charged with homicide confessed.

194 For example, in Mäntyharju a peasant called Risto Kärpänen killed his brother in the early 1750s, and then went into hiding with his relations in the same parish for over ten years without being brought to trial. Eventually he ended up killing his brother-in-law, Yrjö Kärpanen, in 1763. MMA: KymLKa, Saapuneet kirjeet v. 1765, Hovioikeus maaherralle, D 27 a1, no 63.

195 Björn 1991, pp. 141, 155–156.

Figure 2.

The basic features of homicide and control in Ilomantsi and Pieksämäki. The material consists of homicides prosecuted in the period 1748-1807.

Homicide and control at the extremes of the violence axis (Ilomantsi and Pieksämäki)

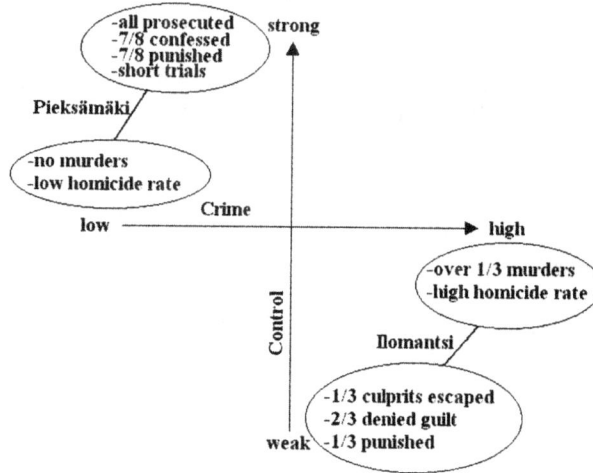

In the greater Pieksämäki area, only one of the principle defendants in a homicide case went unpunished. Two sons of a peasant farmer and three farm hands denied that they had laid hands on a peasant called Heikki Lappi after the latter was found dead on an area of burn-beaten land where he was working. It was not possible to prove that Lappi's death was due to intentional homicide. The circumstances pointed to self-defence.[196]

3. As section 2 implies, seven cases of homicide out of eight were punished in Pieksämäki, but only one in three in Ilomantsi.

4. In the greater Pieksämäki area, there were no premeditated murders. In Ilomantsi thirteen murders (and eighteen manslaughters) were brought to trial. It is probable that a number of homicides also remained undiscovered there.

In Pieksämäki, the sentences were implemented within a relatively short time of the crime. Because the defendants confessed, the trials did not drag on indefinitely.

There are direct correspondences between these differences in control and the features of the crimes. In Pieksämäki, the homicides were generally less violent, often the result of negligence. One of the eight victims who was a close relative of his killer was Heikki Penttinen, the brother of a peasant farmer.

---

196 VMA: VHOA, Alistusaktit, Savon ja Karjalan lääni, v. 1796, Ece 36, no 8; Alistettujen asiain päätöstaltiot, Savon ja Karjalan lääni, v. 1796, Di 31, no 8.

Penttinen attacked his brother with a spade in 1757. The brother, Antti, defended himself, and in doing so struck Heikki on the head with a plough-tail. The blow was so powerful that the latter died within a few hours. At the Pieksämäki District Court, Antti was sentenced to death in accordance with MB XIV. A review of the case discovered extenuating circumstances and interpreted the deed as self-defence. The sentence was commuted, and Antti was sentenced to expiate his crime by paying a half wergeld.[197]

In Pieksämäki, members of the landless population were only rarely involved in homicide. It was not until the end of the century that the culprits began to come from down the social scale:

In 1785, an enraged Gypsy called Kalle Hommonen attacked the wife of one of his own people. In doing so, he accidentally killed the two-year-old child she was carrying in her arms.[198]

The composition of the homicides was quite different in Ilomantsi from that in Pieksämäki. Two thirds (66%) of the principle defendants there either escaped completely, or were acquitted, or then the final sentence was adjourned *sine die,* and they were possibly placed in confessional remand. There were particular reasons for the weak control in Ilomantsi, one of which was a favourite ploy of the local criminals: the defendants attempted to thwart and anticipate the justice meted out by the authorities by denying their guilt or running away. This was clearly more common in Ilomantsi than elsewhere in eastern Finland. The control of homicide was much stricter in the immediate neighbours of Ilomantsi: Tohmajärvi and Pälkjärvi. Even so, homicide was rife in these parishes too.

The forms that homicide took in Ilomantsi were peculiar to the parish. Murders and killings of relatives were much more common there than in more western areas, and an exceptional number of them went unpunished. Murder indictments came to nothing as the cases dragged on from one decade to another, with the accused pleading not guilty or fleeing the country.

Of the *murders* that were committed in the years 1748–67, seven (i.e. 7.8 per year per 100,000 inhabitants) were brought to trial. During the same period, there were a *further* eight belated reports of homicide committed during the period prior to 1748, the earliest of which had taken place even before the War of the Hats (1741–1743). Apparently, the relatives of the victims wished to postpone the investigation of the killings until the administrative situation in the border area became stable after the war. In fact, the time was deemed ripe to prosecute the homicides in the early 1750s,[199] but the last of these cases was not dealt with in court until

---

197 MMA: KymLKa, Saapuneet kirjeet, v. 1757, Hovioikeus maaherralle, D 19 a1, no 57.
198 VMA: VHOA, Alistettujen asiain päätöstaltiot, Savon ja Karjalan lääni, v. 1785, Di 20, no 92.
199 KA: Karjalan tuomiokunnan tuomiokirja, Ilomantsin ja Suolahden osan tk 1751, KOa 20, § 2; MMA: KymLKa, Saapuneet kirjeet, Hovioikeus maaherralle, v. 1751, D 13 a1, no 59/1; v. 1753, D 15 a1, no 10.

the end of the following decade. When the courts had worked through the backlog of unsolved homicide cases from the 1740s, the number of murders also began to decrease gradually, although it still remained relatively high.

The Trouble Spots of the Periphery

The land along the Russian border provided an exceptional amount of freedom of movement.[200] The lax control also fuelled the tendency of the inhabitants to take matters into their own hands over a larger area of Karelia. Due to the fragmentation that had lasted there for generations, this self-help manifested itself in open violence. Antti Kujala, who has studied the records of the district courts during the Great Northern War, discerns a regional connection between a high homicide rate and a tendency to revolt. Violence and peasant resistance were particularly characteristic of the former dependent territories of Karelia that Sweden won in the war.[201] Up to the Peace of Nystad (1721), these territories included the whole of the Province of Käkisalmi, whose inhabitants had no representation in the Diet, for example.[202] Kujala considers the Karelians' propensity for violence to be a consequence of restless and unsettled social conditions.[203] The uncertainty of the situation affected not only politics but also taxation and defence. Unlike in the rest of the kingdom, the administration of the latter matters in Karelia continued on an ad hoc basis for decades even after the Peace of Åbo (1743).[204] A regular system of taxation was not instituted in the region until the 1760s, while the question of defence was only solved in the 1780s. Elias considers both of these elements to be general preconditions for the centralization of state authority in the civilizing process, for only then can the centrifugal attraction of social forces be broken down.[205]

The geopolitical situation of the eastern regions changed as a result of the Great Northern War and the War of the Hats along a zone extending all the way from the central area of Ilomantsi right down to the Gulf of Finland: at the same time, the area of Karelia that was left to Sweden after the war became an integral part of the kingdom, only now it constituted the outermost frontier of that kingdom. Only Pielisjärvi had been located totally along the Russian border before the Great Northern War. And this old frontier parish did not suffer statistically from the violence of its inhabitants as much as those areas that found themselves in a novel geopolitical position. This was so in spite of the fact that Pielisjärvi had traditionally been one of the centres of Karelian peasant resistance.[206]

200 Heikkinen 1988, p. 286.
201 Kujala 2001, p. 170.
202 Cf. e.g. Vampilova 1997, p. 192.
203 Kujala 2001, pp. 178–179.
204 Saloheimo 1980, p. 239.
205 Blomstedt 1984, pp. 297–299; Elias 1994, pp. 345–346, 420–439.
206 Katajala 1994, pp. 349–351.

The Problems of the Periphery in the Pre-Modern World

In an in-depth synthesis of the sources of social power, Michael Mann analyzes and clarifies the concept of the traditional and pre-modern (non-modern) state. Mann characterizes the weak logistics of the administrative infrastructure as one of the main elements defining this form of government. The expression can be interpreted as the fragmentary nature of official communications. When administrative communications break down, the authorities lack the competence to infiltrate the life of the people and it is not possible to focus the surveillance of the population properly.[207] Mann and Anthony Giddens support Weber's conclusion that the creation of the law's monopoly of the use of (violent) force presupposes the ability and the opportunity of the state to handle huge streams of information. The administration must be extremely stable before its grip can fully reach the frontier regions at the furthest ends of the state.[208]

According to Giddens, one of the most essential conditions of modernization is a border guard. Before one can speak of a modern state, its zone-like state frontiers must be drawn up into accurately defined and inviolable borders.[209] Between Russia and Sweden, a modern, accurately drawn, controlled and inviolable border was not established until after the Peace of Åbo in 1743.[210] In practice, it was decades after this peace treaty before the border dividing the states was fixed in the most remote areas of Karelia.

The protection of the border was increased temporarily between the Peace of Åbo and the early 1750s and again from the end of the 1760s, when three companies of the Savo Infantry Regiment were detailed to guard it. During the latter period, an epidemic of the plague that had broken out in Russia was used as a pretext for the measure, but the real reason was one of domestic politics: Gustav III's attempt to seize power. The border was closed altogether in March 1772, but immediately after the success of the coup, the King declared that the epidemic was over and reduced supervision of the border. The closure of the border had aroused fears among the subjects on the Russian side that a frontier war might break out.[211]

Quite apart from the special reasons for the intensification in the guarding of the frontier, it also answered a need in criminal policy; Wallenius, the Crown Bailiff, was aware that even in 1773 deserters and criminals were still hiding in the deserted tracts around it.[212] The administrative control of neither Sweden nor Russia extended to the villages populated

---

207 Häkli 1997, pp. 11–13 and notes. Mann 1986, p. 440–445. On the frontier periphery and control see also Conversi 1997, pp. 217–218.
208 Häkli 1997, pp. 11–13 and notes; Giddens 1985, pp. 49–52.
209 Ibid.
210 Häyrynen 1997, p. 105. Here, Häyrynen means that private persons were not allowed to cross the border without control. Cf. also Jansson, T. 1997, pp. 138, 146.
211 Saloheimo 1980, pp. 303–308; Björn 1991, pp. 144–145; Suolahti 1925, p. 309 ff.
212 Saloheimo 1980, p. 484.

by deserters that had grown up along the frontier, not to mention those in the disputed territory between the two countries.[213] For example, in the 1770s, the inhabitants of Ilomantsi could not say just where the border ran. A line defining the frontier was cleared again during the 1780s, but the forest grew anew to close the clearing.[214] In practice, however, the control of the border crossings must have become stricter since towards the end of the century fewer and fewer criminals managed to flee across it to Russia to escape the judicial consequences of their deeds. After the War of Gustav III (1788–1790), Karelia received its own light infantry troop to guard the border.[215]

Administrative Weakness and Delays

In the period of reconstruction after the War of the Hats, the eastern frontier lands of the realm received new attention, because the political elite in Stockholm began to realize the value of the Finnish territories as an independent buffer against an external enemy. At the same time, there was a sweeping change in occupational and demographic policy that affected every subject of the realm. The coercive mercantile measures that had previously been used to stimulate the economy were replaced by a new strategy, one of increasing the national revenue by encouraging people to enhance their own economic welfare. It became a major aim of the state to increase the size of the population in order that agriculture should expand and thereby augment revenue from taxes. A rich populace would in this way increase the power of the whole state. The demographic and occupational policy gave rise to a number of reforms that gradually introduced a completely new public social welfare system. It was manifested in the creation of a system of loans and parish storehouses, the institutionalization of poor relief and an extension of the network of professional medical care. A redistribution of land and an institutional strengthening of the status of the peasant farmers can also be seen as manifestations of an extensive movement in occupational policy that was inspired by the age of utilitarianism; the policy can be encapsulated in one word: physiocracy.

The execution of the new demographic policy made possible an extensive settlement of the hinterland in Karelia and Savo, despite the fact that the implementation of many of the above-mentioned reforms was delayed for several decades there compared with more central regions of the kingdom.

Relatively, the economic position of eastern Finland did not improve between the mid-eighteenth century and the beginning of the nineteenth because the extensive economic growth that took place affected the whole

213 Cf. Björn 1993, pp. 152–153.
214 Björn 1991, p. 135.
215 Björn 1991, p. 145.

kingdom equally. Savo and Karelia remained the poorest and remotest region of the realm until the rule of Sweden came to an end, an outback peopled by rustics blackened with the smoke of burn-beating, a tract dubbed the Siberia of Sweden.[216] However, the poverty of the region should not be over-dramatized, for in the late eighteenth century, many people in eastern Finland in fact enjoyed an improvement in their standard of living.[217]

Harald Gustafsson, who has collated the findings of research dealing with the political culture of the Nordic countries in the eighteenth century, notes that the administrative decision-making process between the local level and the central government worked reasonably well in the kingdom of Sweden. He concludes that the legal and administrative systems enjoyed a considerable degree of legitimacy among the subjects. However, Finnish historians are fairly unanimous in claiming that the grip of the Swedish government on its citizens, which by international standards was strong, no longer held at the extreme periphery of the kingdom.[218] Initiatives intended to promote economic life in eastern Finland got held up in bureaucratic channels for decades on end. For example, there was not a single city in the wide tracts of northern Savo and Karelia until 1775, when Kuopio was made into a city. Even then, it had to wait for another six years before it actually received city privileges.[219] In Karelia, which had no cities, the ban on trade in the countryside proved impossible to implement, and in 1774 Gustav III revoked the ban in Karelia.[220] According to Toivo J. Paloposki, the objections made by the people of eastern Finland consisted of repeated complaints about the authorities, tax protests, market applications and protests about the border between Savo and Häme.[221]

The mercantile forestry policy that favoured timber-processing for a long time also posed a threat to burn-beating cultivation. The latter was the main source of livelihood of the people of Savo, and the region could offer very few alternative sources because the routes of communication had been cut when peace was made.[222] A fear that the forest resources might be wasted aroused quite unwarranted moral panic at both local and central government levels, as a result of which usufruct of the forest was restricted even before an adequate survey of the special conditions obtaining in Savo and Karelia was made. When the A. H. Ramsay, the Governor of the Province of Kymenkartano and Savo, saw the devastated forests

216 E.g. Blomstedt 1984, pp. 290–292.Saloheimo 1980, pp. 309, 366–370, 470–476; Wirilander 1989, pp. 130–131, 134, 421–479; Pulma 1985, pp. 72–74; Teerijoki 1993; Sirén 1999, pp. 25, 58.
217 E.g. Kaukiainen 1998, pp. 143–145.
218 Gustafsson is also aware of this. Gustafsson 1994, pp. 98–102. See also the earlier Finnish references at the beginning of this section, as well as Heikkinen 1988, p. 56.
219 Viitala 1997, p. 4.
220 Saloheimo 1980, p. 209.
221 Paloposki 1954, p. 115.
222 Kuisma 1984, pp. 246–264.

by the roadsides in 1773, he was horrified and issued an administrative order prohibiting felling and burning altogether. Similar restrictions had long been in force elsewhere in the kingdom. However, the attempts to limit burn-beating cultivation were ineffective as long as there were no alternative sources of livelihood available. The restrictions were revoked in 1781 with the awkward condition that areas for burn-beating were to be inspected beforehand. Extensive burn-beating rights were returned to the people of Savo and Karelia only in 1796.[223]

The fears of the Crown authorities about the destruction of the forests were certainly excessive as far as the fell areas of eastern Finland were concerned, particularly since the populace had no other means of supporting itself. Consequently, in the strenuous efforts of the authorities to restrict burn-beating the people saw an administrative process that was working against them. This naturally did not help to increase the popularity of the authorities among the people of eastern Finland who obtained their living from burn-beating cultivation. In Swedish Karelia, the same trend was intensified by the Crown's unsuccessful commercial policy limiting saw-milling, the exportation of timber to Russia and the peasants' border trade in the goods they produced. The result was that some of the commerce was inevitably channelled into smuggling. The activities of the sawmills in Savo were not restricted in the same way, and sawmilling thrived there.[224] In actual practice, about one half of all the trade carried on by the Karelian peasants was directed (some of it illegally) towards Russia, above all to the region of Old Finland around Lake Ladoga.[225] Old Finland was the name given to the former Swedish territories that passed to Russia in the peace treaties of Nystad (1721) and Åbo (1743).

The comprehensive slowness of administrative communications made the region studied here remote from the point not only of the centre of the kingdom but also of the local administrative parishes. It took two or three months for the post to get to the furthest corners of Karelia from Borgå or Lovisa, and naturally as long again for replies to get back.[226] The geographical distance of Savo and Karelia from the central government was enough in itself to make the region peripheral,[227] but the geographical

---

223 See Kuisma 1993, pp. 57–102; Saloheimo 1980, p. 351; Wirilander 1989, pp. 319, 414–415, 590–592; Blomstedt 1984, p. 291.

224 Saloheimo 1980, pp. 173–175.

225 Saloheimo 1980, pp. 211, 226–228.

226 Blomstedt 1984, p. 296.

227 Periphery status is defined by three local attributes: 1. the distance from centres of power; communications between the periphery and the centre involve high expenses; 2. a difference between the centre and the periphery in one or more attributes; 3. dependence on the centre for political decision-making, cultural standardisation or the economy. The definition is taken from Stein Rokkan's and Derek W Urvin's work: Economy, Territory, Identity: Politics of West European Peripheries. London 1983. The classic study of the relationship between the periphery and the centre is by Immanuel Wallerstein.

size of the administrative units and the poor road network also left some vacuums in local justice and government.[228] A decrease in the number of local government units would have necessitated an ability and willingness on the part of the peasants to pay higher taxes; otherwise it would have meant lower revenues for the taxmen.[229] In consequence, many measures aimed at dividing up the administrative units lagged behind the growth in the size of the population. The sluggish communications in Savo and Karelia also had some side effects on the control of homicide: killings were concealed, and the perpetrators escaped over the border. The unguarded frontier region also offered a sanctuary for bands of robbers, both Russian and Finnish.[230] All these phenomena point to the fact that the hold of the institutions of control continued to be extremely weak at the ultimate fringes of the kingdom.

The Frontier Region Thesis as an Explanation of Violence

The settling of accounts by violence continued to be considered justified in certain kinds of frontier and newly settled regions.[231] Evidence pointing to this has been found in seventeenth-century Scotland, Holland and Småland, eighteenth-century Catalonia and even in the southern border region of the United States in the nineteenth-century, and at different periods also in areas that have been considered otherwise peripheral, such as the highlands of New Zealand, the Andes, western Sicily, and the Lake Titicaca region of Mexico.[232] The characterization of the unstable government of peripheral frontier areas in the pre-modern age has been reduced to two descriptors: a weak defence capability against external threat and an equally weak internal (official) control.[233] The weak defence capability meant that the frontier areas were constantly vulnerable to attack. The lax internal control was a manifestation of the debility of the state's authority. As a result, criminals fleeing from justice congregated in the frontier regions.[234] In the pre-modern era, the side effects of weak control frequently continued to exist in the frontier regions of administrative entities after they had passed into history in the central regions. Such side effects were organized crime (robber bands), the institution of the blood feud and a general tradition of violence. The blood feud survives only as an institution to any great extent where state violence, i.e. the monopoly of the power to punish, has not been strongly imposed. The

---

228 Cf. also Pulma 1985, pp. 30–33; Wirilander 1989, pp. 312–315.
229 Nousiainen 1993, p. 362.
230 Björn 1991, p. 140.
231 Cf. e.g. Elias 1994, p. 158.
232 Larsson 1982, pp. 45–55; Gastil 1971, p. 417; Sahlins 1991, pp. 234–263
233 Conversi 1997, p. 218.
234 Cf. Sharpe 1996, p. 18; Macfarlane 1981; Larsson 1982, pp. 45–55; Gastil 1971, p. 417; Koch 1984. See also Blok 1998. It is the duty of the state to offer protection against both internal and external enemies. See e.g. Karonen 1999a, p. 213.

fact that criminal law did not extend to the frontier region also encouraged criminal gangs to seek out the furthest corners of the premodern state in large numbers.[235]

The American sociologists Raymond Gastil and Shelton Hackney conclude that the classical frustration-aggression model is not capable of explaining the majority of the traditionally high numbers of homicides committed in the frontier regions of the southern states of America. For example, these were not commercially oriented areas of the kind that the model requires, nor were the values of the inhabitants characterized by a spirit of competitiveness. Gastil and Hackney rather seek an explanation for the incredible violence of the southern frontier area in the history of the region and in a cultural tradition of taking the law into one's own hands that went back to the aftermath of the American Civil War with its pillaging veterans. The culture of violence was spurred by the fact that the southern parts of the United States remained a frontier region (and weakly governed) long after the rest of the country. The use of violence was a part of local survival training.[236]

An obvious example of a classical violent frontier region in the early modern age is afforded by Konga in the province of Småland in Sweden. Judicial sources indicate that in the jurisdictional district of Konga approximately 27 homicides per year per 100,000 inhabitants were committed in the early seventeenth century. According to Lars-Olof Larsson, who has studied the history of the region, the inhabitants of the frontier areas of Konga were accustomed to living under the threat of danger to their own or to their family's lives and property. If somebody committed manslaughter – which, according to Larsson, the populace did not consider a particularly grievous sin – the culprit would immediately escape the forces of justice over the border into Denmark. The authorities did not dare to follow the killer into the border region's deep and dangerous forests, which were inhabited by bands of robbers. The state had great difficulty in exerting any effect on the life of the people of the frontier regions: government, the dispensation of justice and the control of people's behaviour did not extend to all parts of the kingdom equally. There was no respect for the law, and the activities of the local community were stamped above all by lawlessness.

Larsson believes that the violent mentality of the people of Konga is explained by the geopolitical position of the district at the periphery of the kingdom on its southern border with Denmark. The inhabitants lived in more unsettled conditions than other Swedes and were in immediate peril whenever a war broke out. When the border shifted further south halfway through the seventeenth century, the geopolitical position of Småland changed. Larsson considers the fact that by the beginning of the eighteenth century homicide had decreased in the jurisdictional district

235 Lenman & Parker 1980, p. 40.
236 Hackney 1969, pp. 906–925; Gastil 1971, p. 417. For criticisms of the Gastil–Hackney argument, see e.g. Loftin & Hill 1974, pp. 714–724.

of Konga to one fifth of what it had been a hundred years earlier to be a clear manifestation of the strengthening in the grip of the authorities that had taken place at the end of the previous century.[237] The frontier parishes of Karelia (and southern Savo) can undoubtedly be included in the list of violent frontier regions, although the number of homicides prosecuted there in the late eighteenth century does not come anywhere near those of the more notorious extreme examples, although in terms of the brutality of the killings eastern Finland certainly does not pall in comparison with them.

Despite all this, the argument that violence is determined by the frontier status of a region is justifiably considered an historical cliché. The most severe criticism lodged against models based on this thesis is that they ignore the fact that not all frontier regions are plagued with blind violence.[238] For example, communal disagreements were not settled especially violently in the seventeenth century in the province of Norland along the border between northern Sweden and Norway (then part of Denmark).[239] The frontier region thesis does not even hold for anywhere near all the frontier settlements in the United States.[240] Attempts have been made to prove by means of these and other examples that it is not the frontier status of a region as such that brutalizes its inhabitants but rather its vulnerability to external threats. This generally means that the region repeatedly becomes a theatre of war. Only after the threat of war withdraws can the populace begin to renounce individual violence.[241] In addition to actual warfare, scholars have also regarded the economic losses brought about by war as factors that contribute to brutalization by undermining confidence in the government and in society.[242]

The frontier region thesis, when supplemented by the threat of an external enemy, nevertheless does provide a reasonably satisfactory explanation for the growth in homicide in Karelia (and Savo). When the defence of Karelia was debated in the Diet in 1760, Gabriel Wallenius, the long-serving Crown Bailiff of Karelia (1750–1800), presented an assessment of his bailiwick. According to Viktor Riissanen, who has studied the administration of Wallenius, the Bailiff (who was later dubbed "the King of Karelia") described the external enemy as a scourge that lay heavy on the land. Here, Wallenius was referring to the wars that broke out every few decades, and which inspired the civilian population to engage in indiscriminate pillaging and killing on both sides of the border. The history of guerrilla warfare with its looting and reprisals had its roots deep in the wars of the Old Wrath (1570–95), the Great Wrath (1713–21), the

---

237 Larsson 1982, p. 20, 47–56.
238 Lane 1997, p. 349.
239 Sundin 1992, pp. 288–289.
240 Lane 1997, p. 349. The violence of the American frontier region was also influenced by local factors such as slavery, racism and settler isolation, as well as relations with the indigenous peoples. Ibid, pp. 349–350.
241 E.g. Sundin 1992, p. 293; Liliequist 1999, pp. 178–179.
242 Johansson 1997, p. 208.

Lesser Wrath (1742–43), and the Rupture War in the 1650s.[243] The acts
of terrorism committed by occupying forces and patrols carrying out reprisal raids from over the border exacerbated the traditionally suspicious
attitude of the Karelians on the Swedish side towards their fellows who
were subjects of Russia.[244] Above all in the Great Northern War and the
War of the Hats, the Karelian frontier parishes typically suffered from
vandalism carried out by bands of guerrilla troops coming over the border from Repola and Aunus (now Olonets). According to Wallenius, the
Swedish Karelians were themselves to blame for this as they had started
the cross-border pillages and through their plundering and killing had
goaded the Russian Karelians into seeking revenge. Informers among
the Swedish Karelians had supplied the enemy with information about
suitable targets.[245]

Wallenius was also aware of the grievous problems resulting from the
fact that the Karelian troops were not made up of regular soldiers. The
most disastrous consequence of this was the fact that the reprisals from
behind the border for the acts of terrorism committed by the Swedish
Karelians were always directed at the local civilian population. This
stemmed from the principle that, with the peasant farmers waging a war
on their own account, the enemy directed their reprisals at the whole
peasant population without discrimination. In this respect, the nature of
the warfare in Karelia differed essentially from that in areas where the
actions were restricted to the military, and the peasants were left in peace
to carry on with their normal way of life while the soldiers fought their
wars.[246] The Karelians themselves did not regard the lack of regular troops
as a problem; indeed, they would have preferred to have compulsory
military service extended to the region under the leadership of some local
peasant farmer. This proposal was rejected, however, and the question of
strengthening the defence capability of Karelia was not addressed until
the 1780s.[247] The external threat decreased materially in the last decades
of the eighteenth century, when the defences of Karelia were strengthened
and the region received its own permanent light infantry regiment.[248]

In his assessment of the barriers to the development of Karelia, the
Crown Bailiff, who possessed a thorough knowledge of his bailiwick,
added that the prosperity of the region was also vitiated by the existence
of an internal enemy: *an enemy within*. By this he was alluding to an
internecine war manifested in the tendency of the populace of northern
Karelia to attack their own people as soon as a war broke out. For the
most part, the Swedish Karelians plundered the property of the richest

---

243 Riissanen 1965, p. 48. On the origins of the enmity between Lutherans and Orthodox,
     the border peaces and the historical roots of the cycle of vengeance, see Björn 1993,
     pp. 135–146.
244 Katajala 1997, p. 45.
245 Björn 1993, pp. 143–144. See also Kujala 2001, pp. 166–170
246 Saloheimo 1980, p. 484.
247 Blomstedt 1984, p. 298.
248 Saloheimo 1980, pp. 307, 495–502.

peasant farmers, burning their farmhouses and killing the inhabitants, and sometimes then even appropriating the farms of their victims for themselves. Historically, this phenomenon was also inspired by social differences: at the turn of the century the peasants and the cottagers had plundered the manors of the gentry, and during the Great Northern War they continued to do so in the name of the Czar. The authorities exacted harsh retribution for this.[249] Moreover, the relations between the Orthodox and the Lutheran sections of the poulace during the wars frequently deteriorated into open hostility.[250]

In speaking of "the enemy within", Wallenius might have been referring to revolts that took place in the distant past, in the years of the Great Famine. Even at the end of the eighteenth century, the estates feared that the inhabitants of Karelia might rise in rebellion if there was a war.[251] On the other hand, Wallenius' view of the inclination of the Karelians to kill one another was clearly coloured by the stories that he had heard of events that had taken place during the War of the Hats. The Crown Bailiff recounted his impressions of what had happened during the period of occupation in 1773 to Anders Henrik Ramsay, the Governor of the Province of Kymmenkartano and Savo, as follows:

> "[…] all in all, in time of war the Karelians have an enemy within. In particular, many slothful persons who live as dependent lodgers and support themselves on Crown lands begin to murder and plunder whatever they can get without discriminating between their own people and the enemy. And now in time of peace, they make bold to say that they hope for war in order to be able to get an even share of property with the rich."[252]

The tradition of violence that burdened the frontier parishes of Karelia halfway through the eighteenth century was indisputably connected with the local composition of the military, which consisted of an army recruited on a man per household basis and was thus made up of ill organized peasants. In consequence, the norms of war and civilian life became badly confused. The soldiers had no hesitation about robbing their own people. Kenneth Johansson has observed the same kind of behaviour in connection with the jurisdictional district of Allbo in the Province of Småland in Sweden during the Kalmar War in the early seventeenth century.[253] Ted Robert Gurr speaks of a similar phenomenon in British and American history; war legitimizes not only military violence but also

---

249 For example, during the Great Northern War, the internal strife had taken on the character of a religious war. Björn 1993, pp. 139, 143–144. For a more extensive treatment of the phenomenon, see Katajala 1994, p. 395 ff.

250 Björn 1993, p. 146.

251 Björn 1993, p. 144

252 Saloheimo 1980, pp. 482–483.

253 Johansson 1997, pp. 201, 214.

personal, everyday violence.[254] In the seventeenth century, the majority of the homicidal violence that appears in the court records of northern Karelia consists of spontaneous killings.[255] This leads one to suspect that two periods of war and occupation in the early eighteenth century with their concomitant local guerrilla conflicts and reprisals exacerbated the brutality of the killing.[256] The people of Karelia, incensed as they were by acts of terrorism, did not escape from this spiral of homicide until a generation had elapsed from the time of the guerrilla wars. The long period of peace that followed the War of the Hats also curbed the Karelians' inclination to settle their differences with fisticuffs. By the time of the War of Gustav III, the cost of the war for the area had become lower than before because the inhabitants of the frontier parishes concluded a separate mutual border peace that held relatively well. Nevertheless, some of the Orthodox inhabitants decided once again to openly throw their lot in with Russia – and this time they were also supported by many Lutherans.[257] There exist, however, some statistical indications that during the *pax russica* in the nineteenth century, the violent heritage of eastern Finland abated altogether.[258]

Although the relative number of homicides decreased at the end of the eighteenth century, the brutality of the deeds was not moderated. This is explained by a deadly trinity: first, the opposition to the authorities that was endemic in local tradition; second, the connection between religious disunity and politics; third, the fact that the region repeatedly became a battlefield of warring states. When these phenomena were combined, there was little chance that there would be any mutual loyalty among the populace. And it explains why it was above all in the frontier parish of Ilomantsi that the historical heritage sowed the seeds of grievous violence.[259]

The violence of the frontier region is considered to reflect a need for self-help. In such circumstances, self-help constitutes an unofficial form of punitive control, the administering of justice by one's own hand, which results from the weak protection afforded to the people by the official system of justice. The violent settlement of differences would seem to

---

254 Gurr 1981; Johansson 1997, p. 207. Dane Archer and Rosemary Gartner have described the relationship between war and violent crime in terms of seven different models; The Karelian propensity for violence can be linked to two such models of social disorganisation and legitimized violence: war transgresses the traditional concepts of law and justice and makes violence into a norm-sanctioned phenomenon. It also legitimates violence in all its forms. On the connection between war and violent crime in various studies, see Johansson 1997, pp. 202–212; Archer & Gartner 1976, pp. 937–963.

255 Matikainen 2002.

256 Cf. Kujala & Malinen 2001, p. 427.

257 Björn 1993, pp. 142–145, 168. Nevertheless there were attacks on Pälkjärvi and Matkaselkä in the parish of Kitee. Saloheimo 1980, pp. 489–493.

258 Turpeinen in Ylikangas 1976, p. 18; Ylikangas 1984, pp. 146–148; also Sirén 1996. On the *pax russica*, see e.g. Ahonen 1986, p. 279.

259 Cf. Kujala & Malinen 2001, p. 427.

have assumed more brutal forms close to the eastern border of Sweden than it did in more central areas of the kingdom. This phenomenon was a result of the fact that the justice system was unable to react sufficiently effectively to the homicides that were committed in the area, let alone other, perhaps less grievous, offences. Thus homicide became partly an extension of the official system of repression: the individual took over the imposition of control, using homicide as the extreme deterrent.

Despite the fact that the eastern frontier gradually became more peaceful, social forces thrust the whole area studied here in a contrary direction in which the pressure to resort to killing increased. This pendulum effect was triggered by an upset in the balance of the ecology that gradually led to a deepening crisis in burn-beating cultivation. The latter not only consumed the relative prosperity of whole generations, but it also gradually swept the entire social stratum of independent peasant farmers into absolute poverty and made them members of the landless class. The beginning of this process coincides in time with the rise in violent crime in the greater parishes of Liperi and Iisalmi.

A Tragedy of Internalized Control

The eastern frontier aspect alone is not the key to the question of the motivational structure of homicide. Questions regarding the inter-relationship between the national border and the tradition of violence have been shown to be part of a larger phenomenon: the weakness of public authority and control at the periphery of the kingdom.[260] Cultural crosschecks have established that taking the law into one's own hands by violent means, self-help and unofficial arbitration are characteristic methods of settling differences in weakly governed societies.[261]

In the greater parish of Liperi in Karelia, the fluctuations in violence followed other laws than those that prevailed in Ilomantsi and Tohmajärvi, which lay in the immediate vicinity of the border. In the Liperi District Court not a single case of intentional manslaughter or murder was prosecuted between 1748 and 1767, although there was one acquittal for manslaughter in 1756.[262] It was given to the local sheriff, Kristoffer Gröön.[263] In the period 1768–1787, however, the relative number of homicide victims calculated on the basis of the number of trials exploded to over seven per year per 100,000 inhabitants. The trend peaked in the five-year period 1778–1782, when the relative number of victims approached seventeen. The killings also became more brutal. During the first thirty-year period (1748–77) not a single murder was prosecuted in

---

260 For a summary of the relationship between public authority, forms of conflict arbitration and a high violent crime rate in mediaeval England, see e.g. Lane 1997, pp. 31–32.

261 Koch 1984, p. 96 "societies with little or no government" (government = the institutionalization of authority positions whose incubents control [...] the behaviors of individuals in the public interest [...]). This refers mainly to a stateless situation, but the idea can also be extended to more complex forms of society.

262 VMA: VHOA, Alistettujen asiain päätöstaltiot, Savon ja Karjalan lääni, v. 1756, Di 2, no 22. The one homicide that took place in the period 1748–1767 corresponds to 0.8 killings per 100,000 inhabitants per year.

263 The word "sheriff" is used to translated the office of *länsman*, who was the local law-enforcement officer, one of whose duties was to prosecute crimes in the district court.

the parish, whereas in the latter period (1778–1807), according to the legal records ten murders were committed.

One particular homicidal crime that was committed in Liperi during the period under investigation offers a dismal picture of the situation. The killing turns out to be a tragic symptom of the administrative crisis that afflicted the parish in the 1770s and 1780s, and which made it into one of the most violent parts of eastern Finland.

On a spring morning in 1782 the long-serving and respected Provincial Barber-Surgeon, Johan Fredrik Geisse, awoke early, walked into the bedroom of his three youngest children in his home at Siikasalmi in Liperi and killed his eight and thirteen-year-old sons with an axe and mutilated his third child to within an inch of his life. Geisse then marched into the kitchen with the axe to attack his adult daughter. The girl managed to avoid a blow aimed at her head, but the blade of the axe struck her neck, opening up a long wound that bled profusely. Geisse also tried to strike his daughter-in-law with the back of the axe, but he missed, and the woman was unwounded. Geisse then ran out and killed himself.

The deaths of Geisse and his children were investigated in a makeshift district court session. This was because the sheriff of the administrative parish of Liperi, Johan Bernsten, and the minister of the parish, Adolf Fredrik Stenfeldt, had recently been dismissed from office.[264]

There had been no warning signs of what was to happen in the home of Barber-Surgeon Geisse. In the doctor's and priest's reports submitted to the court, Geisse was described as leading a pious, quiet life. In his last years, according to both the spoken testimony given by his widow and the doctor's statement, he had fallen into a state of deep "melancholy". In court, the widow stated that he had behaved reasonably normally on the days preceding the deed. During the night, however, Geisse had complained of feeling ill. She had also wondered at something that he had said: "I feel as if my heart were hanging from a tree" (*[mitt] "hjärte voro til som det hangde på ett träd."*). The case was dropped because the culprit himself had died. The motive for the homicide was established as a mental aberration, and the surgeon was granted the right to an honourable burial in sanctified ground.[265] This ended the judicial enquiry into the case.

What was it that made the surgeon's heart hang from the branch of a tree? It is known first of all that Geisse had been experiencing severe financial problems.[266] One gets an inkling of these from the judgment records of the court of appeal: the expense claims that the barber-surgeon had submitted for his official journeys were regularly reduced. However, it was not money troubles alone that had caused Geisse's mental distress. Within a mosaic made up of fragments of evidence one can discern a far

264 VMA: VHOA, Alistettujen asiain päätöstaltiot, Savon ja Karjalan lääni, v. 1781, Di 16, no 50.
265 KA: Karjalan tuomiokunnan tuomiokirja, Liperin tk 1782, KO a 59, § 20.
266 Manninen 1917, pp. 121–122; cf. also Saloheimo 1980, p. 473.

more complicated psychological dynamics than that revealed by the court records. However, in order to examine it, we should first know something about the control of crime in the region.

The local rise in crime in Liperi was heralded by the manslaughter of a farmer called Pekka Sallinen.

He died violently on his home farm in the part of Oravinsalo that lies in the parish of Liperi in 1779. There was only one suspect: a farmer's son called Heikki Tapanen, with whom those living on Sallinen's farm had been constantly in dispute. Tapanen had been seen assaulting Sallinen on the day of his death with an axe and a poker. However, in court the accused denied having laid a hand on Sallinen, which meant that the capital sentence for homicide passed on Tapanen by the lower court could not be upheld in the court of appeal. The case was adjourned *sine die*, and he went free.[267]

Was it a local sense of justice injured by such acquittals that inflamed the smouldering violence among the inhabitants of Liperi? Certainly one individual unsettled homicide case would not have been enough to spark it off, but there were just too many victims of unsolved homicide cases in the years 1767–1772 to inspire public obedience to the law. Moreover, there were more trials of other grievous crimes in Liperi than in any other area of eastern Finland in the 1770s.[268] From the same period date the disturbances about the tenure of lands owned by the nobility (*frälsejord*). The worst turmoil, however, was in Pälkjärvi, not Liperi.[269]

Whereas in the years 1748–66 only one case of homicide was prosecuted in Liperi, in the year 1779 alone there were at least four killings in the greater parish together with its chapelries, two in 1780, and one in the following year. The records for 1782 are darkened by the bloody deaths of Provincial Surgeon Geisse and his two children. In a space of four years, the number of victims of homicide in this parish of 10,500 inhabitants rose to 21 per year per 100,000 persons. In terms of the number of prosecutions for homicide, Liperi deteriorated into being the most violent corner of the region during the 1770s and 1780s.[270]

Just before Barber-Surgeon Geisse took the lives of himself and his children, the sheriff of Liperi, Johan Bernsten, was dismissed for illegal imprisonment, assault and drunkenness. Together with the parish minister, Adolf Fredrik Stenfeldt, he had locked in the local jail a farmhand called Juho Niiranen from Lieksa, who had returned from Russia. There they harangued the young man, accusing him of a killing that had been committed in Aunus (Olonets). They also tied him up and kicked, whipped and stamped on him with their boots.

267 VMA: VHOA, Alistettujen asiain päätöstaltiot, Savon ja Karjalan lääni, v. 1779, Di 14, no 83.

268 Mäntylä 2000, p. 51; Sirén 1996, pp. 164–168.

269 Saloheimo 1980, pp. 284–295.

270 The violence of Pälkjärvi should not be emphasized, however, because of the small population of this parish, which was split in half by the Peace of Nystad. There were only three homicides committed in the parish over a period of six decades.

Juha's fate was probably not unique, but the timing of the authorities was unfortunate. It was probably the disapproving attitude of Gustav III towards forcing confessions out of suspects that had led to an increase in measures to control the arbitrary power of the authorities from the early 1770s on. On top of everything else, the accusation of manslaughter made against Juho Niiranen was false. The sheriff was proved guilty of malfeasance and dismissed in 1781.[271]

The minister, Stenfeldt, had a much heavier burden of guilt to bear than the sheriff: this man of the cloth had repeatedly been seen blind drunk and cursing as he delivered sermons and administered Holy Communion. As a matter of fact, drinking and swearing were Stenfeldt's "full-time occupation", as Ilmari Manninen expressed it in his history of the parish of Liperi. This, the most senior of the local clergy, is known to have assaulted members of his flock frequently on his tours of inspection and in the sacristy of the church.[272]

There were many other symptoms of confusion in the administration of justice. The ill-reputed Crown Jail of the parish was abolished in 1772 because of the chronic numbers of prisoners on confessional remand who had escaped from it, but it continued to function – with an equal lack of success – until half-way through the decade.[273] Nor were all those who held positions of trust locally completely blameless – let alone their relatives. For example, a juror of the Liperi District Court, Olli Haapalainen, was discharged from his duties in 1781 after being convicted of slandering his parents.[274] Another juror of the Liperi District Court, Pauli Lappalainen, died in mysterious circumstances in June of the same year when the process of dismissing the sheriff and the minister was still under way. One suspects that the weakness of official control had been exploited in order to eliminate Lappalainen, for his widow, Kristiina Kaupitar, and a vagrant called Juho Jernberg, who was known to be her lover, were accused at the 1782 district court sessions of killing him They were also indicted for fornication.[275] The trial of the couple for manslaughter was adjourned *sine die* in the district court, but the court of appeal acquitted them of the charge.[276] The autumn district court sessions of that year had to be suspended because of a plethora of cases in order for the judge to get to the next judicial district in time.[277] The quality of the civil servants in eastern Finland has frequently been described as being in the main

---

271 VMA: VHOA, Alistettujen asiain päätöstaltiot, Savon ja Karjalan lääni, v. 1781, Di 16, no 87.
272 VMA: VHOA, Alistettujen asiain päätöstaltiot, Savon ja Karjalan lääni, v. 1781, Di 16, no 50.
273 Saloheimo 1980, p. 274.
274 VMA: VHOA, Alistettujen asiain päätöstaltiot, Savon ja Karjalan lääni, v. 1781, Di 16, no 57.
275 VMA: VHOA, Alistettujen asiain päätöstaltiot, Savon ja Karjalan lääni, v. 1783, Di 18, no 16.
276 VMA: VHOA, Alistettujen asiain designaatioluettelo, v. 1783, Di 18, no 16.
277 Saloheimo 1980, p. 272

deplorable.[278] Certainly, the functionaries and clergy of earlier times in Liperi were no exception to this generalization.

In 1756, a peasant farmer called Heikki Eronen sued the sheriff, Kristoffer Gröön, for assault and causing him grievous bodily harm. In fact, Eronen died within a year of the deed. There was a full proof of the assault, as two eyewitnesses ventured to appear before the court. The sheriff did not deny the deed, confessing that he had kicked, pushed and beaten Eronen and pulled his hair. The only external trace of the assault was a bleeding wound, which the pathologist regarded as unconnected with the cause of death. The Provincial Surgeon, Geisse, who was then living in Rantasalmi, drew up a report of the autopsy, the truth of which is impossible to ascertain afterwards. The sheriff was fined twenty silver *dalers* for assault.[279]

Five years later, in 1761, the priest of the Greek Orthodox parish, Pedri Katanski, was dismissed from office for profane malpractice, including drinking and violent behaviour.[280] Even the provincial prosecutor, A. J. Geitell, eventually ended up in the box in Liperi: he was prosecuted in 1789 for causing a woman to have a miscarriage and breach of the peace of the district court, but he was acquitted in both the lower court and the court of appeal.[281] The denunciation might have been inspired by a grudge felt by the Karelian peasants against him, for in consequence of inspections made by him nearly thirty persons had recently been sentenced to heavy fines at specially arranged district court sessions in Liperi, Kitee and Tohmajärvi for moonshining or concealing a still.[282]

In his study of the pre-industrial legal system in Stockholm, Hans Andersson notes that the contempt for the justice system characteristic of the seventeenth century had disappeared from the legal source material by the beginning of the following century. Andersson concludes that this reflects people's increasing confidence in the system of justice. That in turn increased their willingness to settle disputes in court rather than by fisticuffs. The phenomenon suggests that the protection afforded by the law had improved.[283]

The situation in the outlying regions of the kingdom was still very different in the late eighteenth century. Many of the citizens were suspicious of the justice system, and not altogether without reason. As in Liperi, this

---

278 Cf. Ylikangas 1976, pp. 227 ff; Suolahti 1925, pp. 33–75; Heikkinen 1988, pp. 34–43. This picture is endorsed by Saloheimo to the extent that many of the sheriffs in the province seem to have been prosecuted or discharged. Saloheimo 1980, pp. 241–245, 253–254.

279 VMA: VHOA, Alistettujen asiain päätöstaltiot, Savon ja Karjalan lääni, v. 1756, Di 2, no 22.

280 Jusleen 1798, Till consistorium i Borgo, at prester wid Grekiska församlingen i Swenska Carelen för Embeter fel anses efter Swensk lag, then 8 juli 1761. Saloheimo 1980, pp. 426–427.

281 VMA: VHOA, Alistettujen asiain päätöstaltiot, Savon ja Karjalan lääni, v. 1789, Di 24, no 25.

282 Mäntylä 1995, p. 93.

283 Andersson 1998, p. 63

mistrust is apparent from the district court records of Ilomantsi. The minister of Ilomantsi, Anders Norrgren, was taken to court in the 1750s and 1760s over a burn-beating dispute, and he was charged with peculation. He himself was also the victim of a number of robberies. The sheriffs of Ilomantsi, for their part, were quite frequently involved in brawls in the performance of their duties. One sheriff, Johan Hultin, was fined in the 1750s for hitting a man and pulling his hair. There were also numerous complaints of negligence laid against him, for he was not very keen to apprehend the criminals who plagued the area. The Government of Vyborg complained that he took bribes from them and therefore allowed them free passage in the parish. For example, when Teppana Huurinainen, who was suspected of a triple murder, was at liberty and hiding in the forest, the local inhabitants had good cause to fear for their safety. Hultin also took legal action himself, for slander among other things. His successor, Johan Mandell, was likewise accused of taking bribes on a number of occasions during his period in office. The charges – whether justified or not – were dismissed in court. So many insults were also hurled in the face of Mandell that in 1768 the court issued fines for fourteen different cases of contempt of court.[284] Disturbances in the courtroom were usually caused by those whose cases had taken an unwelcome turn.[285] The values of the authorities and those they governed by no means always coincided.[286] Therefore, the justice dispensed by the courts was not able totally to obviate the violent settlement of disputes.

Just like their colleagues in eastern Finland, research has often drawn attention to "the poor quality and cravenness" of civil servants in Southern Ostrobothnia. The weakness of the authorities has emerged as a particularly significant factor in describing the background to the wave of violence that plagued the region from the late eighteenth century on. However, it is not thought that the miserable quality of the functionaries was the only factor involved.[287] So it is not justified in the case of Liperi, either, to claim that the arbitrary behaviour of the officials was the sole source of the violent inclinations of the local people, for before the 1770s personal disputes had only very rarely ending in killings. Nevertheless, the repeated abuses of the authorities undermined the people's belief in the justice of the administration. Such factors mould popular attitudes to the law; people become more inclined to solve disputes by violent means than by having recourse to the channels of justice.

284 Piipponen 1988, pp. 6, 13–14. KA: Karjalan tuomiokunnan tk 1759, KO a 28, 74 §. In view of this, it is interesting that there were fewer homicide trials during the period when Mandell was in office than before or after it.
285 Katajala 1994, p. 227.
286 Lenman & Parker 1980, p. 40.
287 Ylikangas 1976, p. 28 and note.

The first suspicions of possible offences by Stenfeldt, the parish priest of Liperi, were dealt with in the Åbo Court of Appeal as late as 1779, when a peasant farmer called Erkki Hirvonen, brought an action in the district court against the minister and one Ensign Kyander for a breach of domestic peace. Hirvonen said that in the spring he had been reporting for Holy Communion when the minister had grabbed him by the lapels and dragged him into his chamber. There Kyander had pulled him by the beard and chased him out of the building. A few weeks later, said Hirvonen, the minister had come to his farmhouse in Liperinsalo. There the priest had attacked him, beating both him and his wife and inflicting visible wounds on his aged victims. When later Hirvonen had summoned the priest to administer Holy Communion to him, the latter had refused to do so. And so had his curate.

The minister and Ensign Kyander were acquitted of the charge because there was no legal proof of the deed. Instead, Erkki and Kirsti Hirvonen, who had brought the action, were fined twenty silver *dalers* for making a false charge and ordered to make a public apology at the following assizes. The aged and ill Hirvonens were permitted to atone for their offence with a prison sentence of eight days on bread and water.[288]

Stenfeldt was also acquitted on another charge of assault.[289] It was not until he became engaged in a dispute with his 61-year-old chaplain, Henrik Alopaeus, that the district court and the Cathedral Chapter of Borgå (Porvoo) began proceedings to have him removed from office. The initiative of the chaplain elicited from the long silenced parish an indictment against the minister that was dozens of pages long. Although most of the charges were unproven, there was still a crushing list of crimes for which there was legally valid evidence: repeated performance of his duties when blind drunk, assaulting his verger, drunken association with worthless persons, illegal imprisonment, swearing at the alter in front of the congregation and various acts of violence against his parishioners – these were all testified to by a sufficient number of eyewitnesses to establish a full proof against him.[290] If the offences had not been grievous and of long duration, the tightly knit network of mutual loyalty among the authorities might have discouraged the people from the idea of trying to get a person in an official position dismissed. For example, at the turn of the following century, a couple of similar attempts to have chaplains removed in the parish of Kuhmo partly failed.[291] In Liperi, the parishioners do not seem to have shrunk from availing themselves of the services of Stenfeldt, for all his dangerous reputation, as long as he legally held office.

The Cathedral Chapter of Borgå suspended Stenfeldt from his duties for the course of the investigation, and after sentence was passed no longer permitted him to continue in the performance of his duties. He lost his office. As a member of the estates, Stenfeldt was sentenced to atone for

---

288 VMA: VHOA, Alistettujen asiain päätöstaltiot, Savon ja Karjalan lääni, v. 1779, Di 14, no 107.

289 KA: Karjalan tuomiokunnan tuomiokirja Liperin tk 1780, KOa 55, § 1.

290 VMA: VHOA, Alistettujen asiain päätöstaltiot, Savon ja Karjalan lääni, v. 1781, Di 16, no 50. See also Mäntylä 2000, p. 60

291 Heikkinen 1988, pp. 34–38, also 201–204.

his numerous crimes with one year's hard labour, in the course of which he managed to escape from Kuopio Prison, though he was later recaptured. Adolf Fredrik Stenfeldt died in shame in the fortress of Svartholm in the spring of 1785.[292]

After the disgrace of the highest spiritual authority in the parish, the way was open not only for the dismissal of the sheriff, Bernsten, but also for the desperate death of Provincial Barber-Surgeon Geisse. He was known to have performed the autopsies of the people of the Province of Savo and Karelia irreproachably for nearly twenty years, [293] It was only at the end of the 1770s that he had come to witness a plethora of violent deaths in his immediate neighbourhood, arising from the exponential increase in homicide in Liperi.

The case of Geisse was a subject of discussion for a long time among the people of the parish as well as among the members of the estates throughout Karelia. In a letter to Matthias Calonius, Henrik Gabriel Porthan laid the blame fairly and squarely on the minister, Stenfeldt. It was widely rumoured among the gentry of Liperi that the "melancholy" of the barber-surgeon had become unbearable because Stenfeldt had bribed him to issue a false death certificate under oath. In this way the minister hoped to escape from the suspicion of having beaten one of his parishioners to death. According to Saloheimo, the same interpretation of Geisse's motives lives on in Karelian folklore.[294] If the rumours were true, the bribery was successful. Apart from the above mentioned case of Hirvonen, the judicial sources give no indication that the minister had actually stained his hands with blood.[295]

Barber-Surgeon Geisse may have been driven into a fatal depression by a sense of guilt, although equally well it may have been financial difficulties that triggered his mental disorder. Because of his job, it had not escaped his notice that an increasing number of persons in Liperi began to suffer violent deaths after he had moved into the parish and possibly committed perjury. If Geisse had indeed manipulated the truth about the cause of death of Stenfeldt's victim, he may well have construed the plethora of killings in his home parish as a consequence of his false oath.[296] When performing autopsies, Geisse continued to receive occasional offers of bribes from persons suspected of homicide. As a result, he may have been unable to forget what was the perhaps only act of perjury that he had committed. His pangs of remorse finally became severe in 1779,

---

292 VMA: VHOA, Alistettujen asiain designaatioluettelo v. 1781, Di 16, no 50.

293 KA: Karjalan tuomiokunnan tuomiokirja, Liperin tk 1782, KO a 59, § 20.

294 Manninen 1917, pp. 121–122; Lagus 1898, p. 52; Saloheimo 1980, p. 473.

295 It is also possible that when the rumours spread beyond the locality that Bernsten may have been confused with the above mentioned sheriff, Gröön.

296 The form of the oath in the autopsy reports was as follows: "...hwilket jag ej allenast på min redan aflagde embetsed intygar, utan ock med denna min edeliga förbindelse, så sant mig Gud hielpe till lif och själ, bekräftar." (... which I on my already pledged professional oath and further by this my sworn undertaking attest to be as true as God may help my life and soul attest.) Den 29 Julii Kongl Instr. för Prov Med 8 §, Flintberg 1803, p. 465.

and he reported a peasant farmer's son from Eno who was suspected of manslaughter to the sheriff for bribery. The remanded youth had offered him two roubles, two talents of butter and ten wildfowl in return for making a certificate of death that would acquit him.[297] The false death certificate that Geisse issued for the benefit of the priest was perhaps not the only one of its kind, but on this matter it is possible only to speculate. If the corruption was general, conclusions about the numbers of homicides committed in the northern parts of Savo and Karelia are based on a shaky foundation for the whole period in which Geisse held the office of barber-surgeon, that is up to his death in 1763.[298]

In the light of the concept of justice that prevailed during the age of orthodoxy, it is not far-fetched to conclude that Geisse felt that his heart was hanging from a tree because he was a perjurer. One could even imagine that some mythological belief or some pre-modern European law might ordain that the body of a person who broke the Second Commandment be symbolically desecrated in this way. The man of the church, Geisse's friend who had enticed him into crime, had in the meantime lost his position and in practice also the last sheds of any social respect he may have enjoyed. Geisse, who had the reputation of being a pious person, probably shared the belief of his contemporaries in the doctrine of blood guilt developed by the reformers. The tenets of the doctrine were inscribed in various forms in the instructions for judges, in the Patent of Eric XIV and in the Trial Ordinance of 1614. During the seventeenth and eighteenth centuries, the clergy indoctrinated their flocks thoroughly with this ideology. There were several version of the doctrine of blood guilt. In that of Laurentius Petri in the 1560s it took the following form: [Homicide] is a just reason and cause for the ills that God shall lay upon the land for the shedding of blood. (*[Mandråpare] är rätta orsaken och upphovet till de plågor, som Gud för bluds utgjutelse skull over jorden komma låta.*)[299] A grievous crime that went unpunished aroused the wrath of God upon the country and the locality. The spilling of blood brought divine retribution, God's vengeance upon the whole community in the form of famines, plagues and riots.[300] A celestial agent would eventually intervene in the repression of crime by punishing every member of the community if the justice system was negligent in the performance of its duties in punishing criminals.[301] He who swore an oath always in so doing

---

297 VMA: VHOA, Alistettujen asiain päätöstaltiot, Savon ja Karjalan lääni, v. 1780, Di 15, no 49. Despite this, the young man was acquitted on the basis of Geisse's post mortem report

298 Saloheimo 1980, p. 473. Geisse's name is mentioned for the first time in post mortem reports in Savo and Karelia in connection with a double murder in November 1763. His widespread professional territory was reduced after the new provincial division of 1775. VMA: VHOA, Alistettujen asiain designaatioluettelot, v. 1764, Di 4, no 25. On Geisse's earnings, see also Wirilander 1989, pp. 474–476.

299 Bergman 1996, pp. 33, 40. On the Scapegoat Theory, see also Williams 1996.

300 For further details see e.g. Aalto 1996, p. 136; Ylikangas 2000, pp. 343–344; Anners 1965, p. 11; Thunander 1993, pp. 57–58.

301 Gaskill 2000, pp. 212, 214–215.

also invoked God's vengeance for a false oath.[302] Perhaps Barber-Surgeon Geisse realized that he had offended against the Second and Fifth Commandments in various ways by killing, concealment of a crime, taking bribes and perjury.

If Geisse really falsified the death certificate to help Stenfeldt, the exponential growth in the number of victims of homicide would have been evidence to him of a retribution for which unexpiated bloodshed was calling out. In accordance with a belief that was generally accepted and politically validated, the blood guilt could only be expiated by the blood of the person who had shed it, for the blood of the murdered person continued to flow for as long as the killer went free among the people.[303] Since it was also stated in the Old Testament that God would punish the wrong-doer unto the third or fourth generation, Geisse evidently did not wish his own descendants to experience these merciless further consequences.

Barber-Surgeon Geisse committed a so-called "extended suicide", of which there are but few examples in the history of crime in pre-industrial Europe.[304] The motive for his self–immolation was most probably the ethos of self-punishment, inspired by a misdemeanour that offended against his own ideal of himself and his moral principles.[305] The psychological background factor, the "melancholy", or depression, indicates that he had fallen victim to a conflict between the personal standards that he had internalized and the outer world. Geisse directed the aggressive energy created by this tension mainly against himself. This kind of personal reaction has been thought to represent the emergence of a new culture of guilt replacing the more ancient culture of shame and externally directed aggression. The phenomenon is considered to have gained a footing first of all among the so-called new middle class. It was in this group that the significance of birth as a factor determining a person's future first declined. Consequently, one could no longer blame only circumstances for social or financial failure; the failure lay also with oneself.[306] It is by no means farfetched an interpretation to place Barber-Surgeon Geisse with his financial troubles among a gradually emerging middle stratum of society that was outside the division of the estates.[307]

---

302 Nousiainen 1993, p. 402; Nehrman 1759: XII, 33–34.

303 Flintberg 1803, p. 450.

304 Sharpe 1981, p. 33 points out, however, that suicide in the pre-industrial age mainly took place in connection with homicides within the family.

305 Cf. Berkowitz 1962, pp. 34, 324. The need for self-punishment is stated to be one of the main motives for suicide in modern times.

306 Cf. Mm. Berkowitz 1962, pp. 318, 326; Ferrer 2001, pp. 147–148; Miller 1993, p. 116; Sundin 1992, p. 296.

307 On the subject of shame, see also Braithwaite 1989. The idea of cultures of shame and guilt comes from social anthropology. Jan Sundin, Johan Söderberg and Björn Furuhagen consider the historical development that led to the culture of guilt as being an indication of a decline in the binding nature of personal relations in the social sphere. Sundin 1992, p. 296; Furuhagen 1996, p. 165; Söderberg 1990, p. 246 ff. Cf. also e.g. Elias 1994, pp. 453–456.

The developmental psychologist, Liisa Keltikangas-Järvinen, popularizes the conceptual distinction between shame and guilt by distinguishing them according to their object: one feels shame before others, but guilt, a later and more developed emotion than shame, one feels above all before oneself and one's conscience. The ability to feel guilt delivers one from external sanctions and punishments and makes it possible to set oneself internal ideals. When one acts against these ideals, one feels guilt. But a personality that has not passed beyond the stage of shame has no internal ideals. Then one's actions are governed merely by fear of being caught and social disgrace. If one has no sense of guilt, one's conscience becomes flexible as long as one can be sure of not getting caught.[308] Therefore, it is generally believed that a stable and strong control over one's personal actions is a much more effective deterrent to murder than capital punishment.[309]

> There was an early antecedent of Geisse's death: in 1767, he had himself had to deal with the inquest on two murdered children in Rantasalmi, where he lived at the time.[310] The children's father, a crofter called Pekka Kankkunen, had slain them while of unsound mind. Moreover, in addition to Geisse, two other men in the area of this study ended up committing suicide after killing members of their own families. Pauli Pasanen from Kaavi, also in the parish of Liperi, took his own life in 1786 after killing his brother, who was a man of ill repute. Then the chaplain of Joroinen, Gustav Hielman apparently drowned himself in the Varkaudenkoski Rapids after killing his wife in 1748.[311]

The significance of killing his own children took on quite a different aspect in the mirror of Geisse's soul from the appearance it assumed in the eyes of the rest of the world. It was a misguided attempt to save the souls of his children. Thus it is not possible to treat their killing as homicide in the traditional sense motivated by an intent to injure. The scrupulous moral code internalized by Geisse had become separated from the external deterrent, i.e. the threat of legal consequences. His excessive internalization of the control of his own actions nevertheless led to an outcome that was equally as lethal as in many cases where there is a lack of such control: the death of three people. However, this internalized orthodox Lutheran outlook was foreign to many of those who during the same period committed grievous homicides in the full knowledge that it was worth trying to avoid the legal consequences of their bloody deeds by denying their guilt. Many of these killers had a Greek Orthodox background. A report of a Lutheran dean's inspection of 1780 complains in a prejudiced manner that Orthodox criminals considered breaking the fast and other external features of their religion to be greater sins than real crime.[312]

---

308 Keltikangas-Järvinen 2000, p. 310; also Berkowitz 1962, pp. 307–309.
309 Berkowitz 1962, p. 322.
310 This is evident from a priest's certificate of character written posthumously for Geisse. KA: Karjalan tuomiokunnan tuomiokirja, Liperin tk 1782, KOa 59, 19–20 §§. See also Wirilander 1989, pp. 474–475.
311 MMA: KymLKa, Hovioikeus maaherralle 1749, D 10 a1, 10.3.1749.
312 Saloheimo 1980, p. 436.

Denial of Guilt: the Manipulation of Justice

Denial of guilt can be considered one of the forms of resistance to the authorities and the justice system.[313] This form of defiance was not only understandable but also non-violent in nature, although the deeds associated with it certainly were not. Since denial proved in practice to be an incredibly effective method of avoiding the judicial consequences of crime, it had the effect of maintaining the lack of faith in the ability of the judiciary to act in the public interest. It also increased the tendency of members of the judiciary to concentrate on defending their own interests.[314]

From the mid-eighteenth century on, several royal circulars were sent to the courts of appeal on the subject of speeding up long-drawn-out trials and the implementation of sentences.[315] The problem was an old one: it had aroused considerable discussion ever since the end of the seventeenth century, when the law of the kingdom was drafted. The solution was sought not by changing the structure of the courts but by improving the procedures observed in them.[316] From the Crown's point of view, the length of trials was problematic partly because long periods of remand strained the state's finances. It was also felt that long incarceration caused the prisoners unnecessary suffering. A third argument for speeding up the

313 On the non-violent forms of protest by the peasants in the seventeenth century, see Katajala 1994, pp. 135–138.
314 Cf. Björn 1993, p. 146.
315 Jusleen 1751, Til samteliga Hof-rätter, om rättegångens förkortande i brottmål. Stockholm den 18 oct 1750. Jusleen 1787, Til samteliga hof-rätterne, at utan uppehåll afgiöra thit inkomne besvär, angående wid under-domstolarne ådömde böter. Stockholm den 23 jan 1751; Ugla 1798, p. 234, Til Hof-Rätterne angående arbetsmethoden och rättegångs-sättets förkortande den 11 dec 1766; Modeé 8., p. 7623, Til samteliga landshöfningar, at med all droft och skyndsamhet afgiöra executions-mål samt theröfver hvarje halft år insända förtekningar; af Ugglas 1780, Til landshöfdingarne, at utan uppehåll befordra de til dem från Kongl Maj:t och des nedre revision avgående remisser och bref...den 21 jan 1773; Circulaire til samtelige Hof-rätter, collegier och öfverrätterne, angående brottmålens skyndesamma afhielpande til lagligt slut, then 15 april 1774. On earlier statutes, see Nousiainen 1993, p. 358.
316 Nousiainen 1993, pp. 358, 362–373.

trials concerned general deterrence; the deterrent effect of a punishment was believed to weaken if too long a period elapsed from the time of the crime.[317] The length of homicide trials in Savo and Karelia crucially depended on whether the accused pleaded guilty or not. However, this factor went by and large unrecognized by the King and by the courts of appeal in their attempts to shorten the duration of trials.

In the whole kingdom there were altogether about 300 remand prisoners in 1748. Because they constituted a considerable outlay for the Crown, a royal order was issued permitting them to be used for labour. His Majesty pointed out that the prolongation of remand should not become an extra penalty on the accused. However, the length of remand continued to grow as the number of judicial instances increased when Gustav III decreed that all capital sentences were to be referred to the Council of Justice. Nevertheless, remand was not to be used as an unofficial form of punishment.[318] This condition was satisfied in procedural terms by the expansion of a separate institution: confessional remand (i.e. incarceration for the purpose of extracting a confession).

From the tendency of criminals to deny their guilt we can discern the existence of two separate jurisdictional cultures. Those who committed homicide in northern Savo were relatively speaking more prepared to confess to their crimes than the Karelians, but they too gradually adopted the strategy of pleading not guilty from the turn of the 1770s and 1780s on. A similar growth in denial, linked to an increase in the brutality of the crimes, has been observed by Ylikangas both in Southern Ostrobothnia in the 1780s, and also in some other areas in the early seventeenth century.[319] Seppo Aalto, too, has described a murder case in the 1670s in which a defendant used denial as an intentional survival strategy.[320] Rudolf Thunander, for his part, has examined the sentencing practice of the Göta Court of Appeal over three decades in the seventeenth century. His material contains only fourteen murder trials in which the accused confessed to their guilt.[321] This trend of pleading not guilty to murder, which spread to Savo from Karelia, and possibly also from Southern Ostrobothnia, cannot be considered a phenomenon that transcends history and is independent of time and place; rather, the reason for it must be connected with a particular legal system and culture. While this was naturally above all represented by the legal theory of evidence, also involved was a deeply rooted local folk strategy for manipulating justice, the official

---

317 Cf. Calonius 1800, 1802, 1804, pp. 42–45; af Ugglas 1780, Circulaire til samtelige Hof-rätter, collegier och öfverrätterne, angående brottmålens skyndesamma afhielpande til lagligt slut, then 15 april 1774.

318 Jusleén 1751, Till öfwer-ståthållaren och samteliga Hof-rätter at fångar måge tilhållas til arbete. Stockholm den 18 mars 1748. Nehrman (Ehrenstråle) 1759, III:54, p. 119. Modée 1781, pp. 139: 29.3. 1773, Kongl Göta Hofrätts bref ang. brottmåhls skyndesamma afgiörande.

319 Ylikangas 2000, pp. 45–47.

320 Aalto 1990, pp. 145–148.

321 Thunander 1993, p. 132.

purveyors of which were traditionally distrusted. The manipulation was made possible because loopholes in the establishment of proof had become common knowledge and it was thus possible to predict the practical effects of their exploitation. A concomitant weakening in unofficial control was another reason for the increase in murders.

However, it is not the strength of the punitive deterrent that prevents crime to any great extent; rather, it is the perpetrator's ideas of right and wrong.[322] The origins of crime, particularly homicidal crime, are never influenced by external repression alone; rather they are strongly determined by the complex dynamics of two other variables: first, the features of the perpetrator's personality, the degree of his socialization and the extent to which he has internalized a moral code; second, the society and the social pressures that propel a person into crime.[323] Thus the fear of punishment offers a poor explanation, for example, for fluctuations in the number of murders of members of the same family. For the most part, familial homicides did not differ from other forms of homicide in the extent to which they were denied by their perpetrators in Savo and Karelia – apart from cases concerning the killing of a spouse, in which the culprits generally denied their guilt to the bitter end.

Studies of the psychological make-up of killers in recent times conclude they often lack a vital emotional control force: the ability to feel guilt. Many killers have also failed to internalize the concepts of good and evil.[324] The source of control of one's own actions remains purely external when it is bound only to the expectation of rewards or the fear of punishments, with no internalized conscience to prohibit one from killing another person.[325] Lawrence Kohlberg, who has classified human moral ideas, considers the stage that is oriented around punishment and obedience to be the lowest level of morality. At this stage, a person's actions are regulated purely by fear of punishment. According to Kohlberg, the highest level of thought is represented by a morality based on universal ethical principles.[326] In practice, Elias is of the same opinion.[327] Despite the fact that these views have been criticized for being restricted in terms of time and place, that is for their concentration on modern western cultural ideals, it is nevertheless possible to draw some general conclusions on the basis of them. The psychology of an individual whose personal moral standards are based purely on an external deterrent and not on an internal ethical imperative offers a fertile soil for illegal actions if both the threat of punishment and the unofficial control exercised by the social

322 E.g. Berkowitz 1962, pp. 307, 322.
323 Sharpe 1990, pp. 8–9.
324 E.g. Berkowitz 1962, p. 34; Keltikangas-Järvinen 1978, pp. 32–33.
325 Keltikangas-Järvinen 1978, pp. 32–33.
326 Kohlberg 1984, p. 621 ff. Kohlberg's attitude has been criticized among other things for regarding western values as paramount, but the problem concerns not so much what are regarded as the highest levels of moral analysis as the lowest. Berger 2001, pp. 335–336.
327 Elias 1994, pp. 123, 210.

networks are diluted. Then all three links in the chain of control are broken: the control of the person himself, that of his immediate community and that of society at large. When this happens, the consequences of a diminished risk of getting caught may give rise to an increase in such grievous forms of crime as murder. This is what seems to have happened to a considerable extent in northern Savo and northern Karelia during the last decades of Swedish rule.

The means of the law for proving the guilt of a person who had hired an assassin, for example, were extremely limited. Usually such a person had furnished himself with an alibi for the time of the killing. None of those persons who hired assassins pleaded guilty to their crimes, and therefore it was not possible for lack of evidence to sentence them to the punishment prescribed by law: beheading with mutilation of the body.[328]

A 24-year-old woman from Kitee called Inkeri Laakkonen, who coveted her father's inheritance and was incensed by the district court indictments that she had received, engaged an assassin to kill her father, a deed which neither the authorities nor her father, Antti Laakkonen, despite his pleas for assistance, were able to avert. In all three judicial instances in which the crime was tried, lack of legal evidence against Inkeri Laakkonen, who had bribed the witnesses, made it impossible to sentence her. Nevertheless, contrary to her expectations, she ended up spending the rest of her life in confessional remand in Stockholm House of Correction.

Antti Laakkonen's widow told the court that she had woken up on Boxing Day 1795 a little before midnight with her shoulders feeling wet. She had kindled a light and realized that she was covered in blood. To her shock she saw that her husband had been murdered. The victim's skull had been smashed in with an axe, which was still in place.

The victim's daughter, Inkeri Laakkonen, who was described as violent and malicious in the priest's certificate of character, was immediately suspected of the murder, together with the deceased's son-in-law and namesake, Antti Laakkonen, and a vagrant called Klaus Tolonen. Witnesses testified that the trio had threatened the victim on numerous occasions.

They also told the court that Inkeri Laakkonen had started to hate her father after the latter had refused to comply with the wishes of his daughter and to relinquish his position as head of the farm. Relations had become ever more inflamed when the father remarried after the death of his first wife, the mother of Inkeri. The idea that young heirs might be born of the new union was not to Inkeri's liking.

In the summer preceding his death, the father had reported his daughter and the parents of his son-in-law for assaulting him and his wife. Inkeri Laakkonen had thrown an axe at his head when he blamed her for the disorder in the house. He had also brought an action against her and her husband for theft, because they had taken a heifer, three fyke nets, a ordinary fishing net and other property to the value of fifty *dalers* from the farm.

328 In Pälkjärvi, however, the person who commissioned the murder of Juho Päivinen and the perpetrator gave such conflicting testimonies against each other that the case was ultimately settled on the order of the King by drawing lots. VMA: VHOA, Alistettujen asiain päätöstaltiot, Savon ja Karjalanlääni, v. 1787, Di 22, no 5; v. 1788, Di 23, no 2.

Many witnesses testified that the daughter had vented her spleen on her father in numerous vitriolic curses. These accompanied threats that he would not live long, or that he would not see the following district court sessions, when the family disputes were due to be dealt with. She had made threats to her acquaintances that she would find surely find a man to carry out the murder if she could not do it herself. She had promized half of her father's farm to a female witness if she would get a vagrant called Klaus Tolonen who was going about the village to murder him.

During the course of the autumn the father complained to both the parishioners and the District Judge that his daughter and son-in-law were threatening to kill him. He knew that they had persuaded Tolonen to attempt his murder. The state of open psychological warfare that prevailed is also indicated by the fact that Tolonen had several times held Laakkonen in the sights of his gun without pulling the trigger. It began to be rumoured in the village that Klaus Tolonen had been hired to murder Antti Laakkonen. Despite his pleas, Laakkonen did not receive any communal assistance to protect his life.

Inkeri Laakkonen's open bragging indicates that she did not really believe that the law would be able to solve the crime that she was about to undertake. The young women was apparently firmly convinced that the witnesses would not testify against her in court. After all, it would have made no sense to commit a murder for the sake of the inheritance, because by criminal law a person who commissioned a murder was disinherited together with his or her whole branch of the family.[329] A strong confidence in the weakness of control, both official and unofficial, based on her own personal experience lay behind Inkeri Laakkonen's motives.

Laakkonen was murdered according the timetable stated in his daughter's threat: before the following district court sessions. During the washing of the corpse, she offered one of the witnesses three barrels of rye and two *riksdalers* to keep silent in court about what she saw. Probably it would have been possible to silence the witnesses in some petty crime, but the case being one of patricide the witnesses disregarded material benefits and told the court what they knew of the case.

Because the evidence assembled against Laakkonen's daughter and son-in-law was only enough for a half-proof, the District Court of Kitee and Kesälahti adjourned the conviction of Inkeri for murder *sine die*. However, both the lower court and the court of appeal found that there was sufficient evidence supplied by eye-witnesses to convict her of assault of a parent and sentence her to thirty lashes and infamy.

The Supreme Court confirmed her incarceration in confessional remand under suspicion of murder. The sentence was justified in the rhetorical terms associated with such cases by the fact that she was generally considered guilty in the locality where the crime was committed, and her release would have aroused strong disapproval there. The guilt of her husband as an accessory to murder continued to be adjourned *sine die*.

Even after the trial was finally over, Inkeri Laakkonen stubbornly continued the litigation and, citing her poor health, petitioned for the punishment of 30 lashes to be commuted to imprisonment on bread and water. This petition was granted on the basis of a doctor's certificate. Inspired by this, she also appealed to the King to be released from confessional remand. In order to lend weight to her appeal, she swore her innocence of the crime for which she had been committed to confessional remand. She complained that her heart, which had been broken by her father's death, was utterly crushed by

329 Nehrman 1756, V:II:80.

the murder charges, and she also made appeal to the plight of her children, who had been left without a mother.

Inkeri remained behind bars in Stockholm. His Majesty was not moved to clemency because the evidence against her was considered to be extremely incriminating.

The commissioned murder lay heavier on the conscience of Klaus Tolonen than he had anticipated. More generally, we can conclude that money alone did not provide a motive for committing a crime and was not sufficient to silence the accusing inner voice of the culprit; that usually required a deeper, subjective justification welling forth from personal loss or insult. The clergy's prolonged and eloquent persuasion finally got through to the assassin in August 1796. He confessed to murdering Antti Laakkonen at the insistent behest of Inkeri for a promised reward of over 55 *riksdalers*.

Tolonen stated that in the end he had not received any reward, which is also indicated by the fact that there was no evidence of his becoming suddenly rich around the time of the murder. In court, the assassin exculpated Inkeri's husband, Antti, from suspicion of the crime and said that the latter had tried rather to prevent the murder. Tolonen's evidence may have been false, for one of the villagers told the court that the son-in-law had tried to persuade him to drown his father-in-law when the latter was fishing. The Laakkonen couple may also have had a single goal but differing views as to who should carry out the deed. Again, it is possible that the husband had somehow managed to bribe Tolonen, who was already facing the death penalty, to keep silent about his part in the crime.

Klaus Tolonen informed the court of one further person who had incited him to commit murder, a peasant farmer called Mikko Laakkonen, whose family relationship with the other defendants is not clear from the court records. On the day of the murder, he had plied Tolonen with spirits to expedite the deed. Inkeri herself had joined in during the course of the day with the result that Tolonen was completely drunk when he set off for Tolonen's farm to commit the murder.

Although Klaus Tolonen confessed to the murder, the person who ordered it, Inkeri Laakkonen, steadfastly continued to deny it. Klaus Tolonen was sentenced for committing a contract murder to lose his right hand, to be beheaded, and his body to broken on the wheel. Although he repented, Klaus Tolonen was executed in February 1789.

Inkeri Laakkonen died in childbirth in Stockholm House of Correction in autumn 1798. Before she died she confessed to the murder of her father to the prison chaplain. She also relieved her conscience of the burden of another serious crime: infanticide, which she had committed over ten years earlier at the age of sixteen or seventeen. She did not mention the name of the child's father, simply stating that it had been conceived as a result of an illicit sexual liaison (*oloflig beblandelse*). There is no indication of incest in her account, which would offer a natural explanation for her resentful attitude to her father. Inkeri Laakkonen's infanticide was never reported to the authorities. She said that she had revealed the matter to only a few close friends and relations. On her death bed she repented of all her sins,[330] which according to the religious doctrine of the times was sufficient to save her soul. The chaplain of the house of correction gave her absolution and described the confession to the legal authorities as confidential. At the same time, another woman, from Tammela, who was in confessional remand in the same institution unburdened her conscience of the weight of her sin by confessing to the murder of her husband.

330 VMA: VHOA, Alistusaktit, Savon ja Karjalan lääni, v. 1798, Ece 46, no 4; Alistettujen asiain päätöstaltiot, Savon ja Karjalan lääni, v. 1798, Di 33, no 4; Designaatioluettelot ja alistettujen asiain päätöstaltiot, v. 1797, Di 32, no 1; Designaatioluettelot, v. 1796, Di 31, no 27.

Inkeri Laakkonen's garrulous vaunting before the local people is explained by her own personal history. The undiscovered infanticide and the experience of living with it had most probably filled her with a partly unfounded belief that she would get away with the crime in court. The killing of her child by a young and ignorant girl might have appeared in the eyes of the witnesses – if not in those of the legislators – to be a more defensible act than a transgression of the Fourth and Fifth Commandments tainted by greed and hatred. That is why the unofficial control functioned in this case, and the background to the deed was made clear to the authorities through the statements of the witnesses. It remains an open question whether Inkeri Laakkonen's belief that she would go unpunished had a wider basis in the legal culture of Kitee: the general concealment of homicidal crime.

The willingness to confess to charges under persuasion from the clergy was influenced by features connected with the *modus operandi*, the motivation for the crime and above all the individual psychology of the criminal, the awakening of his conscience leading to possible repentance. The killer might be amazed at what he had done, but then in other cases openly confess that he had acted out of revenge with no attempt to avoid the consequences of his crime.

However, in most cases the motivation for confession was religious: a desire to save one's own soul when close to death.[331] Prisoners committed to confessional remand for theft also did this.[332] In many cases, the accused person died before the report of his confession reached the legal authorities. Murderers were driven to confess by the divine retribution they faced, for according to the religious beliefs of the time confession was a precondition of absolution and eternal salvation.[333] Even the most stubborn criminals in eastern Finland generally confessed to their crimes when facing death, for they no longer had anything to lose in this life. The timing shows that the perpetrator experienced the threat of his own damnation as a far more powerful deterrent than the imperative of solidarity: the idea of blood guilt, according to which the whole kingdom faced perdition because of the misdeeds of one person.[334] Thus it can be claimed that this kind of confession did not really indicate any expansion of the so-called "culture of guilt". In Swedish society at the beginning of the modern age, the development of the culture of guilt was stimulated by severe public sanctions and by the Lutheran clergy's inculcation of a mentality that appealed to feelings of remorse, as well as by the economic progress that lay behind the process of individualization. From this point of view, it is of minor importance that the source of guilt, i.e. internalized control, was created by means of an external threat of punishment in the afterlife, the loss of the salvation of one's soul.[335]

---

331 Ylikangas 1976, p. 211.
332 Koskelainen 2001, p. 128.
333 Cf. e.g. Elias 1994, p. 164.
334 The basic principle of the doctrine is outlined in e.g. Thunander 1993, pp. 57–58; Kekkonen & Ylikangas 1982, pp. 56–57.
335 Cf. e.g. Ferrer 2001, pp. 147–148, 164–168.

Foucault's thesis concerning the gradual emergence of punishments that were directed against the soul appears in a different light when one considers the tendency of criminals to deny their crimes. It is a well-known fact that the primary object of punishment in the western legal system in the pre-industrial age was the body. It was preached that a criminal would forfeit the eternal salvation of his soul if he avoided the bodily punishment by denying his crime.[336] The soul was the "capital asset" that remained when the punished body was destroyed. According to theological morality, the criminal inflicted the punishment on his mind or soul himself, but he did this in the afterlife.[337] Here there is a choice involved: denial or confession. The greatest threat to this doctrinal framework was constituted by the growing number of criminals who lived outside the conceptual world of the Old Testament. Obviously, this group also included a large number of persons of the Orthodox faith, and in some cases it was the thankless task of the Lutheran clergy to try and persuade them to confess.[338] On the basis of the character certificates issued by the clergy, the average murderer was extremely ignorant of the basic articles of faith of Christianity. If ignorance of these articles means that the criminal's view of the afterlife did not coincide with that of the Christian faith, then capital punishment lost all significance as an act of atonement and was thus to be avoided to the bitter end.[339].

E. Nygren, the Sheriff of Ilomantsi, charged a peasant farmer called Juho Savolainen, his sister Helena and his wife Elina Airaksitar, and a settler called Antti Kärkkäinen, who was the betrothed of the victim, with the murder of one Maria Tikka, the widow of a settler, on 18 July 1793. The latter's body had been found in Haukilampi Pond.[340]
Juho Savolainen had told his wife that he had lain in wait behind a fence in order to kill Maria Tikka, who had been working in a burn-beaten field of oats. His motivation was a desire to avenge the wrongs he felt he had suffered from Maria. When he saw her going into the forest to cut hay, he had gone after her together with his sister, Helena. When Maria started working, he assaulted her, pulling her to the ground by her hair and smashing her skull with a rock. Then he and his sister tied her feet together and carried the body to Haukilampi Pond. Then they went to fetch some old planks that had fallen from the roof of a cabin and made a raft of them, on which they bound the body of Maria with willow shoots. They had then rowed the corpse to the middle of the pond and sank it. Juho Savolainen's nine-year-old deaf-mute son, who was a eye-witness to the deed, corroborated the wife's story.

336 E.g. Anners 1965, pp. 18–19.
337 Cf. e.g. Anners 1965, p. 19.
338 The judges appealed to the idea that only the most godless of criminals denied the charges against them. Cf. Anners 1965, p. 199.
339 Cf. Anners 1965, p. 37.
340 The information about the case is based on VMA: VHOA, Alistettujen asiain designaatioluettelot sekä Alistettujen asiain päätöstaltiot, Savon ja Karjalan lääni, v. 1793, Di 28, no 98; v. 1794, Di 29, no 4; v. 1795, Di 30, no 4; v. 1796, Di 31, no 2; RA: HDP 7.12.1795, 7.9.1802.

Even Savolainen was not such a cold-blooded character that he did not begin to tremble all over when Sheriff Nygren arrived at his home to inquire about the whereabouts of Maria Tikka. He displayed exceptional fear when he answered that he had not seen Maria for several days. During the search for Maria, he tried to remove any traces he had left by the pond and sought to sidetrack the searchers further away from the scene of the crime. When the body was found, he had difficulty in speaking and answering the questions that were put to him. In the district court, he said that at the time of the crime he had been clearing land for burn-beating together with his sister Helena at Löyttyvaara, which was some distance from Haukilampi Pond. However, some peasants who had been working in the vicinity of Löyttyvaara testified that there had been no sounds of work being done to be heard in the vicinity, and an examination of the area revealed no signs of recent clearing there. On the day of the crime, Savolainen's clothes had been soaked in blood.

In the days following the killing – before the people of the parish knew anything about the fate of Maria – Helena and Juho were spreading a rumour that the victim's fiancé, Antti Kärkkäinen, with whom Savolainen shared half his farm, had smashed Maria's teeth in with a rock and drowned her in Haukilampi Pond. Helena attempted to hoodwink her listeners into believing that Kärkkäinen was going to try and pin the crime on Juho Savolainen, as the latter was known to feel hatred and a desire for revenge against Maria. The reason for this was known to be the fact that Savolainen had been found guilty of theft in the district court on the basis of a report made by Maria.

When the body was found, the doctor issued a cause of death report. Maria Tikka's lower jaw had been smashed, and several of her teeth had been broken with a hard object. The actual cause of death was a fracture of the skull beside the left temple, which had caused a brain haemorrhage. The victim had died immediately and had subsequently been immersed in the pond.

Juho Savolainen was quite unable to prove his allegations against Antti Kärkkäinen. The Ilomantsi District Court acquitted the victim's fiancé and Elina Airaksitar, the wife of the main defendant, of charges of murder on 14 September 1793. On the other hand, the lower court held that the evidence assembled in the case against Helena and Juho was highly incriminating despite the fact that they denied their guilt and there were no competent eye-witnesses. The guilty parties were sentenced in the lower court to be executed by beheading in accordance with MB XII, after which Juho's body was to be broken on the wheel and Helena's to be burned at the stake.

After an enquiry lasting many years, the Vasa Court of Appeal judged that the evidence against Juho and Helena was extremely incriminating. The accused had clearly taken the life of Maria Tikka with premeditation and malice aforethought. Since, however, they consistently denied doing it and there were no competent eyewitnesses, they could not for want of a legally valid proof be judged guilty of murder.

The court of appeal nevertheless declared that the accused were generally regarded in the locality as having murdered Maria. Therefore, it would be extremely "questionable and publicly reprehensible" to let the accused go free. (At the same time, one Mikitta Jäkin, a thief who was known to have killed his brother-in-law in 1787, was going scot-free around the parish. The court of appeal had adjourned to the determination of his guilt *sine die*.) The court of appeal referred its judgments that Helena and Juho should be placed in confessional remand to the King. Since the only thing that was lacking for a proof that would make a murder sentence possible was a confession, the Supreme Court upheld the judgment and on 25 February 1796 committed

Juho to be held prisoner in the fortress of Sveaborg near Helsinki and Helena to hard labour in the Stockholm House of Correction for a suitable time. The clergy were directed, in accordance with the custom of the times, to try and persuade the accused at regular intervals to confess their deeds and to send a report of their progress in these persuasive efforts at the end of each year

The spouses of the accused petitioned for divorce, but the Supreme Court denied this on the grounds that the suspects had not been committed to confessional remand for life but only for a "suitable" period of time.

In 1802 Helena Savolainen appealed to be released on the grounds that no new evidence of her guilt (in accordance with RB XVII:32) had been adduced. The Supreme Court saw no reason to support the appeal, because she was still considered to be "under the gravest possible suspicion" of the crime. The case would be reopened immediately only if the suspects intended to confess. This, however, did not happen; Juho died in prison fairly soon, while Helena remained silent for years, until she too departed this life.

In dealing with homicide, the system of justice was from the point of view of jurisprudence logical and predictable. The legal premises concerning suspects, however, were not realistic; those who were guilty of grave crimes did not behave in the way the system assumed they would.

Homicide as a Form of Punitive Control

Self-help and Unofficial Justice

The possible rationality of the motivation for homicide has occupied scholars in numerous regards. Spierenburg has applied arguments drawn from social psychology and condensed the development of the nature of personal violence into the modernization model. The axes on the graph of this model are constituted on the one hand by impulsiveness and instrumentality, which distinguish the perpetrator's personality, and on the other by the ritual and rational aspects of the deed, which reveal its motivation.[341] Perhaps the model is better suited to explaining the forms of structural violence, in other words, the reform of the penal system, than to elucidating personal violence. Ritual and retributive violence – in other words, punitive spectacles that demonstrated the power of the king – gave way to rational punishments, like hard labour, aimed at reforming the criminal. Hard labour also had the advantage of benefiting the kingdom.[342] On the other hand, Österberg also sees public execution as a rational, goal-directed measure because of its deterrent aim.[343]

A psychodynamic approach casts doubt on Spierenberg's fundamental concept of a rational motivational basis for homicide. The structural basis for homicide contains an internal logic which is revealed through the contemporary cultural codes, and which exists irrespective of the age;[344] the values of a community are influenced by immaterial benefits as well as by material gain. The views of Donald Black, Jonas Lilieq-uist[345] and Heikki Ylikangas, among others, about the motivation for homicide are functional in this respect; they find that homicide in the pre-industrial age also embodies its own rational logic aimed at maintaining the integrity of society, whether they regard activity stemming

341 Spierenburg 1994, pp. 703–715; Spierenburg 1999, p. 113 ff; Jansson 1998, p. 72.
342 Nousiainen 1993, p. 52; also Garland 1994, p. 96 ff.
343 Österberg 1994, pp. 12–13.
344 Keltikangas-Järvinen 1978, p. 21.
345 Liliequist 1999, p. 185.

from a value-based rationality, for example a masculine code of honour, as the factor determining the Choice of valves, or a goal-directed rationality such as the safeguarding of legal benefits connected with the protection of property. In certain situations these factors require an emotional, even violent, reaction dictated either by the dominant culture or by a sub-culture.[346] The violent settlement of a dispute outside the law is a particularly rational act if it is known that there will be no legal or communal reaction (punishment) to the violence. Even when it is spontaneous, the nature of violence can also be instrumental, that is aimed at achieving a particular goal rather than at hurting another person.[347] That is why, for example, homicides that reinforce a sub-cultural code of honour are sensible acts in terms of the rational values of their own origins, for all that they may also be impulsive and ritual killings.[348]

The American legal sociologist, Donald Black, has formulated a theory about self-help, i.e. taking the law into one's own hands, as a form of social control.[349] Black approaches crime as a kind of self-help, the settlement of differences without the intervention of the authorities. From this point of view, many homicides can be regarded as manifestations of unofficial (informal) control. In the eyes of a person who has recourse to the law, this expression of social control is naturally criminal and reprehensible. Janne Kivivuori presents Black's arguments and applies them to an analysis of homicide in Finland in the late twentieth century.[350] It is also worth considering whether the central arguments put forward by Black can be articulated into a complete empirical entity in a study of homicide in the early centuries of the modern era.

Black considers that personal violence was the normal form of punitive control and self-help in the pre-modern society. Therefore – by a kind of reciprocity principle – violence is common in such societies. Punitive, unofficial control, for example blood vengeance is characteristic of stateless societies. In early states, this same kind of punitive control is expressed for example in duels, which according to the theory of Beccaria were a consequence of the weak legal protection offered by public authority. In the modern state, both blood vengeance and duels have been punished as forms of homicide; indeed, they would satisfy the conditions for murder. This to some extent undermines the traditional view, which regards impulsive killing as being a characteristic of pre-modern man.

However, the monopoly of the legitimate use of violence, i.e. the power to punish, assumed by the state at the beginning of the modern age, was only limited, theoretical and hypothetical. The struggle between state criminal law and self-help never in fact abated during the transition from the mediaeval to the modern age. The law was nevertheless the tool by which the most institutionalized forms of violent self-help were rooted out.

346 Ylikangas 2000, pp. 44–47; Liliequist 1999, p. 189.
347 Berkowitz 1962, p. 48.
348 Cf. for an opposing view, Spierenburg 1994, pp. 704–705.
349 Black 1984 a; 1984b.
350 Kivivuori 1999, p. 75 ff.

A crime that served the needs of control could, according to Black, be an expression of statelessness in all types of societies and communities. However, there are different forms of statelessness. In more recent times, too, violent self-help has been most common in situations where assistance from the law is least accessible. Even today, the conciliatory power of public authority does not, for example, necessarily extend to settling conflicts between persons who are closely related. Irrespective of the form of society, disputes between relatives and spouses are most commonly decided by resorting to unofficial and sometimes violent methods of settlement. There is a parallel situation in many disputes in which the parties involved come from the lowest social strata; conflicts within marginal groups tend to be outside the reach of the justice system.[351] Historically, this phenomenon is manifested in a descent on the social scale of the perpetrators of homicide with the coming of the modern era.

A conceptual framework in which the majority of the motives for killing are viewed as constituting an attempt to implement unofficial control supports the idea of the social contract. Black acknowledges the particular inspiration of Thomas Hobbes and firmly believes that the lack of a legitimate state law leads in practice to a kind of "a war of all against all".[352] Black considers the penal use of the law to vary in inverse proportion to other forms of social control such as compensatory, conciliatory and therapeutic control. Criminal law is stronger (stricter) when other kinds of normative machinery in life are weak, and vice versa.[353]

Black's views lend themselves flexibly to empirical findings about homicide in eastern Finland at the turn of the eighteenth and nineteenth centuries. The judicial repression of homicidal crime in eastern Finland was – characteristically of the pre-modern penal system – haphazard albeit severe. The repressive (deterrent) effect was weak because the system was inefficient and incomplete. It had least effect in the most violent regions. Certain factors involved in the fragility of legal control may have induced the people of eastern Finland to have recourse to inverted forms of social control and to lawless actions.[354]

Factors related to the social situation, control, individual psychology and a situation in life that offers no alternatives all combine to produce killings that are very similar in terms of their motivation and their circumstances.[355] In Savo and Karelia, homicides were most often the consequence of long-standing conflicts. Generally, it was a dispute within a family or a beat-burning partnership that led to the mortal conflict. Other repeated sources of discord included care of an aged relative, sharing of

---

351 Black 1984a, pp. 3–19.
352 It was left to Hobbes' successors to develop this view by pointing out the importance of the immediate community in providing security.
353 Black 1984b, p. 8. However, Black does not claim that the sum of all the above-mentioned forms of control is necessarily a constant that is independent of the environment.
354 Cf. Muchembled 1989, pp. 14–42; Elias 1994, pp. 156–165.
355 Cf. e.g. Keltikangas-Järvinen 1978, p. 19.

the crop and the conditions pertaining to the dissolution or foundation of a partnership.[356] Most commonly, the fatal consequence was the killing of a brother or brother-in-law. Almost as frequently killings were prompted by conflicts connected with marriage, marital fidelity, marital disputes, betrothal and sexual relationships generally. Such conflicts involving family, partnership and marriage accounted for a large number (at least a third) of the motives behind homicide over the whole area. Homicides caused by marriage problems became more common towards the turn of the century, and consequently other killings inspired by internal disputes in a family or partnership decreased in relation to it.

However, the connection with the family does not explain the strong proclivity to homicide in the easternmost areas, because fraternal, marital and partnership disputes were relatively just as frequently the cause of homicides everywhere in the Province of Savo and Karelia irrespective of the absolute numbers of killings. In Kuopio and Iisalmi, the northernmost greater parishes of north Savo, together with their chapelries, where the growth in homicide in general was concentrated, both murders committed in conjunction with robbery and revenge murders became more common during the period of this research. In Karelia, on the other hand, the proportion of revenge murders decreased, but then from the very beginning they had been particularly characteristic of that region. The elimination of criminals by killing them also became rarer. The relative decline in the number of such numerically marginal albeit telling motivations for crime may indicate that such global models of the criminal sub-culture for settling problems were waning. Certainly, the characteristic nature of homicide continued to become more brutal, but it was members of the settled population who now became the perpetrators of the most brutal homicides. There is thus a connection between the extent of criminal sub-culture models for the settlement of problems and the total amount of all homicides, but not necessarily between such models and the characteristic nature of the deeds. The decline in such types of motivation in Karelia was clear. Homicides committed for personal gain, that is murders with robbery and killing for the purpose of obtaining material benefits, correspondingly increased. Instrumental homicide for profit was also common among Karelian women. Again economic ambitions were the main motive when a homicide was caused by a land dispute, for example.[357]

Apart from the high incidence of murders with robbery, revenge murders and contract killings in the east and north, the motivation for most homicides in Savo and Karelia did not vary to any great extent. Therefore, it is not possible to explain the increase in the brutality of the killings merely by analysing the structure of their motivation.

356　Similar causes of dispute were anyway common in family partnerships, Waris 1999, pp. 181, 183, 185.
357　Cf. Ylikangas 19998a.

The Individual and the Law: from Victim to Victor

Behind every killing there lurks a multifarious web of motives. From the most indirect cause there radiate strands that involve the whole spectrum of social life; this means that it becomes impractical and purposeless to reduce the influences to mere numbers, which efface the human being him- or herself.[358] Many premeditated killings could be described in the terms of the frustration-aggression model as acts of revenge for impoverishment, shows of strength after a defeat or the projection of the perpetrator's own inner conflicts on to his fellow men.[359]

The official social control that was implemented through the district courts by the members of the local community sometimes used to label a person accused of petty misdemeanours in his home locality as an irredeemable criminal.[360] When the locals picked out some undesirable as the target of their unofficial control, on the other hand, it was more or less irrelevant to his reputation whether he was adjudged guilty of his offences or not. The testimonial system unintentionally favoured a simple "gateway theory": minor crimes led their perpetrators to commit more serious ones. This phenomenon arose from the fact that, in the course of the trial, the culprit learned the secrets of judicial procedure and evolved a strategy whereby he or she could avoid punishment.[361] A mere plea of not guilty was often enough during the period of this research to ensure an acquittal or an adjournment sine die. For example, Inkeri Laakkonen, Antti Piirainen and Risto Sykkö, who were accused of hiring an assassin, were all recidivists, having been guilty of other serious crimes before they became involved in homicide. However, they had either not been charged with these earlier crimes, or, if they had, not been convicted of them.

Suspicion of theft aroused sentiments of reprehension within the peasant community and was thus highly detrimental to the reputation of the suspected persons.[362] The imputation undermined the respect they enjoyed in the community despite the fact that a charge of theft alone was not enough to deprive them directly of their official rank in society or of their property. However, becoming an object of opprobrium jeopardized a person's social, and thereby his economic, standing in the community, and this in turn had the effect of reinforcing his criminal proclivities.[363]

---

358 On the problem of compiling statistics for different kinds of phenomena, see e.g. Heikkinen 1996, p. 86.

359 See Chapter 9 dealing with evicted tenant farmers, and the case of Erkki Pellikka, who murdered his son, p. 171

360 This labelling means a stigma attached to an individual by the community to mark him or her as in some way deviant. Labelling is effected by social control and its process of selection. On the theory of labelling, see Lemert 1967, p. 141.

361 An observation by Liisa Koskelainen concerning thieves points to the same phenomenon: recidivist criminals are more likely to deny their crimes than first offenders. Koskelainen 2001, p. 125.

362 Thunander 1993, p. 75.

363 E.g. Laitinen & Aromaa 1993, p. 122.

Being labelled a criminal had a detrimental effect socially, and a family of three living in Sonkaja in the parish of Ilomantsi were to become victims of the hatred that it aroused. Antti Sykkö, a peasant who farmed Crown land, his wife Susanna Ahlholm and her eleven-year-old son Mikko all died as victims of a hired killer on a September night in 1757. The case records have been burnt. All that has survived is the judgments of the Åbo Court of Appeal on the various defendants and some separate charges concerning escaped prisoners.[364] I have attempted to elucidate the motives of the parties concerned by a close reading of the judgment books. In the judgment books for the Ilomantsi and Suolahti District Court in the years 1748–1760, I have tracked down all the civil and criminal cases in which the persons mainly involved in the triple murder and their close relatives appeared as plaintiffs, defendants or witnesses in order that I might ascertain the development of relations between the perpetrators and the victims and their positions in the community.[365]

Antti Sykkö had for years farmed a Crown smallholding in Sonkaja together with his father (also called Antti) and his brother Risto, until the last-mentioned began in 1753 to run up debts with some Karelian peasant farmers and the local dean, Anders Norrgren. The debts were incurred in some shady business deals and trading operations, in which the brother, Antti, had no part and was therefore also unwilling to help his sibling in his straitened circumstances. Risto lived in a different home on the farm from Antti and their father. The latter died in the mid-1750s. At the 1755 district court sessions, Antti demanded that the farm be divided so that Risto's portion should go to pay his debts. Risto continued to live on the farm but no longer participated in tilling it.

Even at this stage, Risto had a history of litigation. In 1750 he had been accused by a neighbouring farmer's wife of breach of domestic peace for having insulted her by claiming to have cuckolded her husband. The wife had taken offence at this insult to her virtue and attacked Sykkö on two occasions. The second had taken place on a highway.[366] She was convicted in the court of

---

364 MMA: KymLKa, Saapuneet kirjeet, v. 1758, Hovioikeus maaherralle, D 20 a1, no 31, 57, 64, 71, 73; Rikoskertomukset, v. 1754–1758, Karjalan voutikunta, E 1. VMA: VHOA, Alistettujen asiain päätöstaltiot, Kymenkartanon ja Savon lääni, v. 1757, Di 2, no 46; Alistettujen asiain designaatioluettelot v. 1760, Di 3, no 2; v. 1761, Di 3, no 1; v. 1764, Di 4, no 1; v. 1765, Di 5, no 1; v. 1766–1767, Di 6, no 1; v. 1768–1769, Di 7, no 1; v. 1770–1771, Di 8, no 1; no 77; Di 8, no 1.

365 KA: Karjalan tuomiokunnan tuomiokirjat, Ilomantsin ja Suojärven sk 1749, KO a 17, f 355–356; tk 1750, KO a 19, f. 139, sk 1750, KO a 19, 10 §; 22 §; 28 §; 35 §; tk 1751, KO a 20, 30 §, 32 §, 45 §, sk 1751, KO a 20, f 325 ffol; 330; 332b–333, 336 ffol; tk 1752, § 10; § 17; 26 §; § 27; sk 1752, § 30; § 44; § 53; § 65; 66 §; 70 §; KO a 22, tk 1753, 5 §; § 19, 23 §; 24 §; 30 §, 43 §; 44 §; 45; sk 1753, 4 §; 11 §; 12 §; 15 §; 18 §; 19 §; 32 §; 35 §; 47 §; 54 §; 72 §; tk 1754, KO a 23, 11 §; 12 §; sk 1753; 14 §; 33 §; tk 1754; KO a 23, 31 §; tk 1755, KO a 24, 9 §; 10 §; 33 §; v. 1756 tk, KO a, 25, 25 §; 49 §; 73 §; 74; 90 §; v. 1756 sk, KO a 25, 12 §; 45 §; 55 §; 61 §; ylimääräiset käräjät 1757, KO a 26, 1 §, sk 1757, KO a 26, 19 §; tk 1757, KO a 26, 13 §; 26 §; 32 §; 66 §; ylimääräiset käräjät 12.9. 1758; KO a 27, 1 §; 34 §; tk 1759, KO a 28, 66 §; 74 §; 77 §; 79 §; 85 §; 87 §; 88 §; ylimääräiset käräjät v. 1759, Ko a 28, f 671 ffol; sk 1959, 51 §; 56 §; sk 1760, KO a 59, 15 §, 31 §.

366 The Law of 1734 also recognised the possibility of outlawing a woman. This had not been the case in earlier legislation. Thunander 1993, p. 86.

appeal of breach of peace of the public highway and sentenced to a fine and infamy.[367] Her good name was restored to her when she appealed to the King on the grounds of the suffering caused to the members of her family.

Sykkö was also suspected on several occasions of stealing from local peasant farmers and of damaging their property in connection with certain burn-beating disputes from 1751 on. In the first theft case, he managed to get himself acquitted by taking an oath of purgation.

Risto Sykkö was the defendant in numerous debt cases during the 1750s. His fortune finally ran out in Lovisa, where he was committed to confessional remand in the winter of 1754. The committal was based on charges of the unlawful detention, highway robbery and defrauding of some Russian suppliant monks. He had defended himself against the charges of robbery by claiming that he had thought the monks to be robbers living in the forest. He was committed to incarceration on confessional remand for one year. When he had completed this term of hard labour, the court of appeal adjourned his case *sine die*.[368] He paid dearly for what he had done, and he may well have felt that this was unjustified, because there were indeed dangerous robber bands in the vicinity of Ilomantsi throughout the 1750s.

Immediately after his release, Sykkö was arraigned again at the 1756 autumn district court sessions for his debts and on a serious charge of burglary. Before the court was a financially and socially broken man who had lost his fortune, his rank as a peasant farmer and his reputation and who had very few chances of obtaining even a symbolic restitution of his lost capital, either material or immaterial.[369] The brothers had agreed that Antti would take possession of Risto's share of the farm in return for 200 copper *dalers* and two barrels of rye, but the division of the estate had not yet been carried out. The court records began to refer to him as a dependant lodger, and he was also described in the 1759 winter district court sessions as a vagrant.

At the same time there was a large-scale burglary at the home of Antti Sykkö's father-in-law, Antti Ahlholm, and it was strongly suspected that it had been committed by Risto. The latter had full reason to expect that his brother would continue to turn against him ever more strongly in public, for the brother and his wife had come forward as key witnesses in the burglary case. This is evidently the reason why Risto Sykkö decided to have his brother and sister-in-law murdered. Mikko Sivonen, the son of the wife Susanna Ahlholm and the adopted son of Antti Sykkö, was also murdered.

There were at least three other possible reasons for the murder of Susanna and Mikko. Susanna's father, Antti Ahlholm, was also a petty tradesman,[370] who, according to Risto Sykkö, owed him money for a horse deal. Ahlholm himself denied this in the district court, and it may be that Risto wanted to avenge himself for being reported for burglary by a person who himself was in debt to him – and to do so in the cruellest possible way, for it was well known that Ahlholm had always taken good care of his daughter; on several occasions he had gone to court in prosecution of her financial interests. The purpose behind the killing of Susanna's son, Mikko, might have been to in-

367 Piipponen 1988, p 33.

368 RA: JRR, v. 1755, p. 737; VMA: VHOA, Alistettujen asiain päätöstaltiot, Kymenkartanon ja Savon lääni, Tunnustusvankiluettelo v. 1753–1754, Di 1.

369 The need for personal restitution is recognised as as a factor that incites people to violence, especially when the perpetrator's own social code does not prohibit him or her from hurting others in order to achieve this end. Berkowitz 1962, p. 320.

370 Saloheimo 1980, pp. 233, 236

crease the scope of the vengeance, but it is also possible that the child had to die so than no eyewitness to the deed should survive. Risto Sykkö may also have had an interest in doing away with all the inheritors of the farm, for the disposal of the estate had not yet been carried out. However, Antti Sykkö was survived by one son of his own.

Apparently, Susanna and Mikko were also sacrificed in order that Antti Sykkö himself might be framed for slaying his wife and adopted son. It was probably to this end that the latter's body was cut up into eight parts and hidden in a barn with the intention of disposing of it later. It would then have been possible to spread a rumour that Antti had fled to Russia after his bloody deed.

It was only indirectly that Risto Sykkö stained his hands with blood. When the crime was committed, he was on a fishing trip with a large company of witnesses many miles away from the scene of the murders. Presumably he did not wish to carry out the murder of three close relatives himself because he realized that he would be the first to come under suspicion for it. However, on the basis of circumstantial evidence, the court had strong grounds for suspecting that he had commissioned the murders. It was thought that he had hired, or any rate persuaded, his neighbour, one Teppana Huurinainen, a man of the Orthodox faith who is sometimes wrongly referred to in the court of appeal sources as Hurinoff, to carry out the triple murder. He had been accused of the same burglary in the Ilomantsi District Court as Risto Sykkö.

The life of Teppana Huurinainen is likewise besmirched with charges of theft and litigation. His social background was also perfectly decent, at least nominally: he had tilled a farm on Crown land in Sonkaja together with his brothers Levoska (Leo) and Feodor. His father, Jaakko Huurinaninen, had been one of the electors of the peasant estate in the Diet[371] — and it was rare for a person of the Orthodox religion the rise to such an important position in the kingdom of Sweden. The young brothers were of a hot-blooded nature; a certain farmer's wife had upbraided Levoska for being a robber and a bandit. The errant elder brothers settled down over the years, but Teppana gradually sank down the social scale, as numerous legal case records from the 1750s bear witness: at the beginning of the decade he is referred to on the pages of the judgment books as the son of a peasant farmer or a peasant farmer, but in the latter half he is described as a vagrant.

The first references to Teppana Huurinainen are in connection with a fight between neighbours dealt with at the Ilomantsi District Court winter session in 1752. The fight, in which Huurinainen and his brother had taken part, had arisen over a dispute about the usufructuary rights to some burn-beaten land. In the following year he prosecuted two slander cases in the district court in an attempt to clear his name of suspicions of theft which had been attached to him in many quarters.

First Huurinainen took a young farmer from Sonkaja called Antti Antinpoika Sykkö to court for defamation of character. Antti Sykkö had prosecuted him and his brother in the Ilomantsi District Court winter sessions in 1752 for burglary of his home. In the same sessions, Huurinainen reciprocated by proceeding against Antti Sykkö claiming that the latter had made shameless accusations against him on the road to church. He said that Sykkö had grabbed his knife with the intention of chasing him. He had one witness to support his allegations. He continued his attempts to clear his name and started proceed-

371 Saloheimo 1980, p. 275.

ings against another young farmer who, he claimed, had tried to bring him into disrepute by falsely claiming that he was the thief who had stolen Antti Sykkö's money. In the autumn of the same year, Huurinainen, together with a friend, complained in court that someone had demolished his forest cabin during the summer. In the following summer, he was reported for striking a peasant farmer with the back of an axe because the latter had taken part in a search for stolen property in the home of his cousin Trofim.

In the mid-1750s Huurinainen was associating with a known thief called Timofei Lipitsäinen. A peasant called Prokoi Karhapää accused them of pulling his hair on the highway and taking his bonnet, and Huurinainen was convicted of breach of the district court peace in 1756. He cannot have been very poor at that time, for he paid the fine of forty silver *dalers* immediately.

Huurinainen's attempts to force the people of the parish to treat him with respect had already had exactly the opposite effect; around 1752, in addition to being, perhaps in the beginning unjustly, branded as a thief, he was also stigmatized as immoral. This he found difficult to bear. At the autumn sessions of the Ilomantsi District Court in 1753 together with his cousin Arhippa he complained that because of one malicious denunciation he had been ridiculed and disgraced. The reason for the public ridicule was a case that had dragged on painfully from one district court session to another because of difficulties in proving it. It concerned the harassment of a mentally retarded 22-year-old farmhand called Risto, whose mother had accused Huurinainen of treating her son violently and shamelessly when they were engaged in burn-beating work. According to her, together with his cousin Arhippa, he had torn and cut Risto's hair. She also told the court that the pair had thrown the young man to the ground, fitted a kind of gag to his mouth and that Teppana Huurinainen had urinated (*släpt sitt watn*) down his throat. Teppana denied the accusation strenuously, saying that he believed that one Lauri Nuutinen, who had anyway said bad things about him, had lured the retarded young man into telling an invented story to Pastor Norrgren and to the court. Witnesses at the scene of the crime stated that they had only seen him pull Risto's hair and Arhippa cut a few strands of it. The lower court acquitted Teppana Huuranainen of the other charges in autumn 1753 for lack of evidence, but he was fined for hair-pulling, to which he had in fact confessed. On this occasion, too, he paid his fine immediately.

After the trial Teppana no longer appears as a party in the same cases concerning usufructuary rights as his farming brothers. Apparently, he was no longer actively engaged in burn-beating cultivation. Possibly it was shame that separated him from his brothers.

Huurinainen had also been involved in a confused sexual crime years before this. He had been accused at the end of the 1740s of participation in a rape. The victim was described in the judgment of the court of appeal as a "female person" (*qwins-person*). The principle defendant was the same Antti Antinpoika Sykkö with whom Huurinainen later severed relations, and who was to die by his hand eight years later. It was not possible to prove that the future perpetrator and victim of murder had committed the rape. However, the lower court judge considered that there was sufficient proof of illicit intercourse and fined Sykkö. There must have been some circumstantial evidence of his guilt, for the case was prosecuted by the Sheriff of Ilomantsi together with the victim of the alleged rape.[372]

---

372 MMA: KymLKa, Saapuneet kirjeet v. 1749, Hovioikeus maaherralle, D 11 a1, no 29.3.

What then were Risto Sykkö's motives? Did he become embittered against his brother purely because he had lost his share of the farm to him and consequently his status as a peasant farmer? The life story of Risto Sykkö gives us a glimpse of what financial loss and descent into the very depths of society meant.[373] This classical case of frustration was certainly significant with regard to the course that events were to take. The deterioration in the situation of Risto, who had shown some entrepreneurial bent in his business affairs, was made even more difficult to bear by the fact that his younger brother Antti, who had handled his accounts much better than he had, finally turned against him completely by testifying against him on a charge of burglary and trying to deprive him of his last connection with the peasant farming class. By publicly turning against his brother, Antti Sykkö was taking away not only his material wealth but also the last remnants of his invisible capital: his place in society and any good name that he may have had. These interpretative assumptions of frustration and dishonour nevertheless leave many questions unanswered. Why should Risto Sykkö, who already had the reputation of being a thief, have taken such offence at this particular charge? Also, why was the deed exceptionally brutal, a triple murder apparently carried out with an axe? One suspects that there were other deep psychological motives behind the killing. Perhaps they were connected less with the culprits than with the victim, Antti Sykkö. The charge of rape against him is a strand that ties up the motives of Huurinainen and Risto Sykkö for murdering him and dismembering his body. His appearances in the dock, moreover, were not limited to answering the charge of rape. Like Risto Sykkö and Teppana Huurinainen, he had been accused in the district court of fraudulent horse-trading and once also of theft.[374] His court record was dubious, if by no means exceptional in the locality, and it probably helped to seal his fate. Risto Sykkö would certainly have found it difficult to forgive his brother. What made reconciliation totally impossible, however, was the double betrayal involved in the act: first the breaking of his fraternal bond, and then the fact that Risto did not consider that his brother was any better than he himself was in the eyes of the law, just more fortunate. Antti Sykkö had taken him to court over a crime of which he had himself been suspected. By stealing – probably indeed together with his brother Risto – Antti had forfeited the right to the protection of his property by the law in the eyes of other thieves.[375] A thief could not testify against another thief without breaking the code of silence of the criminal sub-culture, an eastern Finnish version of the law of *omertà*, which transcends time and place.

Even this hardly provides an exhaustive account of Risto's motives. The strongest influences on his actions are to be found in his earlier experiences. A man who had languished in confessional remand for months

---

373 E.g. Spierenburg 1999, p. 113.

374 VMA: VHOA, Alistettujen asiain päätöstaltiot, Kymenkartanon ja Savon lääni v. 1757, Di 2, no 46

375 Cf. Kivivuori 1999, pp. 78–80.

on end and served a year of hard labour in Svartholm fortress no longer wished to put his own life at risk, starving and threatened with all sorts of diseases in the miserable conditions of Lovisa Workhouse. He would rather have the witnesses killed. So, to cover his tracks, both the potential witnesses to the burglary (including the child) had to die, despite the fact that they were incompetent to testify.

It is unlikely that a mere charge of burglary would have turned Teppana Huurinainen into a triple murderer either. The suite brought by Antti Sykkö was but a small link in a chain of cases against him. A person who has suffered enough disgrace no longer has anything to fear from it.[376] Nor is it likely that the most important inducement to commit the murder was the possible reward. From the point of view of the sub-culture, the thefts committed by Antti Sykkö in a way justified the motive (vengeance) for his murder, but Huurinainen was probably influenced more powerfully by the fact that his denigration by the local people had made things difficult for him in his home parish. Already branded as a budding petty criminal of questionable morality and with a proclivity for pilfering, Huurinainen chose the path of serious crime. Antti Sykkö provided a most suitable victim in that at the end of the previous decade he had been among the first of those who started a campaign of denunciations against Huurinainen.

It was in Huurinainen's interest to set up Antti himself for the murders of his wife and adopted son by doing away with his corpse so that it would appear that he had fled the country after killing his nearest and dearest. The idea that he might be suspected of the crime was not necessarily as unwelcome to Huurinainen as it would have been to another person – on the contrary, it may have incorporated a concealed incentive for the killing: the association of fear and power with violence put the criminal on a par with a person who has achieved success in society by normal means. This happens above all when the forces of law and order are incapable of banishing the terrorization that is associated with violence.[377] Even if he should fail in framing Antti Sykkö for the murder of his family, Huurinainen surely believed that the triple murder would silence the public ridicule he had been subjected to. It would make him the most feared man in the locality. He had nothing to lose in Ilomantsi; in an emergency he could easily flee over the border, where in practice the authorities could not track him down. Criminals living along the border had successfully escaped to Russia since time immemorial. Huurinaninen's calculation proved to be exactly right.

Johan Hultin, the Sheriff of Ilomantsi, made no special efforts to solve the triple murder. After the crime was reported to him, he pressed not a single charge on his own account until Antti Ahlholm, the father of the murdered Susanna Ahlholm, denounced Risto Sykkö and a local petty trader and farmer called Mikitta Toroskainen (who was later found to be innocent) of committing the murder. Huurinainen went into hiding, and a hue and cry was raised. A band of men with firearms stormed with the home of a peasant farmer called Iivana Maksimoff from Hattupää, who was suspected of harbouring numerous criminals. The searchers beat Maksimoff in order to force him to reveal the whereabouts of the miscreants. He later admitted in court that Huurinainen had hidden in his barn for two days.

376 Cf. Foucault 1977.
377 Ylikangas 1998a.

116

Antti Ahlholm lodged a complaint at the 1759 autumn sessions of the district court that Teppana Huurinainen's father, Jaakko, had made threats against his life: "Your back shall bend in earnest before you escape the trial." (*Din rygg skulle med alfware böija sig innan du släpp rättegången*). He also complained that Jaakko Huurinainen had egged his son on into committing murder. At the Ilomantsi District Court, Antti Ahlholm also accused the other brother of the victim, Simo Sykkö, of a strange unwillingness to search for his brother's body.

Obviously, Ahlholm was grievously anguished by the dilatory investigation of the crime, because he also reported the sheriff of the parish, Johan Hultin, for dereliction of his duties: the negligence of the official was, according to Ahlholm, manifested by the slackness of the investigation and the fact that he had not apprehended two thieves who were sojourning in the locality. Both Simo Sykkö and Sheriff Hultin were acquitted on all charges in the district court. Ahlholm also left a number of highly incriminating depositions against Huurinainen and Risto Sykkö at the next two district court sessions.

There was something definitely suspicious about the behaviour of the sheriff. A complaint was made by the Office of the Government of Vyborg in 1759 that he had allowed seven Russian deserters and three killers (Huurinainen, Antti Kontiainen and a Russian called Pamfilei Parloff) to go freely about the parish. Moreover, it was claimed that he himself extorted money from travellers. The Government Office pointed out that it would have been easy for him to apprehend the men if he had exerted himself. The Office hoped that the Governor would be able to bring about a change in the way the affairs of the parish were handled.

In spite of Ahlholm's lone efforts, the investigation of the murder gradually petered out. The reason for Hultin's prevarication is unclear; possibly he may have been bribed. According to the complaint made by the Government of Vyborg, Hultin had taken bribes not to report a killer who was facing the death penalty, and who had escaped from Käkisalmi Prison. It was claimed that he had used the runaway to work for him. The sheriff denied all the charges and offered explanations of every charge in the complaint to his own advantage. He was acquitted on all counts at an extraordinary session of the district court in 1759. He evaded the charges of harbouring killers by claiming that they had escaped from Swedish soil to Russia. The board of jurors confirmed this. As far as the negligence is concerned, it may have been a matter of mere impotence. This is indicated by the fact that a change of prosecutor failed to expedite the case.

The web of evidence against Risto Sykkö was woven of strong threads, but the mesh was not fine. He was known to have been at odds with his brother. Before the murder, he had made some strange statements about a future murder trial. According to the evidence, Huurinainen and he had been afraid that Antti and Susanna would denounce them. Although he was miles away fishing at the time of the crime, the district court suspected that he had commissioned the killings. However, he steadfastly denied any involvement in the crime. The board of jurors nevertheless considered that there was sufficient evidence provisionally for a half-proof and the incarceration of Sykkö. He was sent to Lovisa Crown Prison, a place with which he was already very familiar, where the clergy tried to persuade him to confess that he had ordered the murders. When he persisted in denying the crime, he was sent to be cross-examined in the Åbo Court of Appeal, which committed him to solitary confinement (*svårare fängelse*) in the prison of Åbo Castle. His solitude was broken only by the visits of the chaplain to pressurize him into confession and the long periods for which he was suspended to hang by his arms from chains on the castle walls. He still refused to admit his involvement in the murders in any way.

He was sent back to his home parish to await his sentence. The lower court considered that it could not convict Risto Sykkö of commissioning a contract murder without a confession or eyewitnesses, and the determination of his involvement was adjourned *sine die*. The case was referred to the Åbo Court of Appeal, where the judges ruled that the circumstantial evidence and motive were not sufficient for even a half-proof. This was obviously the reason for Sykkö's "consistent and calm" behaviour in solitary confinement. In assessing the legitimate circumstantial evidence, among other things the judges always considered the gestures and changes in the countenance of the accused.[378]

The court of appeal acquitted Sykkö according to RB XVII:33 of being an accessory to murder in May 1758. However, the sentence of the court of appeal concerning the earlier burglary case ordering his expulsion from the parish was put into effect. The court commanded him to leave the locality because of the disapproval that his way of life aroused. He was enjoined to acquire a lawful way of earning a living somewhere else; otherwise he would be treated, according to the statute on hired servants as a vagrant, which in practice meant either being drafted into the army or the labour force for building fortifications, or being placed in the compulsory service of some member of the gentry. After his release, Sykkö returned to Ilomantsi for the winter district court sessions of 1759 to sue Antti Ahlholm for appropriating goods that were his personal property from the estate.

Teppana Huurinainen, who had been fleeing the authorities, was also caught within a couple of weeks and brought to justice. On the basis of strong evidence, he was charged in the district court with having carried out the triple murder. He had no alibi. On the contrary, a sworn witness called Iivana Polviainen had seen Huurinainen on the morning after the murders clearly wounded from some scuffle. Huurinainen tried on several occasions to persuade Polviainen to keep quiet about the meeting. In an extraordinary session of the district court, he was sent back to Lovisa, but he soon escaped from the Crown Prison there through a rotten timber in the palisade on 14 October. He was recaptured in a few days, but once again – and this time for good – he managed to escape from the hands of the law on the way to being cross-examined by the Åbo Court of Appeal.[379]

Ahlholm organized a search for him at his own expense in Ilomantsi. One of the men from there was interrogated at the 1759 winter sessions of the district court in consequence of a report by Antti Ahlholm that he had seen Huurinainen on the highway and not tried to apprehend the triple murderer. The district court judge acquitted the man on the grounds that he would have placed his life in real danger if he had tried to come to grips alone with the murderer, who was armed with an axe.

Huurinainen crossed the border into Russia, after which it was not possible to bring him to court to answer the charge of triple murder. Since he never petitioned the King for safe conduct to return to his homeland, the triple murder

---

378 Nehrman 1759, VI cap.
379 The courts of appeal interrogated prisoners who were strongly suspected of having committed grave crimes if it had not been possible to get them to confess to their crimes. Jusleén 1751, Til samteliga hof- och öfwer-rätterne, angående munteliga förhör. Stockholm den 12 juli 1750.

of Antti Sykkö's family was to remain on the court of appeal's list of unsolved crimes for fifteen years. If Risto Sykkö had confessed to commissioning the murder and Huurinainen to carrying it out, they would both probably have been sentenced by the Supreme Court to be beheaded with their bodies to be broken on the wheel.[380] In accordance with the precept of a life for a life, the number of victims was sufficient to justify two executions.

In fact, Teppana Huurinainen did not die a natural death: he was himself slain in Russia in the early eighteenth century.[381] His killer is not mentioned by name in the lists of the court of appeal. It is not, of course, impossible that he was killed out of revenge. However, in view of his vagrant life-style, it is equally likely that his death was totally unconnected with the murder of Antti Sykkö's family. Nevertheless the triple murder might well have sown the seeds of a grudge between the Huurinainen and Sykkö families. This is indicated by the fact that three years after Teppana Huurinainen's violent death, his cousins, Arhippa and Trofim, beat the sister of the Sonkaja Sykkös so badly that she miscarried and died. As a result of the assault, the two Orthodox men were ordered to take an oath of purgation.[382]

The poor results of the investigation into the murder of Antti Sykkö's family certainly did not increase the traditionally low confidence of the inhabitants of Ilomantsi in the authorities. By a bloody deed, Huurinainen and Risto Sykkö managed to hold to ridicule the same justice system that in their opinion they had each earlier been victims of. After he was acquitted, Risto Sykkö was even theoretically entitled to inherit the brother he had had murdered. Since the judgment in his case was acquittal (based on RB XVII:33), and Huurinainen was out of the reach of the law, the last instance in which the case was handled was the Åbo Court of Appeal; this case, which sheds light from so many angles on the system of justice at the local level, was never referred to the King.

Sykkö had endured solitary confinement in Åbo Castle, for which a half-proof based on circumstantial evidence against the accused was required. The logical consequence of solitary confinement would have been his committal by the court of appeal to confessional remand. Therefore, his acquittal seems somewhat contradictory. The case was dealt with in the period immediately following the coming into force of the Statute on Mitigation of 1756. It is possible that Sykkö's acquittal stemmed from the court of appeal's reluctance to submit a difficult case that was still pending to judicial revision. It is also suspicious that the judgment

380 Cf. Flintberg 1803, p. 208 for a precedent in 1786.
381 The Provincial Governor informed the Åbo Court of Appeal of Huurinainen's fate on 29.2.1772. VMA: VHOA, Alistettujen asiain designaatioluettelo, v. 1772, Di 8, no 1.
382 VMA: VHOA, Alistettujen asiain designaatioluettelot ja päätöstaltiot v. 1776, Di 10, no 89; v. 1777, Di 11, no 23. Some members of the previous generation of the Sykkö family had also died violently; for example, Maria Airaksinen, the wife of one Antti Sykkö had been slain by the Russians in the 1730s. According to Björn, however, she did not die but was shot and remained a cripple. Saloheimo 1980, p. 303; Björn 1991, p. 141. It was possible to order the Huurinainen brothers to take an oath of purgation because juridically the charge was battery, even if it did result in the miscarriage and death of the victim.

registers (*designations förteckningar*) and the judgment records (*utslag*) of the Åbo Court of Appeal for the years 1758–1759 are totally missing from the archives of the Vasa Court of Appeal.

The Culture of Shame and Revenge Murders

In her analysis of the historiography of the concept of honour, Sari Forsström defines honour as a category that plays a central role in maintaining the integrity of traditional societies and communities. In them, the concept of honour was a collective one, transcending the limits of the individual; a person who was guilty of a dishonourable act or way of life was considered thereby to bring shame on the whole community. Apart from a few ritualized exceptions, the only means the community had of dealing with such a situation was permanent expulsion of the individual from membership of it. The tolerance of dishonour would otherwise bring shame down on the whole community. In such collective cultures of shame, the compromising of one's reputation constituted a strong provocation: if one wished to preserve one's membership of the community, one was often required to react violently in order to clear oneself of suspicion.[383] Since the categories of honour and shame determined the integration of the actor in society, it is traditionally recognized that the conservation of personal honour was a reason for the slight rise in violence in the sixteenth century.[384] And it continued to be a significant motive for homicide in Stockholm up to the end of eighteenth century.[385] The obverse of honour, shame, also played a role in many killings in eastern Finland in the eighteenth century. For, example, it was understandable, albeit unlawful, if a person reacted violently, sometimes lethally so, to an imputation against his own or his spouse's morality.[386] Indeed, disputes between men over matters of honour have still not completely disappeared from the spectrum of motivations for homicide,[387] and they probably never will.

In the conservative agrarian society, the respect a person enjoyed determined the institutional circumstances in which he could prosecute his financial and legal affairs. Personal honour was inextricably bound up with the social network, and dishonour was considered contagious. Therefore, if one became the subject of various rumours, it posed a considerable threat to one's ability to prosecute one's legal rights, and the multiplier effect was fatal unless the subject tried to clear his name of the injurious imputations.[388] In the monolithic rural society, shame was

---

383 Forsström 2000, pp. 1–2 and notes.
384 Ylikangas 1971; Österberg 1994, p. 15.
385 Jansson 1998, p. 101; Kaspersson 2000, p. 104.
386 This was the reason why Anders Asp killed Mooses Ihalainen in Tohmajärvi in 1803. VMA: VHOA, Alistettujen asiain päätöstaltiot, Savon ja Karjalan lääni, v. 1803, Di 38, no 48.
387 Kivivuori 1999, pp. 81–84.
388 Söderberg 1990, pp. 246–248.

an extremely useful tool of unofficial control; fear of it helped to bridle lawless behaviour when the legal consequences were not sufficient to do so. In particular, those who were labelled as thieves were excluded from the society of honourable men in the old cultures of western Europe.

The excessive proclivity of north Karelian peasants to stealing from the 1750s to the 1770s, however, casts doubt on the traditional rules of the region governing the stigmatization of thieves. In addition to burglaries, property crimes in Karelia were characterized by thefts of money that had been stashed away to hide it from plundering Russian soldiers in time of war. By the beginning of the nineteenth century, the number of thefts in Karelia had decreased significantly, whereas they had risen in northern Savo.

Despite the commonness of theft, accusations of it when taken to court brought deep personal shame on the person concerned in the regions of burn-beating cultivation; suspicion of theft made it difficult to conduct financial and social transactions with neighbours and others in the village. The strength of the effect is indicated by the fact that denunciation for theft was often countered with a much more serious crime. The accusation of theft wounded the receiver all the more deeply if the accuser was a close acquaintance, friend or relative.[389] Such a base act was to be the final undoing of many persons in eastern Finland, in a way that labelling someone a bandit or a murderer never was. This tells a lot about the moral norms of the community and the nature of unofficial control: recourse to violence did not endanger social intercourse in the burn-beating society of Savo and Karelia, but theft did. The thief was a surreptitious element in the community, and his identity was not always known, whereas the robber always lived outside society. Calling a person a robber or a bandit did not offend him in the same way as calling him a thief because the insult could not be taken literally, particularly if directed at a landed peasant. On the other hand, anybody could be a thief.

A peasant farmer from Ilomantsi called Juho Savolainen and his sister Helena murdered the pregnant fiancée of their partner, Maria Tikka, in 1793 because Juho felt that he suffered greatly on account of a charge made against him by Maria. In 1758 Antti Tyllinen, a farmer from Mäntyharju killed his partner, Erkki Tyllinen, who had reported him for theft, and in the previous year Risto Sykkö had had his brother murdered. In Iisalmi, Juho Snickare, a farmer's son, avenged a conviction for theft that he had received at the 1778 winter district court sessions by slaying the person who informed on him, a farmhand called Bovellan, in the cottage of the district court janitor in front of the assembled people. Only one hour had elapsed since the passing of the sentence. In Liperi, the Provost, Heikki Svan, killed a Russian farmhand called Pedri Guyonoff, who had accused him of stealing his gloves. Inkeri Laakotar of Kitee, who was charged with having her father murdered, was also partly motivated by the fact that her father had reported her for theft. In 1780

---

389 Similarly motivated homicides are still committed in Finland with comparative frequency, cf. Keltikangas-Järvinen 1978, p. 25; Kivivuori 1999, pp. 78–82.

Antti Kuikka, a dependent lodger from Liperi, killed a farmer called Markus Hakkarainen, who had flown into a rage believing that Kuikka had accused him of stealing his property. In 1806 Matti Ärvänen, a crofter from Iisalmi, was suspected of drowning the son of his master, Juho Väisänen, because, suspecting Ärvänen of stealing oats from him, he had organized a search of the outbuildings of the croft. Ärvänen found Väisänen drowned in a fishing seine the following day. His part in the incident was investigated as possible manslaughter or murder. Because it was not possible to determine the cause of death of Väisänen, Ärvänen was acquitted of these charges, although he was convicted of theft.[390]

Apart from Provost Svan and Juho Snickare, the parties involved in these killings were relatively closely related or associated with one another. Those people of Savo and Karelia who murdered their relatives and partners, out of rage at being reported for theft by them, denied the charges of murder, unlike Nikkari and Svan, who did not know their victims well. When the parties were not related, the affronts clearly demanded a more public violent reaction than in the opposite case.

The Savolainens spent the rest of their lives in confessional remand for the murder of the fiancée of their partner. Risto Sykkö was acquitted in the court of appeal of the murder of his brother and his family on the basis of an alibi. Tyllinen was committed to a year's confessional remand in Lovisa Prison, but he was later hanged as a thief. Provost Svan and Juho Nikkari, who had publicly killed their victims to clear their names of suspicion of theft, were beheaded, the latter after having his right hand cut off.

In theory, the stigma of being a thief was most onerous in areas where crime was generally rare. There the thief had to bear his ill repute alone. However, accusations of theft were also avenged with fatal consequences in those parishes where a large number of different crimes were committed and prosecuted. The thieves often maintained their position by terror, by creating a balance of fear. The informer had to be punished so that the deterrent created by the terrorization should not be weakened.[391] However, since in eastern Finland the parties involved were generally fairly closely associated with each other, in most cases the reaction was probably prompted by other considerations. The denunciation of members of one's own family was a form of washing one's dirty linen in public;[392] it was seen as an attempt to exclude a member from the extended social unit, the so-called local community, as well as from the smaller social unit, be this the family, the partnership or the sub-culture of thieves. Recourse to the law for the settlement of such disputes went against the moral code

---

390 VMA: VHOA, Alistettujen asiain päätöstaltiot, Savon ja Karjalan lääni, v. 1778, Di 13, no 30; v. 1799, Di 34, no 30; Alistusaktit, Savon ja Karjalan lääni v. 1799, Ece 52, no 30; Alistettujen asiain päätöstaltiot, Savon ja Karjalan lääni, v. 1780, Di 15, no 57; Alistusaktit, Savon ja Karjalan lääni v. 1807, Ece no 85.

391 E.g. Kivivuori 1999, pp. 78–80.

392 Ibid., also Forsström 2000, pp. 1–3.

of the family, the partnership and the sub-culture. It brought shame on one's relative or partner and was therefore a dishonourable act.[393]

The collective burn-beating culture of eastern Finland, in which an individual's place was defined mainly in relation to others, was at the turn of the eighteenth and nineteenth centuries based on a sense of shame before others and on its converse, honour.[394] It was a culture characterized by strong dependence on others. Informing on a brother or partner was a frightening sign of isolation, for in a collective society a person was nothing without his immediate social network. Thus the murder of an informer implemented and reinforced the norms of the community. Murder was used to maintain the community's conservative power relations. It satisfied the requirements of social discipline, for all that it was a grave crime.[395] The defendants were able to deny the murder of those who informed on them in their trials to the bitter end because they firmly believed that their actions had been justified; it was after all the informers themselves who had been disloyal to them by trying to deprive them of something vital: their reputation and membership of the social network. This kind of rationalization is suggested by the behaviour of Jäkinen, Huurinainen, Sykkö, Tyllinen, the Savolainens and others.

The fact that the killing of another thief helped to reduce the growth of a section of the population that the settled peasant farmer community felt to be a threat was unintentionally expedient in that it had a cementing effect on the integrity of the local community. Accusations of theft only led to retributive murders in areas where theft had assumed the proportions of a social problem. When the identity of a faceless pilferer in the night was revealed, the stigma of a treacherous miscreant was attached to him. If the informer himself was some sort of thief, the dominant culture also in a way benefited from his murder, and the people of the village or parish were not particularly interested in tracking down the culprits. The liquidation of inveterate criminals was a part of unofficial control. It alleviated the failings of lax official control.

> The code of silence may also have operated among violent criminals. Johan Veckman, a cobbler from Kuopio, reported one Johan Nyman, an army musician, for assault in 1806, but Nyman killed the informer, who was present when he was being reprimanded by his superior officer. Veckman's denunciation may have been unforgivable in Nyman's eyes because the informer had previously been found guilty of a far more grievous crime: Veckman had been sentenced to death in the Kuopio District Court for killing the parish schoolmaster, Samuel Kuronen, but His Majesty had pardoned him on the grounds of extenuating circumstances.[396]

---

393 On surmounting the threshold of prosecution in cases of theft, see also Heikkinen 1997, pp. 156–159.

394 Cf. e.g. Taussi Sjöberg 1996, p. 159 on the collective nature of the concept of honour in pre-modern communities..

395 Kivivuori 1999, p. 79.

396 VMA: VHOA, Alistettujen asiain päätöstaltiot, Savon ja Karjalan lääni, v. 1796, Di 31, no 5; v. 1807, Di 45, no 143.

The killing of one's legal opponent was defined in criminal law as manslaughter in breach of the peace. The law specified separately the most common situations in which this form of reactive self-help was employed: a deposition by a witness or statement for the defence or a case that had been concluded with a conviction or a settlement.[397] Killing in these circumstances, it was thought, constituted a considerable threat to the proper functioning of the law. The research material contains only one manslaughter, that mentioned above of Matti Bovellan, that took place in such circumstances as to constitute a breach of the peace of the court. Usually, the killing of an opponent because of a court case was prosecuted as murder. Vengeance was a legally aggravating circumstance, when and if the accused admitted his or her motive.[398] Apart from imputations of theft, other accusations that were considered to bring dishonour might also incite their objects to commit murder. The killings were committed without exception just before the district court sessions.

A farmhand called Risto Viinikainen, who was charged with bestiality, murdered the person who had reported him, one Jaakko Vik, a dependant lodger, in Rautalampi in 1785, but he never admitted to doing so.[399] A similar obduracy was displayed by Mikitta Jäkinen (also written Jäkin), a peasant farmer from Sonkaja, who in 1787 shot his brother-in-law, a petty criminal called Patro Romanoff, after he had levied a distress upon Mikitta's home.[400]

Patro Romanoff was in 1787 an aged dependant lodger, a former crofter, with some small means of his own. He himself was notorious for his numerous appearances in court. Over the years, he had been charged with contempt of court and swearing while drunk, harassment of the sheriff and rape of a farm girl. From the 1740s to the 1760s he had been fined thirteen times for different crimes. His fines alone constituted a tenth of all the fines imposed on persons of the Orthodox faith in the Ilomantsi District Court in the years 1738–1771; all in all he was one of the most heavily fined persons in Ilomantsi.[401] Romanoff met his end on 10 October 1787, when he was murdered by Mikitta Jäkinen.

Some uninvited guests had called on Mikitta Jäkinen the previous day: the bailiff and his assistants, who had come to seize the property of Patro Romanoff. After the distraint, according to the testimony of some sworn witnesses, Jäkinen had become involved in a heated exchange with Romanoff, and uttering the strongest insults he had promised the latter that he would gain nothing from the seizure. In the evening, he had made inquiries of the witnesses concerning the whereabouts of Romanoff and the route he took to his home village of Lokanlahti.

---

397 Nehrman 1756, V:II:68, p. 239; 1734 års lag, MB XVIII:7; XXIII cap; JB XVI:8.
398 VMA: VHOA, Alistettujen asiain designaatioluettelo, v. 1756, Di 2, no 38.
399 VMA; VHOA, Alistettujen asiain päätöstaltiot, Savon ja Karjalan lääni, v. 1785, Di 20, no 12.
400 The description of the case is based on the following sources unless otherwise mentioned: VMA: VHOA, Alistettujen asiain designaatioluettelot ja päätöstaltiot v. 1787, Di, no 9, 96, v. 1800, no 28; v. 1801, no 7; v. 1804, no 65; Alistusaktit, Savon ja Karjalan lääni, v. 1801, Ece 60, no 7.
401 Piipponen 1988, pp. 12, 51, 53; MMA: KymLKa, Rikoskertomukset vv. 1754–1771,E1–E 2, Karjalan voutikunta. Also e.g. KA: Karjalan tuomiokunnan tuomiokirja, Ilomantsin ja Suojärven osan sk 1748, KO a 27, 32 §.

On the morning following the distraint, Patro Romanoff had set out on foot from the village of Lokanlahti for Sonkaja, but by the next day he had not been sighted even in Kokinvaara, which lay between the two villages. One Stefania Simanovna, the fourteen-year-old daughter of a farmer who lived in the village, had seen Mikitta Jäkinen in the morning crouching behind a rock along the road between the villages with a gun in his hand, but when he saw her he disappeared into the forest. At nine o'clock, a peasant farmer called Antti Parviainen had heard a shot fired from a field of turnips in the same direction.

Mikitta Jäkinen was arrested under strong suspicion of having murdered Patro Romanoff. Together with his fiancée, Iro Ihanus, Jäkinen was in the dock to answer the charge at an extraordinary session of the district court on 16 October. While the court was in session, Romanoff's corpse was found buried in a swamp about a mile from Kokinvaara. To judge from marks in the grass, that was where he had been slain as well. He had been struck on the head with an axe, his ribcage had been smashed and, while this alone would have been enough to kill him, the job had been completed by shooting him in the head beside the left ear, with the bullet exiting through the eye. The *modus operandi* indicated "rancour and a butcherous disposition".

Jäkinen obdurately denied the murder. He said that he had been in his burn-beaten field checking on his rye stooks, but some peasant farmers who were working in the same part of the forest denied this. There were no eye-witnesses to the killing, but the circumstantial evidence assembled during the days following the act pointed to Jäkinen's guilt. Two days later, his fiancée was seen washing his bloodstained clothes. When he was apprehended on 12 October, he had, according to the sheriff, trembled and turned red in the face, as he did once again when he learned that Romanoff's body had been found. There were other suspicious features in his behaviour: for example, he had earnestly pleaded with a juror called Jormanainen to keep quiet about what he knew and had forbidden the latter's servants to say anything about the murder at all. Jäkinen had also tried to bribe those who apprehended him with rye and money to let him go free. These were all strictly defined *indicia*, the significance of which the judge had to weigh in his investigation.

In the lower court, the judge and the jury stated that they considered Mikitta Jäkinen's guilt of the murder of Patro Romanoff so patent that that in accordance with MB XII: 1, they passed sentence without the evidence required by law that he be beheaded, that his body then be broken on the wheel and that the clothes he had stolen from the victim, (an overcoat, a bonnet, boots, socks, mittens, a belt and a silver buckle), be returned.

After the death sentence was passed by the lower court, in Kitee on 22 October Jäkinen managed to escape from the guards who were escorting him, but he was recaptured after four months. He was immediately arraigned before the lower court again, this time charged with taking part in some burglaries together with two dependent lodgers. The court of appeal designated the burglary trial as urgent because of the murder sentence. It was not possible to link Jäkinen to the burglaries with legally admissible evidence because none of the stolen property was found in his possession and he denied committing the crimes. He was acquitted of the charge of burglary in both the lower court and the court of appeal. Nor was the assembled circumstantial evidence sufficient for a full proof of his having murdered Patro Romanoff, and the case was adjourned *sine die*. The defendant returned home a free man.

Twelve years later, Mikitta Jäkinen was once again in the dock accused of numerous thefts from the homes and barns of farmers in the locality and in Suojärvi. The bailiff asked that the case of Patro Romanoff's murder should also be reopened at the same sessions on the grounds that new evidence against Jäkinen had accumulated over the years. The witness, Stefania Simanovna, who in 1787 was a minor (fourteen years old) and could not be called to testify under oath, was now a competent witness. She repeated her original story and also remembered that before the killing Jäkinen's clothes had been free of the fresh bloodstains that his fiancée had been seen washing out on 11 October.

It had also emerged that, after the court of appeal freed Jäkinen in 1788, he had made some suspicious references to Romanoff's murder and partly even confessed to committing it to one Ortim Sisonen, who was willing to testify to this under oath. This could be considered a "partial confession" i.e. made outside the court. After his release from prison, Jäkinen had also been seen wearing clothes that belonged to his victim. Moreover, his adopted daughter, Oudotea Röksätär, said that he had followed Romanoff after the distraint. On 9 October Jäkinen had admitted to her that he had murdered Romanoff, and on the next day he had described in detail how he had buried the body.

The justice dispensed by the lower court is the same old story. Again it was not possible to link Jäkinen with the thefts, which were dealt with in numerous district court sessions, but the lower court did consider his guilt of the murder of Patro Romanoff proven by the new evidence; after all, he had confessed to the deed outside the court. Just as in 1787, Jäkinen was sentenced by the Ilomantsi District Court to be beheaded and his body to be broken on the wheel.

During the trial, Jäkinen once again succeeded in escaping, to Russia. He was recaptured three months later. The court of appeal did not possess the full proof needed to convict him since he denied the crime, and there were no eyewitnesses to it. The court still had to adjourn the case *sine die*. However, the circumstances, evidently above all the confession of the crime to several witnesses, were sufficiently aggravating that now, thirteen years after the crime, the Supreme Court empowered the Vasa Court of Appeal to commit Jäkinen to confessional remand for "a suitable period of time".

In 1801, after languishing in prison in Häme Castle (Tavastehus), Jäkinen was on his deathbed and, being of the Orthodox faith, he made a watered-down confession of his crime to a priest of the same religion. He admitted beating Romanoff with a wooden instrument to within an inch of his life on the highway in 1787. For some reason, perhaps to do with questions connected with how his own body was to be buried,[402] or because of a belief in the ultimate justification of his action, this man of the Orthodox faith avoided divulging the whole truth about the method and place of the murder even on his deathbed. It may be that, with the passing of time, his memory had become distorted, and the content of the confession that he had given had become a subjective truth for him.[403] The denial of the real facts may have been a manifestation of an archaic psychological defence mechanism.

402 A murderer's body was broken on the wheel after execution , whereas, depending on the case, a person who had committed homicide was buried in unsanctified land or in the churchyard without rites. Possibly Jäkinen was not aware that the bodies of murderers who died a natural death were not broken on the wheel.

403 For example, in the sixteenth- and seventeenth-century witchcraft trials, the confessions of the accused are thought to have been made – apart from being induced by torture – also as a result of the subjective reality and the system of beliefs of the culprits. Heikkinen 1969, pp. 39, 43.

Modern criminology defines the various neutralization techniques by which the criminal often legitimizes his deed. One of the most common of these is the denial of responsibility; the criminal sees himself as the helpless victim of social forces or circumstances. For example, Huurinainen and Sykkö may have felt this way in eastern Finland in the eighteenth century. It is also characteristic of the criminal to deny his prey the status of a victim; rather the latter is seen as the wrongdoer, and the perpetrator as an avenger. The culprits may also turn to condemning those who condemn them; those who apprehend them are seen as hypocrites, really just other criminals themselves. This was the case in nearly all the murders that were motivated by informing.[404]

> Mikitta Jäkinen clearly felt that his exasperation at the distraint levied by his brother-in-law was completely justified. That is clearly why he did not wish to give a full account of the murder in his dying confession. The exasperation was probably not just a result of the financial loss caused by the distraint but also by the fact that it was one of the most notorious of local petty criminals who benefited from it. To have recourse to the law and prosecute his indebted brother-in-law in court would certainly have been in Jäkinen's opinion a contemptible and hypocritical act from a man who, according to the district court records, in his younger years had insulted the officer of Kitee Customs House by saying "I shit on you and your Crown." *(Jag skiter på dig och din krona).*[405]

The murder of Patro Romanoff put into effect not only a symbolic vengeance but also the community's mechanism of unofficial control by eliminating an undesirable. From the point of view of its perpetrator it was a moral crime, the aim of which was to achieve justice by avenging a wrong, despite the fact that the act was one that from the law's point of view incurred the severest possible punishment.[406]

There were two main factors that affected the form in which aggression was expressed: first, the person's moral standards, which either prohibited or permitted the violent expression of his feelings; second, an external or internal object of the aggression was needed, to which he could attribute the global blame for the various injustices he had personally suffered.[407] A deterrent based on punishment is most effective in controlling and preventing crimes that are committed for gain. On the other hand, such a deterrent is felt to be irrelevant in the case of the most powerfully motivated crimes.[408] The problem of confession was a twofold one. Especially in matters of honour, the desire for catharsis and revenge could become greater than the desire to live. The basically public nature of honour and its defence could also arouse in the killer the desire to confess his deed

---

404 Sykes & Matza 1957. Laine 1991, pp. 77–78.
405 KA: Karjalan tuomiokunnan tuomiokirja, Ilomantsin ja Suojärven osan sk 1758, KO a 27, 32 §.
406 Cf. Black 1984a, p. 1.
407 Berkowitz 1962, p. 308; see also Spierenburg 2001.
408 Törnudd & Anttila 1983, p. 152.

to the court despite the fact that the price was execution (as in the case of Nikkari). The act of vengeance that effected the catharsis would not have become known to people if the culprit had denied the crime. Within the sub-cultures of real criminals, on the other hand, there was no need for this kind of duel of honour in the public arena; their members strove to keep all settlements of differences outside the legal system. Killers who believed in the ultimate justification of their crimes, like women who slew men that had seduced and abandoned them, might also aspire to the halo of martyrs through their sentence – and to this end they might confess.[409]

Nonetheless, in addition to the code of honour, the rationality behind murders of vengeance also lay in the matter of proof. Most of the murderers would scarcely have embarked on their crimes if they had not believed that they would escape conviction. An argument deriving from theories of developmental psychology and cultural anthropology concerning the change from a shame-dominated culture to a culture of guilt in the early centuries of the modern age in Europe has also been applied to the history of crime. Signs of the shift have been discerned in such things as the decrease in the number of crimes resulting from the very slightest slurs on a person's character. A fiery aggressive attitude towards others was gradually reduced to forms of self-punishment. The turning point in this process is estimated to be in the eighteenth century.[410]

The controlling effect of an external deterrent, any more than the denial of charges of murder, do not give us the right to regard the killers in eastern Finland at the turn of the eighteenth and nineteenth centuries as mere savages ruled by their instincts, to use the language of Elias and Renvall. They were no more primitive than modern killers; even today under half of the culprits deny feeling any guilt for their deeds. This trait is often associated with psychological disturbances, above all psychopathy, i.e. a so-called antisocial personality.[411]

An individual's set of values does not come into being by itself; it reflects the attitudes of the culture around it, and it develops through learning. Elias indeed surmised that a culture cannot further the coming into being of internalized control or the conscience (the super ego) as long as the members of a society live under a major physical threat. Only when the living environment has become pacified and been made predictable is a situation created in which the source of control can relocate itself within the person himself. That is why in unsettled societies the basic fear that controls a person's actions is constituted by a threat to his physical person. Elias considers that, in a civilized society, the physical threat is replaced by the shame that a person feels before others. However, the source of the shame is an internal feeling, no longer based on external

409 Cf. Black 1984a, pp. 13–14.
410 E.g. Furuhagen 1996, pp. 155–156; Sundin 1992, p. 296; Lindström 1988, p. 63; Österberg 1991c, p. 70; Ferrer 2001, pp. 147–148; Miller 1993, p. 116.
411 Keltikangas-Järvinen 1978, pp. 26, 36–37.

signs, of a possible inferiority and a fear of loss of social respect.[412] Such a concept of an internalized shame to some extent overlaps with the so-called culture of guilt.

In eastern Finland, a violent reaction was above all characteristic of situations where the actor felt he or she was psychologically, socially or economically threatened. Or then the killing was an immediate reaction to a loss of status in these respects. In the early nineteenth century, Savo and Karelia became the most peaceful region in Finland concomitantly with the deterioration of the crisis in burn-beating cultivation. A generation which had been plunged into absolute poverty perhaps no longer had such economic or social benefits to lose as to make the use of violence to defend them against threats worth the candle; homicide no longer corresponded to either the needs or the moral attitudes of the penniless denizens of the backwoods cabins. This phenomenon dates back to the same decades in which the change in the geopolitical situation of the area brought by the country's autonomy within the Russian Empire meant that the former border region was no longer threatened by large-scale wars.

In many other contexts, too, violence has been associated with change, upheaval, incipient loss and turmoil. Yrjö Kaukiainen has made a similar assumption regarding organized peasant resistance, or revolt: it is those whose position is about to deteriorate who rebel, not those who have lived for a long time in miserable conditions.[413] The same kind of argumentation has been used to explain the spread of modern urban violence. Howard Zehr considers that urban violence is more closely connected with the novelty and contemporaneity of change than with the urban way of life per se.[414]

Outlaws and Bandits

When the members of European communities began to adjust to state jurisdiction, it was not only their tolerance of personal violence that diminished but also their willingness to accept the chaos caused by gangs of bandits. From the sixteenth and seventeenth centuries on, the gradual but successful eradication of organized crime, for all its limitations, reflected an increase in the strength of state control.[415] As long as the movements of bands of brigands were protected by the fear or the sympathy of the people, the state's chances of bringing gangs of criminals to order were meagre; the control was either arbitrary and sporadic, or its method was to offer a pardon to informers and criminals who were willing to enlist in the army. For example, the *bakkerijder* gang that raised havoc in Holland remained active only because it operated in a border area between

---

412 Keltikangas-Järvinen 1978, p. 13; Elias 1994, pp. 492–498; Spieranburg 2001; Thome 2001; Roth 2001; Monkkonen 2001.

413 Kaukiainen 1980, p. 127; Katajala 1994, pp. 339–346; also Ylikangas 1990, pp. 32, 73.

414 Zehr 1976, pp. 98–101, 103–114.

415 Lenman & Parker 1980, p. 40.

four states and several semi-autonomous regions. Each region had its own legislation. It was easy to escape the authorities of one region by fleeing to another.[416] In the eighteenth century it was common for gangs of criminals in many parts of Europe to scatter in this way.[417]

Similarly, the lawless elements of the population congregated in the border region between Sweden and Russia and particularly in the forest area of Ilomantsi and Mäntyharju. There were also lairs of brigands on the other side of the frontier.[418] The authorities tried to expel the vagrants, who lived mainly by crime, at least from Ilomantsi on numerous occasions, but they failed repeatedly. Part of the reason for this was the religious loyalty and solidarity of those of the Orthodox faith, but sympathy for the vagrants was also prompted by a significant economic factor: they constituted a cheap source of reserve labour.[419]

In the 1740s, a village community of outlawed Raskolniks (Old Believers) was established in the forests of Hattuvaara, the remotest corner of the parish of Ilomantsi.[420] In Liusvaara, on the other hand, a different kind of community was established: a congregation of deserters who were not easily assimilated into the native Finnish population. For a long time the settlers avoided contact with the local authorities, for in the mid-eighteenth century their status as subjects of the Swedish Crown was not clear.

Bandits laid waste to Hattuvaara in 1748.[421] In June of the following year, a group of them attacked Liusvaara and plundered the settlers' homes there. They also threatened to kill the inhabitants, and apparently they did slay the aunt of one settler. Even so, not one of those who had been robbed reported the depredations to the authorities, and they only came to light in another connection, when the illegal immigration of Russian subjects into Swedish Karelia was investigated. Andersin, the Crown Bailiff, and Sheriff Hultin, raided the forest frontier villages, and they captured a man from Kalajoki who had fled over the border after murdering his wife.[422]

In such circumstances it is understandable that the killing of criminals became a form of unofficial social control.

---

416 Lenman & Parker 1980, p. 41. However, later research has shown that in Holland in the pre-industrial age, organised crime in the form of robber gangs also gathered in the countryside between towns and not just on the periphery. Egmond 1996, p. 149. On this phenomenon, see also Blok 1998.

417 Foucault 1977; Küther 1976, pp. 138–144.

418 Björn 1991, p. 141.

419 Cf. e.g. Björn 1993, p. 156; Björn 1991, pp. 142–143, also KA: Karjalan tuomiokunnan tuomiokirja, Ilomantsin ja Suojärven osan tk 1750, KO a 19, f. 144b.

420 Björn 1991, p. 109.

421 Björn 1991, p. 141.

422 KA: Karjalan tuomiokunnan tuomiokirja, Ilomantsin ja Suolahden osan välikäräjät 1751, KO a 20, 3–4 §§. Also Björn 1993, pp. 155–156.

Iivana Lipitsäinen, the son of a crofter, who had himself been convicted of various crimes, killed a Russian brigand called Tito Pamfiloff in 1748. The victim did not enjoy the protection of the law, for he was known to be a common brigand who had slain a woman in the locality. Even so a local peasant had given refuge to him and used him as a cheap source of labour.[423]

In 1786 a group of ten inhabitants of Liusvaara in the parish of Ilomantsi were accused of theft and banditry. The enquiry into the case took place in the Liperi District Court, and during the trial a wide range of illegalities was revealed, the most serious of which was murder. The principal defendants are described in the trial records as farmers. Back in the early 1750s, a judgment book had referred to the same men as Russian runaways, i.e. deserters.

The Fedotoff brothers, Feodor, Fedot and Gauriel, who was a deaf-mute, and Foma and Jeulampei Jestafeoff (all of them farmers) together with a Russian deserter called Offan Minninen, made a raid over the border to plunder the farm of Arhippa Ostafeoff in Säämäjärvi. After making sure that the men folk of the farm were elsewhere, they shut the wife and her children in an ice-house. They stole property from the farm to a value of 362.85 roubles.

The victim, Arhippa Ostafeoff, raised a posse of fifteen men to look for the bandits. The search was successful, but it meant crossing the border into Sweden illegally. The capture of the bandits was reported to the office of the Governor General in Vyborg, and he agreed with the Swedish authorities that the enquiry into the raid should be conducted in Liperi, on the Swedish side of the border.

The members of the posse from Säämäjärvi were acquitted in the Liperi District Court of the charge of crossing the border illegally on the grounds that without their prompt action the bandits would not have been caught at all. In this way, the court admitted its own impotence and at the same time provided a justification for the subjects of a foreign power taking over the control of crime from the local authorities without authorization, for all that their action was a necessary one.

According to the court of appeal, the people of Ilomantsi themselves had been untiring in their endeavours to seek out the criminals. However, it was not possible to award them any separate compensation for their efforts, because the value of the property seized from the captured criminals was not enough to cover the costs of the searches. The opportunity afforded by a royal decree to award Crown or district court funds for the apprehension of dangerous criminals was not used.

The investigation revealed that during the 1760s the brigands had also been guilty of numerous thefts in the vicinity of the village. Moreover, the leader, Fedot Fedotoff, confessed in an extraordinary district court session that three years earlier he had drowned a Russian deserter called Konstantin Gregorioff in the nearby Lupulampi Pond and had stolen from his forest cabin whatever small property there was to take. It also came out in the court that the people of Ilomantsi had generally suspected Fedotoff of killing Konstantin after the latter had suddenly disappeared without trace. However, nobody had reported his suspicions to the authorities.

---

423 KA: Karjalan tuomiokunnan tuomiokirja v. 1749, Ilomantsin ja Suojärven osan tk, KO a 17, ff. 75b, 80, 95b.

A former farm maid from Kuolismaa, who was called as a witness, stated that she had been living from the autumn of 1765 onwards in the bandits' cabins in the forests near Ilomantsi along the border, sometimes on the Russian side, sometimes on the Swedish. She related that the inhabitants of these hideaways stole the rye stacks of the local farmers for food.[424]

The settling of accounts between the inhabitants of the bandit huts of the backwoods of Ilomantsi often led to killings which the local authorities had no inkling of. The violent death of Konstantin Gregorioff came to their knowledge only by chance.

Why did Fedot Fedotoff voluntarily confess to the murder of a deserter three years earlier in connection with the investigation of the raid? It is unlikely that his conscience would have prompted him to this sudden candour. Not is it credible that he desired the death penalty, which was the certain punishment for murder. Harsh corporal punishment and a long stretch of hard labour in prison would theoretically, with a reprieve, have been a sufficient punishment for the banditry. Matthias Calonius conjectured that for the people of Sweden capital punishment represented a stronger deterrent than life-long hard labour, although he personally, like Beccaria, was of a different opinion.[425] It is also possible that as a new settler, Fedot Fedotoff was less aware of the effectiveness of denial of guilt in a court case than were the established inhabitants. But this is unlikely; after all, his own associates had previously got themselves acquitted of grievous crimes on numerous occasions.[426]

Through this extra confession, Fedotoff was probably trying to win time for himself so that he could escape from prison. He could assume that, because of the site of the crime, the enquiry into the murder would be conducted in the Suojärvi District Court on the Russian side of the border, and therefore he would have an opportunity of escaping while he was being transferred there.

The confession of non-existent crimes was a problem that prolonged trials unnecessarily throughout the realm of Sweden. This delay was due to the fact that the validity of all confessions had to be examined in the district court of the locality in which the crime was alleged to have taken place. Frequently the suspects would try to escape while they were being transported from one place to another. In order to solve the problem, the King issued a decree permitting the sentencing of multiple crimes in one locality on condition that the accused had already been sentenced to death or maximum corporal punishment.[427] The circumstances proved that Fedot Feotoff's confession of murder was true.

---

424 VMA: VHOA, Alistettujen asiain päätöstaltiot, Kymenkartanon ja Savon lääni, v. 1768, Di 7, no 48.

425 Calonius 1800, 1801, 1802, pp. 42–43. Cf. e.g. Foucault 1977.

426 E.g. KA: Karjalan tuomiokunnan tuomiokirja, Ilomantsin ja Suolahden osan sk, v. 1751, KO a 20, f 336 ffol.

427 Jusleén 1751, p. 193, Til samteliga hof- och öfwer-rätterne, angående delinquenter, som bekänna sig på flera missgiärningar. Stockholm den 2 mars 1748.

Another of the brigands, Foma Jestafeoff, also confessed to murder at the extraordinary district court session arranged for the trial of the raid, possibly also with the intention of escaping. Jestafeoff said that he had killed a deserter from the Russian side of the border called Foma Makkonen (alias Kirtzu) during the War of the Hats. He had also stolen the victim's clothes. Twenty-six years had elapsed between the deed and the confession. In this case too, the locals had suspected the culprit of murder, but because of the conditions of war that prevailed at the time, no-one had denounced him to the authorities. Jestafeoff also confessed that together with two Russian peasant farmers he had shot a Russian deserter called Fedot in Salmijärvi in the winter of 1742 and had drowned his brother-in-law, Isak Ivanoff. Both the lower court and the court of appeal considered the last mentioned confession a fabrication. The investigation into the double murder would have had to take place in Salmijärvi on the Russian side, and Jestafeoff might have tried to escape on the way there.

Foma Jestafeoff had a black enough reputation without any fabricated confessions. He had been charged in 1751 together with his brother Jeulampei of the murder of three inhabitants of Ilomantsi that took place during the War of the Hats. [428] After the murder, Jeulampei had also threateningly proclaimed that a Swedish head, that is the head of a Swedish Lutheran, was worth no more than the head of a dog.[429] The Ilomantsi District Court and the Åbo Court of Appeal acquitted the Jestafeoff brothers of the murder charges for lack of proof. The truth of the charges was nevertheless patent.[430]

The *modus operandi* of the raid on Säämäjärvi at the end of the 1760s has a spectral, *déja vu* quality about it, for the brigands living around Ilomantsi had earlier, in the early 1740s, travelled to Säämäjärvi to extort money by violence from the inhabitants, one of whom was a peasant farmer called Arhippa Kuismoff. At that time, some of the peasant farmers of Ilomantsi had sheltered the bandits.[431] This makes one suspect that the main motive for the 1767 incursion was ultimately linked to a kind of cycle of revenge that may have had its origins in the bandits' raids on Liusvaara at the end of the 1740s, or even earlier in the depredations that reprisal patrols carried out during the last internecine war, the Lesser Wrath.[432] Indeed, the roots of the conflict might go back even further, for apparently the parents of Foma and Jeulampei Jesafeoff had been expelled from the parish of Selk in Russia back to the father's birth place in Liusvaara in the 1720s.[433]

428 KA: Karjalan tuomiokunnan tuomiokirja v. 1751, Ilomantsin ja Suojärven osan sk, KO a 20, f. 336 ffol; MMA: KymLKa, Saapuneet kirjeet, v. 1753, Hovioikeus maaherralle, D 15 a1, no 10/2.
429 Björn 1993, p. 143; Saloheimo 1980, p. 39.
430 MMA: KymLKa, Saapuneet kirjeet, v. 1753, Hovioikeus maaherralle, D 15 a1, no 10, 15.2.1753.
431 KA: Karjalan tuomiokunnan tuomiokirja, Ilomantsin ja Suojärven osan tk 1750, KO a 20, f. 144b.
432 Cf. e.g. Björn 1993, pp. 142–143.
433 However, I am not certain of this identification. See Björn 1991, pp. 110–111.

Four of the bandits were sentenced to death in the extraordinary session of Liperi District Court. Five female relatives of the main miscreants were sentenced to pay for their crimes of aiding and abetting and the possession of stolen goods with severe birching. In the court of appeal, two of the death sentences were commuted, and only the death sentences on Fedot Fedotoff and Jeulampi Jestafeoff were upheld. What weighed the scales against these two were their reputations, which were already stained with killing and robbery. The Åbo Court of Appeal commuted the death sentence passed on Foma Jestafeoff in the lower court to maximum corporal punishment and life-long hard labour. He was not sentenced to the legal consequences of the murder that he had confessed to because it had happened during the War of the Hats. Under the terms of the Peace of Åbo made on 15 August 1743, crimes committed against foreigners in time of war came within the scope of a general amnesty. His nationality was to some extent a matter of interpretation: he or his father had come illegally from Russia to live in Ilomantsi. Despite the commuting of the death penalty, Foma Jestafeoff had little time to live: he died in Lovisa almost immediately after suffering his corporal punishment.

***

The history of crime in Finland is full of descriptions of killings that enact unofficial control. They are homicides the main aim of which may be to punish the miscreant or rid society of him. For example, in Southern Ostrobothnia, where there was a wave of exceptional violence in the early nineteenth century, which has been studied by Ylikangas, occasional illegal executions were carried out by the people if the criminal succeeded in escaping the punishment prescribed by the law. The punishment of crimes by the community was a reaction of individual persons to the weakness of the authorities.[434] Antero Heikkinen, too, has described of the murder of a thief in Kuhmo in 1810, which bears witness to the most violent forms of unofficial control that a criminal might face. The control was carried out by members of the local community. Both in the burn beating community of Kuhmo and in Southern Ostrobothnia, this kind of weeding out of the community's unwelcome elements was characterized by the tendency of witnesses to remain silent about what had happened.[435] In northern Karelia and in parts of northern Savo, too, the killing of those who were guilty of crimes was to a great extent a matter of self-help and the need for repression. [436] Such incentives to homicide were most apparent in cases where the victim was a thieving peasant farmer, a vagrant or an army deserter who was feeding himself from the local grain stores. The killing of vagrants was not to remain a characteristic only of the violent mid-century period in northern Karelia, either. Some of the killings of

---

434 Ylikangas 1976, pp. 239–251.
435 Heikkinen 1988, pp. 116–164; Ylikangas 1976, pp. 242–251. See also Lappalainen A 2001.
436 Cf. Black 1984a, p. 1.

members of the lowest stratum of the landless population certainly never came to light; they did, however, emerge in Ilomantsi and Liperi in connection with the investigation of quite different crimes.

In Europe, certain communities, like Gypsies, outlaws and pirates, traditionally and consciously put themselves outside the law and organized society.[437] The Romanies who travelled around the northernmost parts of Savo were such a section of the population. From the 1770s on, more and more (six in all) killings that took place among the Gypsies were prosecuted in courts of law. At the same time, there was also an increase in the number of homicides committed by the indigenous section of the population there. The violence of the Romanies did not reach northern Karelia – possibly because the outlawed element of the Karelian population may have kept the Gypsies out of northern Karelia or prevented killing within the group – although in Ilomantsi alone at least three Russian bandits or Finnish army deserters were slain.[438]

The homicides committed by Gypsies were all connected with the settlement of differences within their own group. They also happened in parishes in which crime of any sort, let alone homicide, was rare. In the first trials dealing with lethal brawls among the Gypsies, the parties involved were women. However, this certainly does not represent the true situation, for killings committed by men could be passed over as blood feuds without the matter being brought to the attention of the authorities. Irrespective of the form of the society, it is the lowest social groups that are regarded as being most loath to have recourse to the law for the settlement of their disputes. When the conflicts are then resolved within the group, the unofficial social control frequently takes on a form that is criminal in the eyes of the judiciary,[439] and this in turn requires the authorities to take a hand in matters. The latter, on the other hand, are inclined to let criminal sub-cultures settle their own disputes. Thus the greatest threat to criminals emerges from their own people, and this was also the case with the Romanies.

Beata Danielintytär, a Gypsy widow, stabbed another Romany woman in Leppävirta in 1771. It was only in connection with the investigation of this case that it emerged that two Gypsy men called Valtin and Timoteus Kristianinpoika had taken the life of one of their own, Jonatan Swartz, in Iisalmi. The two men and Beata all ran away, but the population tables indicate that the latter was caught and executed in Leppävirta in 1774. A fifteen-year-old Romany girl called Juliana Glasberg, who was travelling around Leppävirta with her people also stabbed her companion, Helena Ristontytär, being enraged by the latter's intention to change her fiancé. The King commuted the death sentence

---

437 Lenman & Parker 1980, p. 40.

438 Only one Gypsy was killed by a member of the indigenous population of Karelia. His death, too, was connected with an internal settling of accounts between criminals. The killer himself was a peasant horse thief from Tohmajärvi, who killed a young Gypsy boy over a disagreement about stolen booty. VMA: VHOA, Alistettujen asiain päätöstaltiot, Kymenkartanon ja Savon lääni, v. 1764, Di 5, no 38.

439 Black 1984b, p. 3.

passed on Glasberg in the lower court and the court of appeal to birching and two years hard labour. In the following decade in Pieksämäki, the two-year-old child of a Gypsy woman died when he was struck accidentally by the fist of a Romany man called Kalle Hommonen in a fight.[440]

A Romany called Fredrik Palm was murdered in Pielavesi (in the parish of Iisalmi) in 1806, but the culprit was never finally discovered. A dozen or so other Gypsies were dragged up before the court and charged. At about the same time, in Liperi, a seventeen-year-old Gypsy called Adam Larm refused to take part in stealing some grain, as he had been incited to do by his companions, and instead warned the owner of their intentions. One of his companions attacked him for his "grassing", but Larm stabbed his assailant. The court of appeal considered that it was a case of self-defence in a genuinely life-or-death situation.[441]

Organized gang crime is often regarded as a social factor that increases individual violence. However, the connection between violent crime and organized crime is a complex one.[442] For example, bands of bandits and vagrants may pose a threat to public security when they incite larger social groups to react violently. It would appear that the nomadic bands of Romanies did not incite people to this kind of defensive reaction, but that the Russian bandits who lived along the border did. In northern Karelia the violent resolution of personal conflicts was also encouraged by tradition.[443]

440 VMA: VHOA, Alistettujen asiain päätöstaltiot, Kymenkartanon ja Savon lääni, v. 1775, Di 10, no 4. MMA: KymLKa, Saapuneet kirjeet, v. 1772, Hovioikeus maaher-ralle, D 34 a1, no 96. VMA: VHOA, Alistettujen asiain päätöstaltiot, Kymenkartanon ja Savon / Savon ja Karjalan lääni, v. 1775, Di 10, no 72; v. 1785, Di 20, no 92.

441 VMA: VHOA, Alistettujen asiain päätöstaltiot, Savon ja Karjalan lääni, 1807, Di 45, no 13.; v. 1806, Di 43, no 108.

442 Bäckman 1996, pp. 37–39; 100–107.

443 Riissanen 1965, pp. 48–49; Kujala & Malinen 2001, p. 427; Katajala 1994, pp. 395–396.

Homicide as an Extension of Conciliatory Control

Settling Differences in the Family

Familial Homicide in Europe and in Eastern Finland during the Last Years of Swedish Rule

Mediaeval Europe has traditionally been regarded as a strongly communal culture. Individuals were essentially the representatives of their social roles and dependent on their extended families for their safety. Family and kinship relations offered legal, economic and social protection against a violent environment at a time when the institutions that provided legal protection, like the state, were weak. It was essential to belong to a family in order to ensure one's personal safety. The price of strong family affiliation was weakness in the public sphere. Society was forced into the confines of family and kin. The obligation to avenge a wrong maintained the spiral of vendettas between families.[444]

The growth of the power state, which directly offered the individual rights, privileges and the protection of the law, weakened the traditional institutions, especially the family. When the ruling elites of the states assumed a monopoly of the use of violence (the power to punish), the opportunities for conducting a blood feud evaporated. As violence within the family or the kin abated, the networks of extended kinship relations shrank both in size and importance, for the state monopoly of the power to punish decreased the need of people, other than the nobles, to take refuge in extended families. It was only with the establishment of the authority of the state that it became possible for the individual to enjoy his or her rights, privileges and the protection of the law. In monopolising the legitimate use of violence, the state also assumed responsibility for the protection of individuals, but where the authorities failed to carry out this

---

444 Voionmaa 1915 (1969), p. 48; Gillis 1996, pp. 1275–76; Lane 1997, pp. 10–13; Ylikangas 1994. Cf. also Myhrberg 1978, pp. 1–2. The power of the kin survived longer within the aristocracy than among other groups. Winberg 1985, pp. 48–50; Lappalainen 2001

responsibility, commitment to the family remained strong. At the local level, families continued to vie with the state in offering their members protection and attempting to preserve their influence – and in doing so they maintained the local sub-culture of violence.[445]

Among others, Lawrence Stone, Edward Shorter and Jean-Louis Flandrin have painted a dismal picture of European family life in the early modern era: according to them it tolerated a considerable amount of intra-family violence. Wife-beating and infanticide are described as practically everyday phenomena. On the other hand, Jim Sharpe is one who questions such a gloomy concept of the family, pointing out that the proportion of killings within the family out of all prosecuted homicides was in fact very small in mediaeval and pre-industrial western Europe. Shorter answered this criticism by claiming that this was caused by the cool emotional climate within the family, which was a consequence of the historical situation; the functions of marriage were for a long time mainly connected with property arrangements. The family was not a private institution, and personal relations were not intimate. Nor did the family then have the monopoly of affects that was later attached to the modern family. In the household, the basic unit of agrarian communities, the spouses were indispensable to each other economically and in terms of the distribution of labour. The family constituted a kind of fortress against the outside world as a result of the bonds of practical necessity, property and inherited status. Therefore, deadly violence within this community was out of the question. The predominant inter-family and inter-clan violence was only transformed into intra-family violence with the advent of the modern age.[446]

In England, the ratio of intra-family manslaughters and murders rose to 13-18% of all homicide in the seventeenth century, and continued to rise steadily. At the same time there was an exponential increase in the number of infanticide trials. At the end of the eighteenth century, the proportion of killings within families rose to over one third in some places.[447] In Am-

---

445 Gillis 1996, pp. 1275–1276. However, even in mediaeval times most of the homicides were not vengeance killings, which today would be considered murders; rather they resulted from simple spontaneous disputes. E.g. Lane 1997, p. 19; Sharpe 1991, p. 38. For an extensive review of the literature on the power of the kin and its waning significance at the turn of the Middle Ages and the modern age as well as an outline of opposing views, see Cressy 1986, pp. 39–69; also Winberg 1985, pp. 10–31.

446 E.g. Sharpe 1981, pp. 34–35, with references to the above mentioned factors. There were, however, exceptions to this: for example, in Toulouse in the early eighteenth century, two thirds of the homicide cases prosecuted took place within the family. Moreover, Cockburn, among others, has criticized the documentation of familial homicides in the sources and considers that they were strongly characteristic of earlier times. Cockburn 1991, p. 93 ff. Cf. however e.g. Spierenburg 1994, p. 705; Lane 1997, pp. 16–17.

447 Lane 1997, pp. 28–29. For the debate on this subject, see also Kaspersson 2000, p. 22 ff.

sterdam the killing of family members and other relatives, servants and close companions had risen from just over one tenth of the total amount of homicide to nearly a half by the latter half of the eighteenth century.[448] On the other hand, in Sweden prosecutions for violence between family members were still very rare in the first half of the nineteenth century.[449] In pre-industrial Europe, at most one in four homicides is estimated to have taken place within the family.[450]

In British research dealing with family violence, the family is assumed to be the nuclear family, and therefore its findings cannot be applied to areas where the nuclear family was not the only family model.[451] For example, the family institution in the Province of Savo and Karelia was traditionally conceived of as an economic unit, and the number of persons it included depended on such factors as the amount of labour required for burn-beating cultivation. Kirsi Sirén, Elina Waris and Kari-Matti Piilahti have complemented the work of older Finnish historians like Väinö Voionmaa, Eino Jutikkala and Arvo Soininen in demonstrating the connection between the extended family and cultural factors, the realities of economic survival and demographic pressures.[452] In practice, the most common form of the family in northern Savo and also in northern Karelia was the nuclear family, although the fraternal joint (extended) family was almost as common.[453] The joint family was in principle almost totally independent of the clan, because the family or the partnership could be supplemented with the introduction of fresh male labour from outside the clan, and correspondingly its members were free to leave it.[454] A logical consequence of the relatively large size of the family organization in Savo and Karelia was that, by western European standards, an uncommonly high number of the homicides committed there during the period studied in this research took place within the family or the kin.

Altogether a third, at times rising to a half, of the killings prosecuted in homicide trials in the Province of Savo and Karelia took place within the family or the immediate kin. And two thirds of the murders were of close relations. In northern Karelia in the period 1748–1777, in 23 (47%) out of a total of 49 prosecuted cases of homicide, the victims were near relations by birth or marriage of the killers. In the second half of the period under investigation (1778–1807), 24 killings within the family or kin were

---

448 Thus only some of these were actual family members. Spierenburg 1994, p. 710. The relative growth was mainly caused by the fact it became much rarer for acquaintances or strangers to be victims of homicide.

449 Sundin 1992, p. 271.

450 Spierenburg 1996, p. 64.

451 For a summary of comparative studies of family structures in this period, see e.g. Waris 1999, pp. 32 – 41.

452 Björn 1993, p. 112; Voionmaa 1915, pp. 150–152; Piilahti 1999; Sirén 1999, pp. 46, 60, 73–75, 90–96, 143–147; On the Finnish historiography of the concept, see also Waris 1999, pp. 37–40.

453 Wirilander 1989, pp. 86–89.

454 Björn 1993, p. 112; Voionmaa 1915, p. 50.

brought to justice in comparison with a total of 68 victims of homicide overall that came to the cognisance of the law during the same period. In the Savo region of the province during the first thirty-year period, thirteen (36%) of the total of 36 homicides were committed within the family or the clan, and in the latter period fifteen (33%) out of 45.[455]

What makes the familial killings of the Karelians exceptional is their high frequency per 100,000 inhabitants per year rather than their relative proportion of all homicides, although this was also fairly high. In studies of some other European countries, it was not until very recent times that the proportion of victims of family violence relative to the total number of homicide victims rose to any considerable extent, when homicide generally decreased. However, during the period of this study, northern Karelia, with all its intra-family killing, remained an area characterized by a relatively high homicide rate.

This special connection between homicide and family relationship in Savo and Karelia is also partly related to another characteristic feature of the killings, one that was, judged by international standards, exceptional: premeditation. An absolute majority of the parties involved in premeditated killing (i.e. murder) in eastern Finland were related to each other through marriage or betrothal or biologically. In northern Karelia during the period studied here, 27 (60%) of the 45 murders, were committed within the family or the clan, while in northern Savo the equivalent figure was eleven (73%) out of fifteen.

In pre-industrial England, the most common form of homicide within the family was the killing of legitimate children.[456] In eastern Finland, on the other hand, courts far more often tried cases of homicide arising from disputes between close adult relatives. Particularly in the case of murder, the conflicts behind the majority of the cases in the area of this research involved family or kinship relations in one way or another. The principal motives for killing sprang from quarrels within family partnerships or

---

455 Thus the number of homicides of relatives relative to the increase in the size of the population declined. No extensive and detailed systematic statistical study of the family structure in northern Karelia and northern Savo during the period of this research has been carried out, but it is probable that particularly in northern Karelia the proportion of familial homicides exceeded the proportion of extended families proper out of all households. For example, Björn has estimated the average size of an Ilomantsi family in 1800 to be seven persons, and the figure did not differ to any great extent between the two main religious groups. The households of social groups below the peasant farmers were smaller, as both Björn and Sirén, among others, have shown. In northern Savo the proportion of familial homicide trials was considerably lower than the proportion of joint families out of all types of family structure. Cf. Wirilander 1989, pp. 88–89.

456 Sharpe 1981, p. 37. The statistical method employed by Sharpe has aroused criticism, because generally infanticide is not classified as ordinary homicide. However, Sharpe speaks only of infanticides within the family, i.e. the killing of legitimate children. Cf. Stone 1985; Spierenburg 1996, p. 73. The present study has included all proven homicides, murders and lethal assaults committed against legitimate progeny, of which there are, however, surprisingly few.

from disputes about material benefits: the ownership of property or the division of an inheritance. An equally significant source of disagreement concerned factors connected with the founding, composition, maintenance and dissolution of a joint family. Wounded honour caused by a legal denunciation was another very frequent source of fatal dissentions among close relatives.

Martin Daly and Margo Wilson have conducted longitudinal and horizontal comparisons which show that the rate of homicides within families is generally inversely proportional to the sum of all homicides. At the same time, the absolute incidence of homicide within the family varies less between countries or cultures than it does for other types of homicide.[457] In northern Karelia, this generalization does not hold true, for there both the total number of homicides and the proportion of intra-family killings in them were high. Both also actually decreased at the same time. Nor is the prevalence of extended families in itself the sole factor that increased homicide. In that case, one would expect violence to have been a characteristic of northern Savo in earlier times as well, but this is not so.[458]

The number of potential victims of homicide is highest when the size of the family is increased by members who are not related to it by blood ties. Longitudinal studies have shown that the risk of blood relatives being slain is considerably lower than that of those who have become family members by marriage or other ties.[459] In eastern Finland, too, in the period studied here, an increase in the size of the family entailed an increased risk of its members' being killed. On the other hand, in northern Karelia particularly, blood ties did not lessen the risk of a family member becoming a victim.

Fratricide in Different Types of Society

The mythologies of many cultures depict fratricide as an archetypal form of homicide: the parties involved are often presented as the primeval enemies in the history of the mankind. The antagonism between brothers was exacerbated into a mythical archetype of competitive aggression by rivalry for an inheritance or for the favours of the opposite sex, or in a contest of prowess. It was only with the advent of the agrarian community, however, that a fertile ground for the growth of fratricide myths like the story of Cain and Abel was created. In tribal hunting and gathering communities, brothers had no motivation to vie for the inheritance of the family's insignificant possessions. In such tribal cultures, relatives are considered as the most valuable property of the "individual", a protection

457 Daly & Wilson 1988, pp. 284–286. The comparison is based on global, partly historical, material.
458 The concept of extended family is used here in the broadest sense, cf. Voionmaa 1915.
459 Daly & Wilson 1988, pp. 22–24.

against the hostile world outside the clan. For this reason, fratricides are rare among primitive peoples.[460]

In agricultural societies, the degree of intimacy and the forms of interaction between people are mainly based on kinship. The major reason for fatal disputes between blood relatives is considered to be fraternal rivalry for the family's limited property, and particularly the possession of the land. It is believed that conflicts between brothers or other male relatives are most acute in two types of situation: in organizations in which social status is patrilineal, and in systems of inheritance in which the estate, such as a farm, is not divided.[461]

Fratricide almost totally disappeared in western countries during the pre-industrial era. This was because the close interrelationship between siblings was broken off at a relatively early age: members of the family had to move out to enter the service of others. Fratricide was already extremely rare in the early modern age in England,[462] let alone in later industrialized societies; in them the patriline no longer determined the future prospects of the descendants as it did in agrarian communities.[463] In the households of western Europe in the early years of the modern age the servants replaced brothers as the principal victims of homicide.[464]

In their description of the psychology of the evolution of fratricide and other forms of familial homicide, Daly and Wilson note that many rules for western civilization no longer hold true in non-European cultures. For example, in the latter blood relatives are not excluded from victimization, i.e. selection as victims of homicide. Among tribes that lived by cyclical cultivation, hunting and gathering, over thirty per cent of the victims may be relations of the perpetrators, mainly adults. Attempts have been made to explain the proclivity of traditional agrarian societies to commit familial homicide through the interaction of family members based on the organization of labour. In such models, the household is founded on kinship-based cooperation and patrilocal residence.[465] The obverse of familial solidarity is fierce competition, which particularly characterizes fraternal relations because the land resources are possessed by families. Fratricides are common (from 7.5% to over 10% of all homicides) and especially so in those agricultural communities where only one of the sons inherits the farm and the others must leave and seek a living elsewhere. [466]

---

460 Daly & Wilson 1988, p. 17, 31.
461 Daly & Wilson 1988, pp. 29–33.
462 Sharpe 1981, p. 37.
463 Daly & Wilson 1988, p. 31.
464 Cf. Sharpe 1981, p. 38.
465 Children killed by their parents account for only 5% of the victims. Daly & Wilson 1988, p. 29.
466 Daly & Wilson 1988, pp. 29–30. It should, however, be noted that the system of justice necessarily has an effect on the form of the crime. The deed is punished in a quite different way if homicide within the family comes within the province of private justice from the way it is penalized under the public penal code.

Fratricide in Eastern Finland

In Stockholm, the loosening of family and kinship ties began in the seventeenth century concomitantly with a growth in the population. At the same time, the ability of the kin to offers its members benefits like property, status or career opportunities weakened.[467] This happened despite the fact that in individual cases material values did not necessarily determine family affiliation. The use of the courts of law for the settlement of family disputes increased considerably throughout the kingdom of Sweden in the course of the eighteenth century.[468] This was a result of a continued increase in the number of surviving heirs resulting from the higher birth rate relative to mortality. The growth in the size of families caused problems for the transfer of property within the family and between generations.[469]

In eastern Finland, kinship and family continued to regulate the individual's life later than in the western parts of the kingdom.[470] Even so, one can assume that the population explosion at the end of the eighteenth century weakened the internal coherence of the kin and altered the networks of local contacts there too, in addition to making the ownership structures of the countryside and the traditional social division into estates problematic.[471] When the number of close relations and siblings grew far beyond the earlier norm, the opportunities for future generations to maintain the economic and social position of their parents weakened disastrously. The joint families of adult brothers could not grow infinitely as the land available for clearance began to run out even in the remote regions. Even a large farm could not always support all the sons and their spouses, and it became more and more difficult for some of the brothers to maintain their position as landed peasant farmers. Kirsi Sirén has shown that there was a considerable increase in the number of landless households in the regions of southern Savo and Kymenlaakso during the last decades of the eighteenth century.[472]

Of homicides of *relatives*, those in which the victim was a brother or brother-in-law accounted for nearly a quarter (23%) in northern Karelia and 14% in northern Savo. In northern Karelia, 9% of the homicide trials handled cases in which the victim was a *brother* of the killer, and in northern Savo 5%. In *all* homicide trials in northern Karelia about 16% of the victims were relatives of the perpetrators *and of the same generation* – brothers, brothers-in-law and sisters-in-law. The corresponding figure in northern Savo is a half of this (7.5%). In the light of the findings of Daly and Wilson, the

---

467 Jansson 1998, p. 44.
468 Gaunt 1987, p. 139; Odén 1991; Odén 1994.
469 Gaunt 1987, p. 136; Sirén 1999, p. 34.
470 Sirén 1999, p. 78 ff.
471 Kauppinen 1997, p. 110; Sirén 1999, p. 87 ff.
472 Sirén 1999, pp. 9, 58–60, 87 ff; Waris 1999, p. 133.

relative figures for homicides of brothers and brothers-in-law particularly in northern Karelia are huge by global standards. The peak period of trials of familial homicide and in particular fratricide in Savo and Karelia was probably somewhere between the beginning of the eighteenth century and the 1770s. This is indicated by two factors: first, familial homicide particularly of persons of the same generation had already begun to disappear by the third quarter of the eighteenth century in eastern Finland;[473] second, in the seventeenth century and during the Great Northern War, the parties involved in homicide trials were only rarely related.[474] (It should be noted that it is possible that a smaller number of the familial homicides in the war years of the seventeenth century and the early eighteenth century were actually brought to trial than was the case later.)

With one exception, the fratricides in Savo and Karelia were all committed by farmers who at some stage in their lives had run their farms as family partnerships, by former farmers or by men registered as the sons of farmers. The social spectrum of homicides of brothers-in-law was wider; in six cases, the involved parties were designated as dependent lodgers. Some of these, however, were living in the households of their brothers-in-law and were probably members of an informal partnership, but the strict statute on hired labour of 1739 denied partners the right to an official rank equal with that of the farmer.[475] On the other hand, there was not a single homicide trial in which sisters were involved as either of the parties involved, although one married woman registered as a dependent lodger murdered her sister-in-law in Pielavesi over disputes concerning a farming partnership.[476] There were also cases of brothers-in-law killing their sisters-in-law in quarrels over the conditions pertaining to the foundation of a partnership or other matters connected with the use of common property.[477]

---

473 In northern Karelia, there were seven cases of men slaying their brothers in the period 1748–77, while during the following thirty years there were only four despite the increase in the population. In northern Savo there were only two in each half of the period studied.

474 Matikainen 1995, pp. 55–56; Matikainen 2002; Kujala & Malinen 2001, p. 432. The latter estimate the proportion of familial homicide at 16%.

475 Cf. Wirilander 1989, pp. 92–95. The recording of social rank in the judicial sources varies. Sometimes the same person is recorded as a dependent lodger and sometimes as a peasant farmer. This clearly reflects the recorder's view of the person's share in a partnership or their position in a joint family.

476 Kristiina Kukotar murdered the wife of her husband's brother, Katariina Moilatar, in Pielisjärvi in 1807 because of disputes about the care of their sick father-in-law and the division of property. VMA: VHOA, Alistettujen asiain päätöstaltiot, Savon ja Karjalan lääni, v. 1808, Di 46, no 4.

477 Olli Ihalainen killed his sister-in-law, Helena Hyvötär, in Liperi in 1777. VMA: VHOA, Alistettujen asiain päätöstaltiot, Savon ja Karjalan lääni, v. 1777, Di 12, no 57; an Orthodox man from Ilomantsi, Ondrei Savinainen, ended some partnership disputes by murdering his brother's widow with her own axe in 1805. VMA: VHOA, Alistettujen asiain päätöstaltiot, Savon ja Karjalan lääni, v. 1807, Di 45, no 4.

Such motives were symptomatic of all the homicides of brothers or brothers-in-law that were prosecuted in eastern Finland, of which eight took place in northern Karelia and two in northern Savo. The most common cause of friction in fraternal relations was the founding of a partnership or a change in the composition of the household.[478] According to Waris, the right to expel a member from the joint family was invoked only in extreme circumstance, especially if the head of the household was still alive.[479]

> Mikitta Karreinen, a tenant farmer of land owned by a noble (*frälsejord*) stabbed his younger brother, Feodor, to death on 1 December 1754 in Kovero in the parish of Ilomantsi because the latter together with his mother had moved out of the brothers' joint home to live in the household of one Iivana Toroskainen in the same village. Apparently the father was no longer alive. When Feodor came to collect his mother's belongings from Mikitta's house, the latter stabbed him as he stood outside the door, and he died the following day.[480]

The peasant family model in eastern Finland, which permitted several adult brothers to remain in the household to till the land, also gave the adult sons a better chance to maintain their social rank than a model in which only the eldest son remained. If they did experience a loss of social rank, this could also could be alleviated by an opportunity to till the outlying lands of the farm as a crofter.[481] Veijo Saloheimo concludes that the growth in the number of adult males living in Karelian families was a clear sign of overpopulation. In the mid-1760, there was no longer enough land to provide as many men with farms of their own as there had been thirty years earlier.[482] Wirilander again considers that the only thing that kept the larger extended families together was economic advantage, and that they broke up immediately if prospects of an alternative way of life presented themselves. He further believes that life in joint families was confrontational rather than harmonious.[483]

When the growth in the number of farms and farming partners reached its final bounds, the price of a family model that guaranteed a flexible division of resources was fratricide. Homicide within the family, and particularly fratricide, were particularly characteristic of jointly cultivated farms, irrespective of whether the parties involved were partners in the enterprise or not. Mona Rautelin has estimated that the high incidence of familial homicide in eastern Finland was connected with the temporary growth in the size of families, which was a consequence of the expected

---

478 Cf. also Heikkinen 1988, p. 72.
479 Waris 1999, p. 52.
480 MMA: KymLka, Saapuneet kirjeet, v. 1755, Hovioikeus maaherralle, D17 a1, no 9/1.
481 Wirilander 1989, pp. 94–98, also Heikkinen 1988, p. 71.
482 Saloheimo 1980, p. 461. For Savo, see also Wirilander 1989, pp. 85–86.
483 Wirilander 1989, pp. 88–89; on points of friction between members of family partnerships, see also Waris 1999, pp. 135–141, 167–169.

redistribution of land in the Land Division Statute of 1775.[484] Indeed, fratricide decreased in northern Karelia at the same time as the size of families diminished and the general redistribution of land following the Land Division Statute got under way in the southern parishes of the province.[485] It is to some extent contradictory that fratricide in eastern Finland decreased at a time when the population growth was at its highest, and the numbers of the landless were rising. This kind of social dispersion, or disorganization, usually gives rise to other forms of homicide.[486] And this in fact is what happened in the northernmost pockets of the area under examination, like Iisalmi, Kuopio and Liperi. However, as the increase in population caused a growth in the number of landless households, the rationale behind the traditional fraternal disputes of the agrarian society gradually disappeared. The points of friction between brothers decreased when the relationship between them changed.

In the eastern Finnish family model, the scope for disputes between brothers and brothers-in-law was wider than in industrialized communities, which were mostly made up of nuclear families. Other forms of cooperation naturally led to different kinds of conflicts than those based on kinship ties.[487] If we limit our examination of homicide to nuclear families in eastern Finland – to the first generation in direct lineal ascent or descent and to spouses – the proportion of homicides committed against other members of the family for the years 1748—1807 was 16—22%, going down to almost the same level as in England at the beginning of the modern age.

Eastern Finland, too, had its share of fraternal rivalry, which was the main motivation for fratricide in traditional or stateless communities, during the period of this research. Nevertheless, it is not possible to draw a direct parallel between the motives for different types of homicide, for the justice systems of the societies compared – a public punitive system vs. the private settlement of differences – differ too much from each other.[488] In primitive communities, no reparation or punishment was necessarily demanded for the murder of a relation; rather it was morally classified as

---

484 Rautelin 1997, p. 195. On the growth in the size of families, see Wirilander 1989, pp. 85–92, Sirén 1999, pp. 88–89.

485 The joint family system survived relatively well in northern Savo and northern Karelia until the crisis in burn-beating cultivation of the nineteenth century, but these joint families often consisted of several different households, at least in some places. E.g. Wirilander 1989, pp. 82–90; Björn 1993, p. 118.

486 Rosenfeld & Messner 1991, pp. 53–54; Berkowitz 1962, p. 313.

487 Cf. Daly & Wilson 1988, p. 293. The risk of being killed by a relative can also be assumed always to be relative to the opportunities available for committing the crime, i.e. the amount of interaction between siblings. In areas where nuclear families predominated, the amount of opportunity within the family is a constant (once fluctuations in the number of children are eliminated), whereas in joint families the risk of internal conflict grows with the size of the family.

488 See e.g. Utriainen 1985, p. 9 ff. for differences between primitive communities and those governed by statute law.

a sinful act.[489] The Karelian proclivity for fratricide should not be attributed primarily to fraternal competition, because the family model did not directly require younger sons to leave the family household on the death or retirement of the father, as was generally the case in western Finland, where fratricide was nevertheless marginal.[490] It would appear beyond dispute that the profusion of fatal fraternal disputes is to be explained by two factors: first, demographic pressures, and second, the amount of interaction and the division of responsibilities between the brothers. It is connected with the traditional organization of work and the forms of cooperation in the economy of burn-beating cultivation. Such fraternal conflicts had already diminished in western Europe when cyclical forms of agriculture there passed into history.

Mona Rautelin considers that lax unofficial control made the investigation of familial homicides in court more difficult in the 1790s. Eyewitnesses to killings that took place in the home were usually disqualified or otherwise unwilling to testify in court.[491] J.S. Cockburn discerns a similar phenomenon in earlier times.[492] The grip of official control on homicide within the family has traditionally been weak. Families strive to resolve their differences among themselves as far as possible and to avoid recourse to public institutions. For settling internal conflicts, they prefer voluntary forms of control such as arbitration, criticism or even suicide and violence.[493] The father as head of the household is only rarely mentioned in trials dealing with homicides arising from conflicts within family partnerships in eastern Finland. For example, the triple murder of his brother and the latter's family arranged by Risto Sykkö took place soon after their father had died. One suspects that, in general, fratricides mainly happened in households that lacked a patriarch to settle disputes and in which the division of the estate had not yet been carried out.[494] Moreover, burn-beating partnerships were also usually based on an unofficial agreement; only rarely were they legally validated.[495]

In Savo and Karelia, the group most inclined to fratricide was the Orthodox community, whose members committed five of the eleven cases of fratricide prosecuted in the area of this study, although it was only in Liperi and Ilomantsi that they accounted for a sizeable proportion (about 20%) of the population. Olli Matikainen has conjectured that some folk institutions of justice, like the vendetta, that had disappeared from western Europe continued to flourish in the Orthodox culture for quite a

489 Utriainen 1985, p. 10.
490 Cf. Ylikangas 1976, pp. 100–104, 149–158.
491 Rautelin 1997, p. 196.
492 Cockburn 1991, pp. 94–95.
493 Black 1984b, pp. 3–4, 22–23
494 Cf. Heikkinen 1988, pp. 71–72; Waris 1999, pp. 41–52. On inheritance practice, see Sirén 1999, p. 79 and notes.
495 Heikkinen 1988, pp. 70–71.

long time, at least down to the sixteenth or seventeenth century.[496] Thus a certain sense of tradition may have maintained the propensity of Orthodox Karelians for fratricide and other serious crimes of violence. The phenomenon may have involved some kind of eastern cultural heritage. Such conjectures are, of course, impossible to verify because so far there has been no systematic study of violent crime among the Russian Karelians in the eighteenth century. For example, the records of the Collegium of Justice of Old Finland, which are held in the Finnish National Archives, offer an enlightening and untapped source of material for this.

Apart from cultural models, fraternal enmity among the Orthodox on the Swedish side of the border is explained by factors pertaining to habitation. The Orthodox were unwilling to move in search of a living to areas completely inhabited by people of another faith. At the same time, on the smallest farms, which were not large enough to not be divided among all the inheritors, there was little opportunity for solving disputes between brothers by legal means, while on the holdings that were owned by the nobles there was in practice no such possibility at all. In parishes where there were many such holdings, the farmers who owned their land or tilled Crown land also had few chances of extending their farms.[497] Nor was it possible to channel the excess population from the Crown farms into holdings on land owned by the nobles, because the number of persons inhabiting the latter could not officially be increased.[498] However, in Ilomantsi it was not the farms owned by the nobility where homicides tended to be committed, but Crown lands in Sonkaja, the main village of the parish, while in Liperi it was in Sotkuma, an Orthodox enclave.[499] Perhaps there was also a connection between the fact that the farms owned by the nobility avoided the worst wave of homicides and the exemption of those who farmed them from the obligation to provide a soldier for the army, a burden that has been shown to have lain heavily on the population of northern Karelia during the years of war.

The violent equation between land and family model is corroborated by findings from Iitti in the southern part of the area dealt with in this study, where as many as seven familial homicides were prosecuted in the period 1748–1774, including two patricides and killings of a sister-in-law and a sister arising out of partnership disputes. On the nobility-owned holdings of Iitti, burn-beating cultivation was still of considerable economic significance in the second half of the century.[500]

---

496 Matikainen 1995, p. 43 and Matikainen 2002.

497 There were three main types of land: *frälsejord* was owned by the nobles, to whom tenant farmers paid their taxes; *skattejord* was owned by the farmers themselves, who paid taxes to the Crown, as did those who farmed Crown land (*kronojord*). Tenant farmers on *frälsejord* paid for their tenancy in day labour. However, they, like farmers of *kronojord,* owned the right to farm the land and the right to pass it on to their children.

498 Cf. e.g. Saloheimo 1980, p. 340.

499 For the villages on land owned by the nobility in the parishes of Ilomantsi and Pälkjärvi, see Saloheimo 1980, pp. 288–289; On the Orthodoxy Statute, ibid. p. 418; Björn 1991, p. 125.

500 Sirén 1999, pp. 22–23.

Despite these reservations, one can suggest that perhaps a different model of land ownership and history of settlement go some way towards explaining the fact that fratricide never spread from northern Karelia into northern Savo. It may well be that the prevalence of ownership by the gentry, extensive burn-beating cultivation with its need for large tracts of forest, and the existence of adult, fatherless brothers and brothers-in-law who lived under the same roof – or generally of any households where several nuclear families of the same generation lived together – all created an equation to which with exceptional frequency the solution turned out to be violence. This was liable to happen particularly when there were strong settlement pressures and the land available in the backwoods was known to be running out. In such circumstances, denunciations of theft made by relatives could also easily evoke a violent response – after all, they were one way of getting rid of the other party from the farm.

Conjugal Homicide

Over a tenth of the homicides committed in the area under investigation involved couples.[501] In northern Karelia, there were twelve assassinations of spouses or life partners, of which five were committed during the first half of the period studied here (1748–1777). In northern Savo there were nine such cases, of which five took place in the earlier part of the period. In northern Karelia six of the nine, and in Savo three of the eight victims were men. This limited sample permits one to tentatively suggest that Karelian women had a high tendency to kill their spouses. It is known that in seventeenth-century England and France, for example, two out of three victims of homicide in marriage were women.[502] The burning desire of Karelian women to do away with their husbands for some reason or another flared up in the 1770s. At the same time, the proportion of women involved in other kinds of homicide also increased. The methods used in of all types of homicide also generally became more brutal.[503]

Killings of a spouse were, both generally and in the period dealt with in this study, unconnected with social rank; the social status of those involved extended from dependent lodgers to the lower clergy.[504] There were more trials concerning the killing of a spouse in northern Karelia than in northern Savo. In relative terms, most charges were made in Tohmajärvi

---

501 Here, conjugal homicide includes not only killings of wedded partners but also two murders of a fiancée and one of a fiancé. The proportion of homicides involving couples in other kinds of relationship is not revealed by the sources. The relatives of woman who died prematurely frequently demanded an inquest into the cause of death by the district court, in consequence of which charges of homicide far exceeded the number of deaths that actually turned out to be violent in the end.

502 Gillis 1996, pp. 1282–1300; Sharpe 1981, p. 37.

503 The peak in conjugal homicide was reached in the late 1780s. It may be that, as this phenomenon declined in northern Karelia, it shifted west into northern Savo.

504 Sharpe 1981, p. 45.

and Pielisjärvi. In Pieksämäki there were none, and in Ilomantsi, where violence was otherwise rife, the first killing arising from suspicion of a spouse's infidelity did not take place until 1789.

The main incentive for the more premeditated murders of spouses was the desire to obtain some advantage through the crime, mainly the opportunity to form a new relationship, but for women also the attainment of economic benefits. The murder of a husband could also combine both these motives if the new male partner was of a higher social rank than the deceased. In addition, long-standing family violence and everyday domestic squabbles led to spontaneous acts of manslaughter.

The unofficial control of extra-marital relations in Savo and Karelia cannot be described as particularly strict. For instance, none of those charged with killing their spouses had previously been charged with adultery. Only after the killing of the spouse was the community moved to report the perpetrator for adultery as well. Denial of guilt was particularly frequent in cases of marital homicide, and not one of those who were suspected of adultery confessed to killing his or her spouse. This was contrary to the situation that prevailed in the Göta Court of Appeal in the seventeenth century, in which those accused of similar *crimes passionelles* invariably confessed and were duly sentenced.[505]

Even so, there was a clear attempt by the lower courts of eastern Finland to to put a strict curb on such crimes; they frequently convicted those accused of murdering their spouses on purely circumstantial evidence without any legally valid proof. This reversed burden of proof was sufficient for a legal death sentence on two occasions. In these cases, appeal was made to the fact that the accused was unable to show that anyone else could have been guilty of the crime. However, the chances of getting away with killing one's spouse in the superior courts were excellent. Because of the great amount of time that the parties spent together, it was easy to find an opportunity, whether during burn-beating work or at night, when no witnesses were likely to turn up.

Antti Kosonen, a married farmer who had taken such a shine to his farm maid, Leena Toropatar, that it had been widely rumoured for some time in Tohmajärvi that they were committing adultery, walked free of a charge of killing his wife. She was found slain in a sauna in 1787, and Kosonen and Leena Toropatar were indicted for murder and single adultery. The lower court ruled that the circumstantial evidence constituted a sufficient proof, although both the defendants denied laying a hand on the victim. Both Toropatar and Kosonen were sentenced according to MB XII (and in the case of the latter also MB XIV) to have their right hands cut off and to be executed, after which Kosonen's body was to be broken on the wheel and Toropatar's body was to be burned at the stake.

---

505 Thunander 1993, p. 132.

The couple staunchly denied both killing the wife and committing single adultery, and the court of appeal did not possess the legal evidence necessary for a conviction. The murder case was adjourned *sine die*, and the conviction for single adultery made by the lower court was held to be not proven. Nevertheless, the court of appeal responded to local pressure and punished the couple for their grievous moral offences and crimes of violence by expelling Toropatar from Kosonen's service and forbidding any contact between them.[506]

In view of the fact that a relatively high number of adulterers were charged with murdering their spouses, it is paradoxical that crimes of passion proper were very rare; in only two homicide cases is the motive directly connected with jealousy.

A widow called Helena Tuppurainen, who lived as a dependent lodger, was believed to have met her death in Pielisjärvi in 1794 because the mistress of the farm suspected that her husband was sleeping with her. It was thought that the mistress of the household had hired another female dependent lodger to hit her on the head with an axe.[507] Then a peasant farmer called Antti Tiirikainen killed Antti Raatikainen, another peasant farmer, in Kuopio after he surprised him in bed with his wife. Tiirikainen's eyewitness testimony and those of several members of the household were not sufficient to prove the adultery of the wife and the victim. Tiirikainen, on the other hand, was incarcerated in "confessional remand" under suspicion of intentional manslaughter.[508]

Because of the difficulties in obtaining a proof, the number of convictions for conjugal homicide was even lower than the average. It was not this weak external control that incited the perpetrators to commit the crime, however; the real seeds of marital conflict lay elsewhere: in the fact that in the eighteenth century it was very difficult to get even a disputatious marriage dissolved. Traditionally, there had to be really good reasons for divorce among the peasant population, and getting a divorce in eighteenth-century Sweden was in practice a process that was both difficult and brought shame on the partners involved.[509] The fractious couple might also be pressurized into living under the same roof against their will by the local priest.[510] Instead of divorce, spouses, especially wives who suffered from physical abuse, sometimes fled to Russia.[511]

---

506 VMA: VHOA, Alistettujen asiain päätöstaltiot, Savon ja Karjalan lääni, v. 1788, Di 23, no 10, Alistettujen asiain designaatioluettelo, Savon ja Karjalan lääni, v. 1787, Di 22, no 101.
507 VMA, VHOA, Alistusaktit, Savon ja Karjalan lääni, v. 1795, Ece 32, no 20.
508 VMA, VHOA, Alistusaktit, Savon ja Karjalan lääni, v. 1808, no 8.
509 For further details see Aalto 1996, p. 33
510 KA: Karjalan tuomiokunnan tuomiokirja, Ilomantsin ja Suojärven osan sk 1750, KO a 19, 8 §; tk v. 1753, KO a 22, 44 §. The creators of Protestant doctrine had nevertheless permitted divorce in order to provide the victims of continued family violence with an opportunity of escaping from an impossible family predicament. Gillis 1996, pp. 1278, 1298.
511 Piipponen 1988, p. 25; Saloheimo 1980, p. 88.

The strategic importance of marriage for the family declined considerably in the seventeenth century with changes in the form of government of the state, but the peasant marriage model also survived in the eighteenth century mainly as a contract based on economic interests between the two families. To some extent, blood relatives tried to see to it that the wife was treated properly, but it was the duty of the married woman to conform to the prevailing norms and submit herself to the will of her husband and the domestic discipline imposed by the old master of the household – and by the old mistress![512] Thus the rough disciplining of wives was not necessarily felt to be reprehensible. Beatings rarely led to legal proceedings unless the victim was in immediate danger of her life. However, the fact that the relatives of a dead wife might occasionally summons the husband to appear before the court at the inquest, for example, is an indication that the family did try to look after the wife's interests. It may also have had something to do with inheritance.

The strict regulation of marriage and monogamous sex in pre-industrial Europe is considered to be a significant factor in conjugal homicide. Extensive statistical surveys have shown that the level of divorce correlates negatively with that of homicides of spouses. This observation has led scholars who study the history of the family to conclude that divorce is related to the efficacy of the state's monopoly of violence, its arbitrational and punitive power, for the risk of a domestic relationship breaking up violently grows if public authority cannot guarantee the safety of a quarrelling spouse or offer a judicial process whereby potentially dangerous family conflicts can be settled by legal means. The opportunity for divorce increases the security of women with chronically violent husbands and thus prevents conjugal homicide. The highest negative correlation obtains between the levels of divorce and premeditated conjugal homicide. Divorce became common in Europe in the late nineteenth century, and only then did the legal protection of battered wives improve in practice, because divorce afforded them an escape from living in constant danger of their lives from their violent husbands.[513] The lax grip of official control over marital violence is also to some extent part of an eternal phenomenon that transcends culture and is independent of divorce; that at least seems to be the conclusion that some modern battered wives come to when they react to the constant violence to which they are subjected by killing their tormentors.[514] However, the possibility of divorce alone does not prevent such homicides; they can only be obviated by striving to control violence within the family.

Anna Mutatar, the wife of a farmer, killed her recently wed husband, Ossippa Piirainen, with the back of an axe on the burn-beating lands of Sokuma in the parish of Liperi on 12 July 1779. On the next day, she returned home without her husband and told enquirers that Ossippa had left the burn-beating area without her knowing.

---

512 Cf. e.g. Aalto 1996, pp. 32, 36.; Sirén 1999, pp. 111-114, 130-133, 141; Waris 1999, pp. 102–103; also e.g. Cockburn 1991, pp. 93–94.
513 Gillis 1996, pp. 1291–1300.
514 Kivivuori 1999, pp. 71–72.

The parish priest rounded up the congregation to search for the missing man. Piirainen's body was found in Lake Viinijärvi with his head smashed in. Anna was imprisoned and indicted for conjugal homicide. At the autumn district court sessions, the widow tried to place the guilt on another inhabitant of the village, Feodor Bajarinen, who had killed his brother and fled to Russia, and whom she claimed had had a fight on the burn-beating land with Piirainen.

Urged by the clergy, Mutatar withdrew her accusation during the trial itself and confessed to taking her husband's life. As a reason she gave his constant roughness and violence. She said that when he had started to beat her yet again, she had finally lost her temper and hit him hard on the head with the back of an axe. When he was unconscious, she struck him with the axe two more times. After making sure that he was dead, she stripped the body and dragged it to Lake Viinijärvi. On the basis of the confession, the Liperi District Court found her guilty of the manslaughter of her husband and sentenced her to have her right hand cut off, to be beheaded and her body to be burnt at the stake in accordance with MB XIV:1. The sentence was confirmed in the superior court.[515]

The prototypical method of murdering a spouse has tended to be poisoning, which aroused strong moral panic in Victorian England, and indeed elsewhere in western Europe at that time. This type of crime was branded a female and insidious way of getting rid of an unwanted husband. It was felt to be a considerable social threat that endangered the whole institution of marriage.[516] We can bypass here the socio-cultural background factors that aroused this kind of fear. However, there were a number of poisoning cases in eastern Finland in the eighteenth century, and it was in conjugal murders that this method was most strongly suspected of being employed. There is no correlation between indictments for poisoning a spouse and the sex of the accused.

A dependent lodger called Iisakki Sorsa of Tohmajärvi, who was suspected of the infanticide of a child that his female servant had had by him, was charged with poisoning Maria Korvonen in 1759. The same charge was made against Maria Mononen, the wife of a farmer from Kitee, in1762. She was also accused of committing adultery with a farm hand. Maria Kuokatar, a dependent lodger from Pielisjärvi, together with her peasant farmer lover, was also charged with poisoning her husband. Gabriel Silfver, a saddle maker from Kuopio was likewise indicted for poisoning his wife in 1794. Poison cases sometimes involved traditional suspicions of witchcraft.[517]

None of the charges of poisoning or accusations of witchcraft could be legally proved. In court it might be shown that the suspected poisoners had procured substances like arsenic, or mercury, or the deadly "Åland salt"

515 VMA: VHOA, Alistettujen asiain päätöstaltiot, Savon ja Karjalan lääni, v. 1780, Di 15, no 7; RA: Rådsprotokoll i justitieärenden, den 18. nov 1779.

516 Robb 1997, p. 178 ff.

517 MMA: KymLKa, Saapuneet kirjeet, Hovioikeus maaherralle, v. 1759, D 21 a1, no 45; v. 1763, D 25 a1, no 80.5. VMA: VHOA, Alistettujen asiain designaatioluettelot ja päätöstaltiot, Kymenkartanon ja Savon / Savon ja Karjalan lääni, v. 1763, Di 4, no 28; v. 1794, Di 29, no 107; v. 1796, Di 31, no 53; v. 1774, Di 10, no 4; v. 1775, Di 10, no 13; v. 1791, Di 26, no 7.

from Sortavala market, for example, and that the victims had reacted to these poisons in the expected way. However, such circumstantial evidence even when backed up by the motive of a notoriously disharmonious marriage was not sufficient to provide a full proof even in the lower court. This was a consequence of the crucial role of the determination of cause of death in establishing the essential elements of the crime. The technical indications for diagnosing death by poisoning may have already existed,[518] but the possibility of conviction foundered on two points: first, the poison could have entered the dead person's system in a wide variety of ways that had nothing to do with the accused; second, the autopsy report generally included a proviso that it was not possible to show with absolute certainty that poisoning was the only cause of death. The difficulties the courts had in assembling sufficient evidence for a proof are all the more surprising when one takes into account the fact that the charges of poisoning that were tried in the Göta Court of Appeal in the seventeenth century were invariably confessed to. And in those days as many as half the homicide cases tried involved poison charges. The defendants pleaded guilty in these cases because they knew that the cause of death could be determined and the charge made to stick.[519] It remains an open question whether the difficulties in obtaining a proof increased the amount of unrevealed crime in the eighteenth century. And it is equally impossible to speculate whether the invariable acquittals of poisoning charges encouraged the expansion of this type of crime.

On the other hand, the conflicts behind the spontaneous manslaughter of a husband or wife were very mundane; any everyday chore like cooking a meal or tilling the land could lead to a fight. In some marriages, blind domestic violence could be triggered by some completely random incident. Nor could the assailant him- or herself always offer any rational explanation for what had happened. Nevertheless, spouses and other family members lost their lives despite the fact that both the victim and the community were often warned of the danger by the murdrous threats of the husband or wife. The protection offered by the law against domestic violence was extremely limited. A battered wife, daughter or mother might seek refuge with a neighbour, but a man did not run away from home in such circumstances; this was obviously contrary to the masculine sense of honour.[520] Women were guilty of violence more rarely than men, but female violence was not unknown

> In Rantasalmi, a local crofter brought the body of his brother-in-law, Matti Ikäheimonen likewise a crofter, to the church for burial at the end of September 1773. He said that he had accidentally drowned on 26 September. After the funeral, the neighbours told the sheriff about their suspicions that Ikäheimonen had died violently. The body was exhumed, and Barber-Surgeon Geisse performed an autopsy. In his report he stated that there were several lethal wounds to the head, neck and body of the deceased.

518 Calonius, Föreläsningar i processus criminalis, pp. 44–45. Cf. also Spierenburg 1996, pp. 93—94.
519 Thunander 1993, p. 131–132.
520 On the improbability of prosecution in such cases, see also Sharpe 1981, p. 32.

The family of the dead man had tried to cover up the circumstances of Ikäheimo's death in order to protect the killer, the victim's own wife, Kristiina Natutar. The widow was charged with the manslaughter of her husband and attempting to dispose of the body by submersion in water. When the hushed-up crime came to light, Kristiina Natutar admitted to the court that she had violently assaulted her husband on the day of his death. The fatal conflict between the couple had started when the husband had asked for food after a hard day's work and the wife had refused to make it. In her fury she threw him to the ground, beating him with a stick and lashing him with a leather belt. When he got to his feet, she jabbed him in the mouth with a stick, drawing blood. When she then threw him out of the cottage, he fell and injured his neck on a mash trough.

Natutar said that Ikäheimonen had fled from the cottage to the lake, staggering and crawling from weakness. She had followed him and dragged him by his clothes into the freezing water, although all he could do any more to defend himself was wheeze. She gave her almost unconscious husband several lashes of a whip on his bare back, and leaving him at his last gasp, went back home. Ikäheimonen was found dead the following day in two ells of water.

The priest's character certificate described Natutar as "hot-tempered and petulant" and claimed that she alone was to blame for the failure of her marriage with Ikäheimonen, who was known to be a "pious and gentle" man. Natutar was sentenced in the district court in accordance with MB XXXIX: 2 to be executed for homicidal assault on her husband. The court also found that she had battered her husband on several previous occasions and cursed him without due cause. She was also accused of the constant slandering of her mother-in-law. This charge was proved, but no separate sanction could be imposed for the crime in addition to the capital sentence. The further charges of strangling her husband and intentionally concealing his corpse that were brought against Kritsiina Natutar in the district court were overthrown for lack of evidence. Had they been proven, the crime would have fulfilled the conditions for murder. Natutar's brother, with whom she shared the croft, was fined for intentionally concealing a crime. He had not revealed the assault on Ikäheimonen in court, and he had lied to the clergy about the circumstances of the victim's death and demanded that the body be buried before it was examined.

The Åbo Court Of Appeal commuted Kristiina Natutar's death sentence on the grounds of "circumstances" to a full wergild (a blood money fine) in accordance with MB XXVII:2 and XXXIX:2. The former chapter of the law concerned unintentional manslaughter and the second section of the latter stipulated the punishment for violent manslaughter in which the victim did not die immediately from the violence. The court of appeal's reprieve was thus based on the criminal law code. There could have been no other justification for mitigation than the cause of death: it was not possible to show that the wounds received by Ikäheimonen were absolutely lethal, and the accused had denied strangling her victim.[521] In this case, the reversed burden of proof based on an incomplete confession was not imposed in order to allow a capital sentence to be passed. Apparently this was because the cause of death was not absolutely certain.

521 MMA: KymLKa, Saapuneet kirjeet, Hovioikeus maaherralle, v. 1774, D 36 a1/1, no 16.1; VMA: VHOA, Alistettujen asiain designaatioluettelot ja päätöstaltiot, Kymenkartanon ja Savon lääni, v. 1774, Di 10, no 40; ibid. Alistusaktit, Kymenkartanon ja Savon lääni, v. 1774, Ece 3, no 40.

Conjugal homicide took place mainly among the Lutheran community. Despite the high incidence of other kinds of homicide among the Orthodox, only two or three of those suspected of murdering their spouses were of that faith. The increased proclivity of Karelian Lutheran women for premeditated murder suggests that their position within the family changed during the eighteenth century. Heikkinen, among others, has concluded that female violence increased as women's freedom of action became greater.[522] Their increased propensity for murder may also reflect the growing control of the clergy over the family life of their parishioners. As a consequence of this, people were prevented with increasing zeal from seeking ways of settling disputes amicably, for example by separating. The development may have been caused by classic frustration, stimulated by the demographic ferment, for when the number of children in the family grew, the daughter's chances of coming into an inheritance correspondingly weakened. In the eastern Finnish system of inheritance, daughters had no familial right to inherit real estate.[523] It may also have been a consequence of an increase in the regulation of family life, or possibly also an unintended side-effect of the contemporaneous relaxation in sexual discipline, which changed the nature of the control of adultery and infanticide.[524]

Getting married was difficult in the most sparsely populated areas of eastern Finland because the forbidden degrees of consanguinity were strictly defined by the law. In the end, the rapid growth in the population of the outlying regions that began in the late eighteenth century made it easier to find a spouse, but the loss of social status that was happening at the same time weakened the economic possibilities for getting married.[525] Apart from one, the motives of all the women who hired murderers are connected either directly or indirectly with their conjugal relations. We can claim, for example, that a woman who eliminated a rival for the favours of her man was indirectly motivated in this way.

A farm maid from Kuopio called Elina Räsätär murdered her former betrothed with an axe in 1790 because he had first slept with her after promising to marry her, but then reneged on his pledge and married her niece. She killed him when he was sleeping.[526] Anna Jack, a farm maid from Mikkeli, gave exactly the same reason for a double murder she committed in 1763.[527]

One explanation for the high incidence of murders committed by women that is linked to the system of justice is the fact that the judicial testimonial practice became common knowledge. This was the case first of all in places where there had previously been numerous acquittals or adjourn-

---

522 Heikkinen 1988, p. 123.

523 Sirén 1999, p. 78; Voionmaa 1915, p. 371; Heikkinen 1997, p. 156.

524 Cf. Anners 1965, p. 320.

525 Rautelin 1997, p. 191; Wirilander 1946, pp. 32–44.

526 VMA: VHOA, Alistusaktit, Savon ja Karjalan lääni, v. 1791, Ece 17, no 8.

527 MMA: KymLKa, Saapuneet kirjeet, v. 1764, Hovioikeus maaherralle, D 26 a 1, no 29.

ments *sine die*. The number of murders committed by men increased at the same time. In this connection, too, it must be reiterated that the laxity of repression encouraged crimes motivated by personal advantage more than those with other motives.[528] The coincidence of exploitation of the loopholes in the testimonial system and the hiring of assassins by women also corroborates well-known findings which show that the forms of aggression most characteristic of women are indirect. The form that the aggression takes is determined by culturally defined sexual roles.[529] With no external threat of punishment, women's built-up pressures erupted in killing – until, that is, they became generally aware of a new "surrogate punishment": confessional remand.

One hypothesis offering an explanation for the violent proclivities of some Karelian women may be found in the pronounced importance attached to physical strength and the possible instrumental attitude to children as a source of labour in the regions where burn-beating cultivation was practised. The birth rate rose, and the number of children in the family grew considerably from the 1750s on; thus the number of male children, who were necessary in order to ensure the survival of the household, increased.[530] In consequence, it may be that girls were ill treated,[531] and that the needs of children generally were neglected.[532] This in turn may have hardened many a woman by the time she grew up and left her with an undeveloped capacity for empathy.[533] Such circumstances in childhood and adolescence explain the development of the so-called "classical criminal personality". In recent times, it is believed that adults grow up whose morality, tolerance of frustration and control of their own actions are weak as a consequence of such environmental factors.[534] Also well known are the views of historians who claim that the insecurity and unpredictability of living conditions prevent the creation of the affect control that inhibits aggressive impulses.[535] A child who has been emotionally rejected and physically chastised cannot learn to trust the people around him or her.[536] The socialising process has a crucial effect on the kind of values and norms that a person regards as socially acceptable and

---

528 Cf. Black 1984a, pp. 8–14.
529 Lagerspetz 1998, pp. 275–277; also e.g. Berkowitz 1962, p. 299.
530 Saloheimo 1980, pp. 63–67; Wirilander 1989, pp. 50–55; on the position of children in landless and landed families, and generally, see Waris 1999, pp. 65–66, 117–121.
531 Cf. also Jutikkala 1988, p. 104; Sirén 1999, p. 134. A scrutiny of the information in the population tables about infanticide in eastern Finland shows that considerably more illegitimate girls were murdered than were boys. Cf. also Lane 1997, p. 22 for an estimate of the number of murders of girl children.
532 Cf. e.g. Berkowitz 1962, p. 303.
533 Cf. e.g. Keltikangas-Järvinen 1978, pp. 33–34.
534 E.g. Berkowitz 1962, pp. 303–306.
535 Elias 1994, pp. 449–451.
536 Berkowitz 1962, p. 312. For example, Jussi Pajuoja has discerned similar features in the childhood of a murderer called Matti Haapoja. Pajuoja 1986, pp. 308-312.

on the way they are internalized.[537] The harsh domestic discipline that was emphasized in the upbringing of children during the first centuries of the early modern age may have had the side effect of socialising children into a culture of violence and fear of external punishment alone without any internalising of self-control. Then social control could only be maintained by means of harsh external sanctions. In such circumstances, alterations in the effectiveness of the external deterrent – for example, the sanctions of criminal justice – significantly affect crime.[538] The forms taken by homicide in eastern Finland confirm this theory, which in the historical sense was to a great extent elaborated by Elias.

This cross between the civilization model and the mentality-historical model is open to certain objections. Women did not begin to commit homicides in the way envisaged by the model in northern Savo, where the circumstances in which they grew up in many respects resembled those in northern Karelia. An assessment of the extent to which general local features of marriage, the weak position of women and particularly daughters-in-law in the family or the intensive tutelage of the people undertaken by the clergy encouraged or discouraged aggression in women would require a separate study of its own.[539] It is significant that military occupation constituted a more permanent threat to the Karelian region, which lay on the border. Thus in Rantasalmi, which lay close to the frontier, but which was otherwise spared the vicious circle of homicide that characterized the frontier region, there were two cases of women violently killing their husbands. The married Karelian women who became perpetrators of violence from the 1770s on had not even been born in the years of the Lesser Wrath, but the latent, insidiously aggressive survival strategies of the women of the area may nevertheless have evolved from their insecurity at living under occupying forces from one generation to another. In court, Lutheran wives in northern Karelia often showed energy and enterprise, even though these were directed towards morally dubious ends.

In Pielisjärvi, one Anna Brita Toliander had her husband, Anders Lackman, an overseer, murdered on an October night of 1789. Anna had engaged Antti Piirainen, a peasant farmer from the village of Pankajärvi, to carry out the murder. Toliander's survival strategy, a conscious plan of action, was to exploit to the utmost any possible advantage offered by the judicial system in order to delay the course of justice. She misled the enquiry, bribed witnesses, made cooked-up allegations, appealed against every sentence she received and repeatedly petitioned for clemency. Indeed, the only thing lacking from the range of her stratagems was escape from prison.

---

537 Ferrer 2001, p. 147 ff; Giddens 1993, pp. 89–114.
538 Ferrer 2001, pp. 147–157, 164; Elias 1994, pp. 451–452.
539 Sirén 1999, pp. 133–134; Waris 1999, pp. 101–102, 108–109, 187; Pylkkänen 1990, p. 213.

The son of the couple testified against his mother in the Pielisjärvi Lower Court, stating the she had been threatening to kill her husband for a long time. To this end, she had all summer long been giving food to Antti Piirainen, whom she then hired to commit the murder. He had recently settled in the vicinity of the farm run by Lackman. On the day of the killing, the son said that he had been bidden to convey an order from his mother to Piirainen to turn up at the hayrick of the farm in the evening and to hide himself in the hay. The boy had seen the assassin in possession of one of the murder weapons, a birch pole. The son's story was corroborated by a later confession made by Piirainen. During the enquiry, Piirainen admitted that Toliander had given him salt, foodstuffs and other goods throughout the summer in order to persuade him to murder Lackman. When the neighbours expressed their wonder at this upkeep, Toliander had claimed that it was in return for Piirainen forging pick-locks for her husband's chests. The explanation was false because Piirainen had no skills as a blacksmith.

The circumstances preceding the murder were highly incriminating for Toliander. Shortly before the deed was carried out, the farm maid had heard her discussing the preparations for the murder with Piirainen. And on the day before she had seen her urging Piirainen to carry out the killing. On the evening of the murder, the inhabitants of the farm testified that Toliander had trembled as if she had the ague. Unusually, she had hustled the servants off to bed at seven o'clock, claiming that it was nearly eleven. In the night, the servants heard her get dressed, leave the house and stay out for so long that they fell asleep again.

When it was discovered in the morning that the overseer was missing, Toliander tried to prevent any search in the vicinity of the hayrick and the river bank, claiming that these areas had already been combed. The witnesses knew that she was lying. When the search was extended to the hayrick, she tried to hide the birch pole which had been used as one of the murder weapons. And she tossed up the hay with particular care in a place where blood was later found. When blood was also found in a ditch by a field, she claimed that it was from her menstruation, and to back up her claim she secretly smeared her clothes with lingonberry juice. On the basis of the testimonies of sworn witnesses, Toliander's defence was deemed to be invalid.

Toliander tried to lead the searchers astray at every stage of the investigation. Lackman's body was soon found in a nearby river. Toliander prevented one witness from comparing the hay found in the folds of the clothes on the corpse with the bloody silage in the hayrick. The woollen bonnet of the deceased, which he was known to have been wearing on the day of his death, had already been found covered in blood in a chest in the farmhouse.

Antti Piirainen, who was suspected of having been hired to carry out the murder, had once previously been acquitted of a homicide: he had been suspected of killing and robbing one Matti Määttänen, the son of a farmer, on Midsummer night of the previous year, and also of committing burglary in the autumn of that year. Määttänen's body was never found, but there was every reason to suspect that he had died a violent death. He had disappeared completely without trace after spending Midsummer's Day with Piirainen, who was then found to be in possession of property belonging to him, property which he had tried to hide. The acquittals of charges of murder and robbery encouraged Piirainen to undertake ever more premeditated crimes.

There was also a lot of circumstantial evidence that pointed to Toliander's guilt, above all previous attempts on the overseer's life, as well as her motive, which was well known in the community: her publicly declared desire to lay her hands on his property. However, her lethal intentions did not reach the cognisance of the district court before she had succeeded in achieving her long-standing ambition to have her husband murdered. She was known to have nurtured an inveterate and irreconcilable hatred for him, and she had frequently cursed and threatened to kill him in public. As she sharpened knives and axes, she ruthlessly said she was doing so because she intended to do away with her husband. It was also shown that she had previously tried to take his life. The victim's brother, who was a priest, had on that occasion succeeded in saving Lackman's life. When the attempted murder failed, Toliander was so angry she bit her husband's finger.

The witnesses stated that the wife had also tried to kill her husband by witchcraft.[540] When she saw that sorcery was not effective as a murder weapon, she had tried to obtain poison from a Russian merchant. It was also known that she had tried to enlist the services of a mounted border guard and the son of another person living in the locality in disposing of Lackman.

Because Toliander persisted in denying the charges, the enquiry was thorough-going. The birch pole that was used as one of the murder weapons was found to have been cut from a place where Antti Piirainen had been just before the murder. The space where the tree had been cut was covered with moss and twigs. Paper in which the bribe of silver *dalers* was wrapped was found on the road leading from Lackman's home to Piirainen's cottage. A skin of liquor which had been left by Toliander to give the murderer Dutch courage had also fallen there. In Toliander's sauna more coins were found hidden in a bark basket. Piirainen admitted that he had thrown the coins on the path when he had run away. The scattering of the money might have been connected with some folk superstition. The investigation also revealed a bloody axe belonging to the dead man in Piirainen's possession.

When Antti Piirainen was arrested, he confessed to the brother of the victim, Chaplain Johan Lackman, that he had murdered the overseer. He also said that he had acted alone, but he denounced Anna Toliander as the person who had engaged him to do it. Piirainen had also told a witness that he had had a part in the murder but that the first blow had been struck by someone else.

Anna Toliander resolutely held up the enquiry from one district court session to the next.[541] In contravention of the correct legal order of procedure, she contrived to make depositions alleging that five of the witnesses had taken part in the murder. She also accused the other inhabitants of the farmhouse of theft on the night of the murder and brought a bribery action against the witnesses, which was held to be groundless. On the contrary, she herself was found guilty of bribing her own witnesses.

On the grounds of all the above mentioned evidence, the lower court found the guilt of both Anna Toliander and Antti Piirainen fully proven. Piirainen was incriminated by persuasive circumstantial evidence and the confession he had made to the priest. Against Toliander there was only powerful circumstantial

---

540 Witchcraft and sorcery were occasionally suspected as the cause of death by the courts. For example, Olli Karvinen of Liperi was caught removing a body from a grave and cutting it up in order to practise sorcery in 1797. The enquiry into this case also revealed that he was suspected of causing the death of a farmer's daughter called Anna Turutar some years previously. The charges were dropped as Karvinen died while the enquiry was still pending. VMA: VHOA, Alistettujen asiain päätöstaltiot, Savon ja Karjalan lääni, v. 1797, Di 32, no 74.

541 RA: (HDP) Rådsprotokoll den 19 mars 1792, no 4.

evidence and the vague insinuations made by Piirainen. On the basis of MB XII:1, XIV:1, XXIV:2-3 and LXV, the pair were sentenced by the Pielisjärvi District Court to have their right hands cut off and to be beheaded, and for Piirainen's body to be broken on the wheel and Toliander's to be burnt at the stake. The sentence was contrary to procedural law, but based on incontrovertible circumstantial evidence; any other conviction would have offended the sense of justice of the public in the district court and could have jeopardized the undisturbed proceedings of the court. Before the court of appeal could pass sentence, the clergy had to try and persuade Toliander and Piirainen in Kuopio Crown Prison to confess to the crimes that they were charged with. Piirainen died in prison while the case was still pending in the court of appeal.

Even in the last district court sessions, Toliander made two more allegations of serious crimes. She accused Jakob Stenius, the minister of Pielisjärvi, of treason during the war of Gustav III, and the sheriff of the parish, Crohn, of insulting the name of His Majesty and particularly his recently issued Constitution. An extraordinary district court session was arranged in Pielisjärvi in order to ascertain the truth of the allegations. It was later shown that this was in contravention of the legal order of procedure; in 1778 His Majesty had specifically ordered that only the King himself should try and prosecute offences against the royal person. The charge against Crohn was proven. He had disparaged the text of the Constitution when two men who had been ordered for military service had read a section out of it to him. Appealing to this section, the men had claimed that their arrest was in contravention of their civil rights. Gustav III later pardoned the sheriff on the grounds that his offence was slight.[542]

The charge brought by Toliander against Jakob Stenius was a much more serious one. She claimed that the minister had negotiated with the enemy during the War of Gustav III, entered into correspondence with the Russians that was harmful to the state and given information to them about the roads and the positions of various localities. She also said that the minister had encouraged his parishioners to disobey the lawful authorities and incited them to surrender to Russia. Toliander's denunciations were certainly inspired, if not directly by the Anjala Covenant, at least by the numerous trials for treason and espionage and for seditious activities to further Finnish independence that were held in Savo and Karelia as soon as the peace treaty came into force.[543] The clergy in northern Karelia had a tradition of stirring up the people to rebel against the rule of Sweden in time of war.[544] However, the information against Stenius was patently false.[545] Despite the fabricated eyewitness evidence Toliander presented, the court of appeal found the allegations made against the minister groundless and acquitted him. He was found to have been a loyal and obedient subject at all times.

Toliander's part in the murder of Lackman was referred by the court of appeal to the Supreme Court, which found that she could not be implicated in the murder without a confession and eyewitnesses. Nevertheless, the court held that her guilt was "in practice proven", and that only the confession

---

542 RA: (HDP) Rådsprotokoll den 30 nov 1792, no 9.

543 E.g. RA: (HDP) Rådsprotokoll i justitieärenden år 1790, 11.1. 1790; 13.4.1790; 19.4.1790; 5.7.1790; ibid, år 1791, 29.3. 1791. See also Soininen 1954, pp. 294–295.

544 Katajala 1994, p. 396.

545 On the anti-state attitudes of the clergy of the parish of Pielisjärvi during the War of Gustav III see e.g. Saloheimo 1980, p. 490.

of the accused was lacking for a full proof. The royal court committed the widow to confessional remand "for a suitable period" (*på behagelig tid*) on the grounds that her discharge would cause public disapproval in the locality of the crime. The court also justified the continued incarceration of Toliander by the fact that her character displayed "an exceptional malice and a murderous disposition" (*sällsynta ondska och mordiska sinnelag*). In addition, this woman, who had commissioned a murder, was sentenced for her defamatory and humiliating charge against Minister Stenius to thirty strokes with a pair of birches, infamy and a public apology.

Toliander appealed against the sentences she had received, petitioning for the confessional remand and birching to be commuted. Her attempts were in vain. Even after the Supreme Court had published its judgment in 1792, Toliander appealed to have the murder case reopened. She claimed that she had found "new evidence" and tried to delate several participants in the crime who had not previously been interrogated. This petition did not succeed either. Two years later she again petitioned for pardon from the confessional remand, and this move too proved fruitless. The judges of the Supreme Court considered that the nature of the case did not justify the release of Toliander, whom they described as hard-boiled. Nor was the court able to find any extenuating circumstances for her denunciation of the local minister. When Toliander learned that, in order to save the state further expenditure, the corporal punishment was to be administered in Stockholm, she had a petition drawn up to have the birching commuted to imprisonment on bread and water. The Supreme Court was reluctant to accede to this because of the ruthlessness of the crime and other aggravating circumstances, but when two doctors testified that birching would put her life in danger, the punishment was mitigated to a full prison sentence of 28 days duration on bread and water.[546] Toliander was not allowed to travel to her home parish to present her public apology to Stenius in person; she had to do so in Stockholm to a representative delegated by the priest.

Piirainen had already become personally acquainted with the inefficiency of the legislature from a previous case. Anna Toliander would not have resorted to hiring a murderer if she had not calculated that she would escape punishment for the crime she had commissioned; indeed she had openly bragged of her plans in public beforehand. Before Toliander, killers in northern Karelia had been committed to a "suitable" period of confessional remand very rarely – only once during the period dealt with in this study.[547] This form of sanction probably came to Toliander as a surprise.

546 RA: HDP den 12 jan 1795, fol 32 ff; den 13 juli 1795.
547 Before Anna Toliander, only Olli Harinen of Tohmajärvi had been committed to a long stretch of confessional remand for patricide in 1783. Inkeri Laakkonen of Kitee, who had her father murdered, was not committed to confessional remand until a number of years after Toliander's crime. Just like Antti Piirainen, Inkeri Laakkonen also had one unsentenced homicide, in her case an unprosecuted infanticide, on her conscience before this case of patricide. In the adjacent parish of Ilomantsi, Mikitta Jäkinen's case on a charge of murdering his brother-in-law had just (in 1778) been adjourned *sine die*. It was not until 1801 that sufficient evidence was assembled against Jäkinen to have him committed to confessional remand. These cases have been described above.

Infanticide[548] as an Instrument in Conjugal Disputes

Disputes between couples sometimes ended in the death of the fruit of the union, their common child. In Iisalmi, a farmer paid to have his six-month-old baby daughter killed in order to avenge himself on his wife.

> Hannu Leivo, a farmer who was known to be given to the excessive consumption of strong liquor, stabbed his six-month-old daughter, Benedicta, to death in the middle of the night. A farm hand had heard Leivo say before stabbing the girl in the neck with his knife: "Now, Margaretha Luckarinen [= Marketta Lukkarinen, his wife], will give me some liquor." When the mother awoke to the cries of her child, he hurled the baby into a hollow in the earth floor in front of the stove. The mother fainted from the shock of seeing her daughter wounded in the neck. She did not recover consciousness until the following morning, by which time the child had died. It may be that Leivo murdered his child in a fit of drunken delirium.
>
> Leivo gave himself up voluntarily and was taken to the district court, where in the presence of his incessantly weeping wife he admitted stabbing his baby. He said he had meant to murder his wife first but had then decided to slay his own baby Benedicta. In justification of his act, he said that children did not need absolution or repentance of their sins in order to go to heaven, unlike his wife Marketta, who was "a greater sinner".[549] He thus proclaimed his own conception of the atonement for sin, which corresponded with the doctrine of the church. Beneath the religious arguments there lay not only the enmity he felt for his wife but also a sentiment of mercy (which he perhaps used as a pretext) and the affection of a father for his child. Leivo stated in court that he had loved the slain child. He admitted that he repented of his deed and said that he wished "to atone for his blood guilt and to willingly follow his daughter into the next world". This indicates that in his own way Leivo was aware of the significance attached to the ritual of execution as an act of atonement between the condemned man and God.[550] In the courts of all instances, Leivo was sentenced to have his right hand cut off, to be beheaded and to have his body broken on the wheel.[551] Leivo was the only one of the parents in the area investigated here who was executed for killing his child.

In Kuopio a baby girl of the same age became an instrument of the strange hatred her mother felt for her husband; this grew so strong that it exceeded the love that the mother felt for her child; in July 1767, one Maria Tuhkutar, the wife of a dependent lodger from Kuopio, threw her baby daughter around so roughly that she died. The motive that was recorded in court was a desire to hurt her husband. This case illustrates just how high was the threshold of family privacy that had to be surmounted before

---

548 The term here is here limited to the killing of legitimate children within the family; it does not include the murder of illegitimate babies, for example.

549 Cf. also Jansson 1998, p. 53.

550 Cf. Liliequist 1992, p. 92 ff; Thunander 1993, pp. 72–73

551 VMA: VHOA, Alistusaktit, Savon ja Karjalan lääni, v. 1807, Ece, no 93; Alistettujen asiain designaatioluettelot ja päätöstaltiot, Savon ja Karjalan lääni v. 1807, Di, no 93.

familial violence became a matter for the law to deal with.[552] Similarly, the details of the fractious marriage of Maria Tuhkutar and Elias Skopa also demonstrate how great the danger was that infanticide could remain outside the cognisance of the courts altogether.

It was not until Maria herself brought an action against her husband, Elias Skopa, at the autumn district court sessions in 1767 for repeated drunkenness, assault and striking his own mother that he in return reported his wife for repeated acts of violence. He also accused her of general maliciousness and recklessness (*argt och överdådigt sinne*). The most serious accusation made against his wife concerned their six-month-old daughter. According to Skopa, on 11 July Tuhkutar had deliberately thrown her baby to the ground with such force that she was now moribund. The allegation was so grave that Tuhkutar was immediately arrested and the case was adjourned for a year and a day in accordance with MB XXXIX:2 and XXIV:1 to await the fate of the child. The baby died at the end of January.

In an extraordinary district court session in the winter the mother was sentenced to death for killing her child in accordance with MB XIV:1. In the lower court, the testimonies of several witnesses and the general circumstances were considered sufficient to convict her. There were no eyewitnesses apart from the disqualified husband.

The load of evidence against Tuhkutar's character was a heavy one. She was notorious for her "irascible and spiteful" nature. At this point, the lower court considered it apposite to record that she was, nevertheless, of sound mind. The records of the enquiry do not show the grounds for the statement of her full responsibility. Among other things, she had falsely claimed in the village that her husband committed incest with his own sister and had slept with other women. It was also shown that on numerous occasions she had beaten her husband, a man known for his mild disposition, black and blue and had drawn blood. During the previous summer she had left her husband's household and roamed around the parish with one of her children for eight weeks.

When Tuhkutar was overcome by rage, her urge to destroy was powerful. She had once chopped up both her own and her husband's clothes with an axe and thrown them together with the axe, some cowbells, a shoe last and other household goods into the river. She had also torn up a brocaded bonnet and intentionally smashed the family's butter churn, several milk tubs and a pot and thrown them in the lake. On another occasion she had buried her husband's plough share in a swamp and broken all the stalks of the flax crop. At the same time, she had amused herself by throwing stones at the cattle in the woods and driven her own cattle out of her croft without milking them.

In a fit of temper and "for the sole purpose of hurting her husband", Tuhkutar had also thrown sticks and stones at him and other people, poured the farm's milk onto the ground, slaughtered the sheep for the birds to eat, given several pecks of grain to the pigs and torn down the bark roofs of her husband's croft and the outbuildings. At the same time she had broken up part of the stove of the cottage and burnt the doors of the buildings. According to the statements of witnesses, she had also thrashed her three-year-old son black and blue with a stick in front of visitors out of pure malice for no reason.

552   On the same phenomenon in England, see Cockburn 1991, pp. 93–94.

Maria Tuhkutar put the blame for her baby daughter's parlous state on her husband, claiming that he had maltreated the child to within an inch of her life. However, she was later forced to admit that she herself had flung her child to the ground and had done so quite intentionally. Tuhkutar was found in court to be guilty both of outrageous and malicious behaviour and of the murder of her child. In both the lower court and the court of appeal the relevant section of the criminal code was MB XIV:1. The only motive for the deed was hatred of her husband, and the method was dashing the baby against the ground from above her head. The child, who before this maltreatment, had been particularly lively and vigorous, afterwards suffered from pains and remained sickly until she died in January.

In his autopsy report, Barber-Surgeon Geisse stated that Tuhkutar's violence had hastened the premature death of the child. However, it was not possible to show with absolute certainty that the injuries were lethal because several months had elapsed since the maltreatment. The court of appeal found that the capital sentence passed on Tuhkutar by the district court was legally valid and just, but the royal court commuted the death sentence on the grounds of "extenuating[!] circumstances". Instead she was sentenced to maximum corporal punishment. In addition she was committed for five years to a house of correction. The real justification for commuting the sentence of Maria Tuhkutar could not have had anything do with the actual circumstances of the crime; it must have been connected with the essential elements of the voluntary manslaughter of a family member: the uncertainty about the cause of death expressed in the autopsy report.[553]

The text which describes the strife between Tuhkutar and Skopa follows a tendency characteristic of the trial records: dichotomization. On the basis of the enquiry, one party is described as innocent of disputation, "of a calm and peaceful nature", while the other is pictured as a "vindictive" quarrel monger. This feature of the records makes it difficult to discern whether there were also conjugal homicides in marriages in which both parties were fractious. To judge from the sources alone, this situation hardly ever pertained – perhaps only when a battered wife, like Anna Mutatar of Liperi, killed her husband. This, however, is probably not the whole truth of the matter.

In northern Karelia in each of the two periods, 1748–1777 and 1778–1807, only three cases of the infanticide of legitimate children were prosecuted.[554] In the earlier period, there were also three such cases in northern Savo, and in the latter period one.[555] Even when the threshold preventing the prosecution of lethal violence against one's own children was surmounted, the upper courts were loath to pass capital sentences. MB XXX:3 stipulated a wergild and infamy as the penalty for lethal chastisement; if the guilty party was indigent, the fine was converted to

553 VMA: VHOA, Alistettujen asiain päätöstaltiot, Kymenkartanon ja Savon lääni, v. 1769, Di 7, no 55.

554 In the second period there were four victims after Barber-Surgeon Geisse murdered his two children in 1782.

555 In this area, too, there were four infanticides in the period investigated, after a crofter called Kankkunen also murdered his two children in Rantasalmi in 1767..

corporal punishment. Moreover, in cases of intentional homicide, the category of the crime was in practice frequently lowered by one degree in the upper courts because of slight uncertainties connected with the cause of death.

Two fathers, who were later judged to be irresponsible for their actions, each killed two of their children with axes. When mothers killed their legitimate children, the cause was either the mother's mental aberration or her exhaustion with looking after her babe at night, or poor nourishment or excessively harsh physical chastisement of the child. In northern Karelia there were five such cases and in northern Savo two.

> The Ilomantsi District Court dealt with the murder of a four-week-old baby girl, which the mother, Kaarina Lepätär of Eno, was found guilty of committing with full malice aforethought. Lepätär died in prison before the final sentence was passed, but her guilt was considered proven because she had confessed to the crime. Her body was ordered to be buried on the gallows hill.[556] Again in 1791, a mother called Kristiina Sivotar, the wife of a soldier, killed her baby after she woke up to its crying one January night and lost her temper. Sivotar was reported to the court for killing her six-month-old son on the basis of a testimony by an under-age witness. The baby had been hit on the head with a spinning wheel, but it was not possible to prove the mother's guilt because she denied doing it. The cause of death was stated to be heavy blows with a blunt instrument. The case against the mother was adjourned *sine die* in the district court, and the court of appeal acquitted her completely.[557]

A child could also be wasted to death by neglecting to take proper care of it.[558] The border line between negligent abandonment and voluntary manslaughter might be a fine one.

> Eeva Hirvotar, the widow of a crofter, left her ten-year-old son, who was tired of travelling, by the wayside on a freezing February night in Heinävesi. She herself continued her journey to her croft, which was situated nearly two miles away. In the morning, the master of the croft brought the frozen boy into the cottage, but he died as soon as he got inside. The lower court considered that Hirvotar's negligence merited a half wergild (a blood money fine) for unintentional manslaughter, but, very unusually, the court of appeal raised the fine to a full wergild. The heavier punishment was justified by the "grievous negligence" shown by the mother.
>
> The increase in the severity of the punishment was influenced by various factors: Hirvotar claimed that she was too tired from the journey to go back and get her son in the evening. Despite this, several witnesses stated that when she got to the cottage she was quite fit. Nor was she in any hurry the following morning to fetch her son from the forest road. When the crofter scolded her for her indifference to the boy's death, she said it was better so because "it wouldn't be necessary feed the boy and take him around with her any more".

556 VMA: VHO Alistettujen asiain päätöstaltiot, Savon ja Karjalan lääni, v. 1777, Di 12, no 33.

557 VMA: VHOA, Alistusaktit, Savon ja Karjalan lääni, v. 1791, Ece 18, no 64; Alistettujen asiain päätöstaltiot, Savon ja Karjalan lääni, v. 1791, Di 26, no 64.

558 Jutikkala 1988, pp. 101–102.

In fact, the increase in the penalty was based above all on the character of the accused: she was described as showing a callous indifference towards her child.[559] The harassed mother viewed the matter differently: perhaps she really thought that she was delivering her son from an earthly pilgrimage that the years of crop failure had made into a wearisome one.

The position of the stepchild has traditionally been regarded as so weak that the word itself has become a symbol of neglect. It has been shown in European research that the myth of the cruel stepmother has a strong basis in reality: parents generally treat their stepchildren badly and indeed even with ruthless malice.[560] Behind this phenomenon lies the notion of kinship. Possibly jealousy of the spouse may also be involved.

On the evidence of the trials, the chastisement of stepchildren in eastern Finland only rarely got so out of hand that it resulted in homicide, but stepchildren were more likely to be victims of lethal chastisement than the children of both parents. Two women and one stepfather were given commuted sentences of one wergild for lethal assaults on their children, and one stepmother drove her under-age child out to beg and consequently to die.[561] It is also probable that some cases were hushed up. However, this was certainly not due to any excessively harsh punishments, because the penalties assigned for the unnecessarily violent chastisement of stepchildren were relatively light.

A case in Sweden in 1776 set a precedent for penalizing this type of crime. A stepmother was sentenced to three weeks on bread and water for burning a large area of the skin of her eight-year-old stepdaughter with a hot iron. She had also been reported for the manslaughter of two of her own children. The King ordered that the child be removed from her stepmother's care.[562]

The Tohmajärvi District Court sentenced Anna Burman, the wife of a dependent lodger, to death for the manslaughter of her two-year-old stepdaughter, Helena, in 1801. She had frequently been seen beating and shaking the girl, and witnesses said that she had displayed unrelenting hatred and bitterness towards her stepdaughter. The child was intermittently ill from the injuries caused by her stepmother. The father had tried to save his daughter from this inhuman treatment by taking her away to be cared for by her grandmother, and the stepmother had threatened to murder the child if he ever brought her back. However, Anna Burman may have needed the girl as a scapegoat to vent her anger on. This sort of relationship is indicated by the fact that she fetched her back herself after a few weeks and continued to beat her in the same way. Helena's feeble strength gradually gave way under the constant violence, and she died half a day after her stepmother had thrown her in into a freezing river in May.

559　VMA: VHOA, Alistettujen asiain päätöstaltiot, Kymenkartanon ja Savon lääni, v. 1767, Di 6, no 34.

560　E.g. Jutikkala 1988, p. 85.

561　Anne Tarkotar, the wife of a blacksmith, beat her husband's five-year-old son to death in Kitee in 1762 (VMA: VHOA, Alistettujen asiain päätöstaltiot, Kymenkartanon ja Savon lääni v. 1763, Di 4, no 12–13).

562　af Ugglas 1794, p. 34, Til n n hofrätt, angående hustro N N:p straff för våldsam förfarande med sin stjufdotter. Den 12 juni 1776. Flintberg 1803, p. 477.

The autopsy revealed that the child had received extremely heavy blows all over her body. The cause of death was determined to be a necrosis of her inner organs, which, however, could not be unequivocally proved to have originated from the violence perpetrated by her mother. Therefore, the court of appeal commuted the death sentence given to Burma by the lower court to a full wergild. This was in turn converted to birching.[563]

In certain individual cases, those members of the family who were subjected to domestic discipline found themselves in a kind of prison, confined to a vacuum where there was no legal protection of the inviolability of mind and body. In the eyes of the law, a wife, a daughter-in-law and the servants had to succumb to the patriarchal rule of the master. To some extent, parents were allowed to continue exercising their right to inflict physical punishment even in cases where the use of this power went beyond reason.[564] The code of behaviour of the time did not really permit outsiders to interfere even in the most merciless cases of child battering. Similarly, husbands who were victims of their wives' violence also found themselves in a humiliating domestic trap, in which they felt it demeaning to seek for outside help. The threshold of legal action was often surmounted only when a repeatedly battered spouse (of either sex) or a child died violently. Because of the high infant mortality, the opportunities for concealing the killing of one's own offspring or a stepchild were good, although the prosecuting authorities did attempt to investigate the cause of death of any child that died. The number of enquiries into unexpected child fatalities and cot deaths in the district courts far exceeded that of actual homicides. The low number of homicides of children and wives may, however, point to the fact that there was no extensive abuse of power in domestic life.

Breaking the Fourth and Fifth Commandments

Most of the familial homicides in eastern Finland were committed against members of the same generation – generally in situations where the old patriarch of the household had died or given up running the farm. The crimes that were regarded as most terrible – patricide and matricide – were few in number in the region dealt with in this study.[565] This type of crime was apparently quite foreign to the judicial culture of the whole western world in the early centuries of the modern age. Thus there were hardly

---

563 VMA: VHOA, Alistettujen asiain designaatioluettelot, Savon ja Karjalan lääni, v. 1801, no 77; Alistettujen asiain päätöstaltiot, Savon ja Karjalan lääni, v. 1802, Di 37, no 6.

564 Piipponen 1988, p. 6.

565 Norell 1800, p. 129, Till N hof-rätt angående straffet för den som dräpa eller förolämpa och oqväda faderfader, fadermoder, moderfader och modermoder och deras föräldrar, den 17 juli 1795 (precedent in 1747). On the ban on burial, see Nehrman 1756, III:III:8, p. 198 (See Just. rev. bref den 18 febr 1729.)

any infringements of the fourth and fifth commandments in such countries as England, the western regions of Sweden or western Finland.[566] During the period covered by this study, in northern Karelia there were two patricides and one killing of a father-in-law, and in Savo one matricide and one homicide of a mother-in-law.[567] These killings had little in common with each other – apart from the family relationship of the participants. The motives for the patricides are not clear apart from the previously described case of Inkeri Laakotar.

> The motive for the murder of his stepmother by Antti Karjalainen of Kerimäki was the undesired marriage of his stepsister. There was no apparent motive for the matricide committed by Reko Kosunen in Leppävirta in 1766 other than the notoriously violent bad temper of the perpetrator.[568] There were also some attempts to conceal parenticide just like other cases of familial homicide. In 1752, the body of Juho Kaskilampi, a crofter from Mikkeli, had to be exhumed when it was revealed that the deceased's own son had killed him.[569]

According to Waris, the legislature was extremely reluctant to interfere in the power relations that existed within group families. The father represented a figure of authority whose position was called in question only in exceptional cases.[570] On the other hand, the position of other members of the family, which was in some respects legally insecure, may have led to a contrary trend, for despite the fact that there were few parenticide trials in northern Savo and northern Karelia, there were a great many cases of the insult and battery of parents – in the years 1754—51 ten cases per year per 100,000 inhabitants. The amount of assaults and abuse of parents is exceptionally high there compared with the regions of southern Savo and Kymenlaakso or western Finland, or indeed Sweden.[571] Mäntylä has also drawn attention to this phenomenon.[572] The laws of the realm stipulated death as the punishment for assaulting a parent and a fine for insulting one. These harsh sanctions were directly based on Mosaic Law; in the

---

566 Sharpe 1981, p. 37.
567 In addition, a peasant from Liperi was reported for the manslaughter of his father-in-law, but the autopsy revealed no wounds in the body of the deceased. There was also a trial for one attempted murder of a father-in-law in Kitee in 1792. VMA: VHOA, Alistettujen asiain designaatioluettelot jä päätöstaltiot, Savon ja Karjalan lääni, v. 1787, no 16; Alistusaktit, Savon ja Karjalan lääni, v. 1792, Ece 33, no 37.
568 VMA: VHOA, Alistusaktit, Savon ja Karjalan lääni, v. 1797, Ece 41, no 2; Alistettujen asiain päätöstaltiot, Kymenkartanon ja Savon lääni, v. 1766, Di 6, no 30. In addition, in Kerimäki in 1755, one Kaarina Haveritar was tried for concealing the homicide of her mother, but the charge was overthrown, and she was granted to right to bring a counter charge.
569 There is also evidence of attempts to conceal this form of crime. The body of a crofter called Juho Kaskilampi, which had been buried in the normal way, was exhumed in 1752 when it was revealed that he had been killed by his own son. MMA: KymLKa, Saapuneet kirjeet, v. 1752, Hovioikeus maaherralle, D 14 a1/1, no 44/1.
570 Waris 1999, p. 51.
571 Koskivirta 1996, pp. 103, 105–108; Liliequist 1991, pp. 7, 10–13.
572 Mäntylä 2000, p. 54.

Law of the Land such crimes had not been separately distinguished. The law reform of Gustav III repealed the death penalty as a punishment for parental assault. This in fact merely confirmed previous practice: no death sentences for parental assault were implemented in the eighteenth century, and there were very few in the seventeenth century either. In cases where the death penalty was applied, the condemned persons had a long list of other serious crimes on their consciences.[573]

David Gaunt has conjectured that children began to treat their parents worse as the annuity (*sytning*) system (whereby aging parents retired from actively running the farm but were allowed to live on there and received a small income) became more common. Gaunt considers that this practice, which was used during the eighteenth and nineteenth centuries, was a consequence of the increasing and systematic withdrawal of aging couples from running the farms. In was in the economic interests of the person who inherited the farm that the old folk should live on for as short a time as possible.[574] However, the quality of the relationship that existed between parents and children was not necessarily determined by material interests alone. In eastern Finland, the annuity system could not have been a major reason for parents taking their children to court, because retirement was a rather rare phenomenon in the burn-beating cultivation regions, where in practice the father's authority continued for the duration of his life. However, in northern Karelia the annuity system did spread at the end of the eighteenth century.[575] The large number of cases of assaulting or abusing parents in Savo and Karelia may have been a side effect of conflicts that foreshadowed the future division of the estates at a time when the number of the parents' offspring had grown.[576] However, even if these disputes were violent, they did not pose a threat to the parents' actual lives; on the other hand, squabbles over a future estate often came to a head in a far more final way for other members of the family: the sons and daughters who were the potential beneficiaries.[577] At this time, many a peasant farmer's child was threatened with expulsion from his status as a member of the estate into which he had been born.

Certainly, in two cases of parenticide the motive may indeed have been to limit the number of future beneficiaries: in Inkeri Laakotar's hired murder of her father, which took place soon after he had remarried, and the killing of his stepmother by the young Antti Karjalainen of Kerimäki, which was prompted by the undesirable marriage of his stepsister.

The nuclear family was not to any great extent distinguished by intergenerational homicides; in other words, it was not characterized by either form of victimization – the killing of children by their parents was just

573 Thunander 1993, pp. 158–160; Odén 1994; Odén 1991, p. 100; Warpula 2002.
574 Gaunt 1987, p. 139; Waris 1999, pp. 111–113.
575 Saloheimo 1980, pp. 461–462.
576 Odén 1991.
577 Kristiina Kukotar, the wife of a dependent lodger, murdered her sister-in-law Katariina Moilatar in Pielisjärvi in 1807 because of disagreements about the care of their ill father-in-law. VMA: VHOA, Alistettujen asiain designaatioluettelot ja päätöstaltiot, Savon ja Karjalan lääni, v. 1808, no 4.

as random as parenticide. During the period of this research, two fathers took the lives of their children in northern Karelia, while in northern Savo no such cases were prosecuted in court. Both of the Karelian men who killed their adult sons, the above-mentioned Mikko Sivonen of Liperi and Erkki Pellikka of Nurmes, embarked upon their actions when their sons had displayed either real or imagined disrespect for them.

Erkki Pellikka, a dependent lodger living in Höljäkkä in the parish of Nurmes, murdered his sleeping son Tuomas with an axe in autumn 1800. He immediately gave himself up voluntarily. In court, he could not at first give any explanation for his deed, saying merely that he was tired of life because for a long time he had failed in whatever he had done. When he was specifically asked, he denied that he had killed his son in order to shorten his own life. He thus dispelled the judges' suspicions of a suicidal murder. However, he seemed to have a powerful need to answer for his deed in the way prescribed by criminal law, because he strongly denied being of unsound mind or suffering from a mental aberration. He could not have been executed for his crime if it was found that he had been suffering from diminished responsibility. In the interrogations, he reiterated time and time again that he was only tired with himself and tired of life. The minister of Nurmes reported that he was reputed to be reticent and introverted. In their assessment of his mental state, the District Court of Nurmes and the Vasa Court of Appeal eventually declared him responsible for his actions.

Pellikka's lonely existence was perhaps the cause of his lasting depression. His wife had left him ten years earlier, when their daughter had got married. As the enquiry continued, he admitted that he had resented his son's leaving the household and taking a job as a farm hand elsewhere. Afterwards, according to Pellikka, his son had not shown him his former obedience or helped him with his work.

All the statements by the witnesses argued against this subjective interpretation of the situation. When the son, Tuomas, had moved out the previous spring, he had taken his father to live with him in his new place of service. None of the inhabitants of the farm could say that the relations between the father and son were particularly fractious; on the contrary, they claimed that Tuomas had looked after his father as well as possible. A couple of days before the murder, it was testified that Pellikka had said that it was not possible for him to go on living as before, but he must not harm the inhabitants of the farm. When Pellikka was interrogated about the meaning of these cryptic words in court, he said that he had been referring only to himself and not to the murder of his son. It may be that Pellikka's soul was troubled by the loss of his authority, his son's successful bid for independence, which he was unable to influence. According to him, his bitterness erupted from a feeling of being abandoned and disappointment with his life. There is no denying the power of this emotion, although the testimonies of the witnesses give one to understand that his interpretation of the relationship between him and his son was mistaken. The customary law of the peasants, however, also recognized a son's need to break free of his family ties and leave his home while his father was still alive.[578] In a modern examination of Pellikka's state of mind, his reserved and taciturn behaviour together with his reported motive would lead one to suspect a mental disorder. Indeed, it did so in his own day, too, but nevertheless he was declared responsible for his actions.

---

578 Sirén 1999, p. 79.

The effectiveness of the penal certainty in controlling criminality depended crucially on the motive for the killing. In some cases, and above all in murders committed for gain, the weak level of repression quite clearly gave rise to crime. On the other hand, the scope of repression was irrelevant when the motivation was sufficiently strong, for example revenge or the defence of one's reputation. And there were some types of homicide with their own particular motivation where the mechanism in fact had the opposite effect. Thus in suicidal murders, embarking on the crime presupposed a firm conviction that the future punishment would be of the harshest kind. That was why a suicidal murderer often tried to confess his crime in such a way as to ensure that he would *certainly* be executed as a result of it and at the same time strove to disguise his real motive: his self-destructive drive. The attempts to conceal this kind of motivation made the enquiry into the crime more difficult, and it is not at all far-fetched to suggest that Erkki Pellikka may have killed his son for exactly this reason.

The motivation that distinguished suicidal murder from other types of homicide led to exactly the opposite result from that planned by the legislators in 1754 in ordaining an extremely harsh punishment for such murders: in Sweden proper they continued to increase. As a result, the death sentence, which was stipulated as a punishment for the crime began to be considered almost senseless. Moreover, it provided opponents of capital punishment with an extremely opportune ideological weapon in their campaign. It was not until the reign of Gustav III that the legislators realized that the death sentences passed on suicidal murderers merely satisfied the death wishes of the perpetrators and at the same time dissipated the general deterrent effect that this form of punishment was supposed to have. The death penalty for suicidal murder was repealed in a royal circular in 1787. Maximum corporal punishment and life-long hard labour were prescribed as the penalty for this crime.[579] This in principal removed the rationale for homicidal murder, but in practice it often only led to the real aims of the killers being concealed in court. The combination of infamy, corporal and capital punishments that had been prescribed as the penalty for suicidal murder in 1754 remained in judicial use even after it had been repealed, and it was used to penalize other extremely grave crimes up till the early years of the nineteenth century.

In order to obtain the kind of death sentence he desired, Pellikka had to deny in court any death wish he may have had, although he openly admitted that he was tired of life and disappointed with himself. He did not appeal against his death sentence. He offered public repentance before he was executed and his body was broken on the wheel.[580]

---

579 RA: Rådsprotocoll 26.1.1787. Flintberg 1803, p. 208.

580 VMA: VHOA, Alistusaktit, Savon ja Karjalan lääni, v. 1800, Ece 57, no 54; Alistettujen asiain designaatioluettelot ja päätöstaltiot, Savon ja Karjalan lääni, v. 1800, Di, no 54.

Summary

The proportion of trials of both murder and familial homicide out of all homicide trials in Savo and Karelia was exceptionally high.[581] Even in regions as close as Southern Ostrobothnia, or in the capital, Stockholm, the distributional structure of homicide was fundamentally different. Familial homicide, murders and grievous killings perpetrated by women were in some ill-fated correlation not only with one another but also with the deficient repression of crime that existed in the region. Relatives were disqualified from testifying in court against each other, and were anyway inclined to keep silent. Thus it was extremely difficult to prove such crimes.[582] The degree of premeditation in homicide in eastern Finland was intimately connected with the fact that the parties involved were usually closely related and of the same generation.

When one compares the high proportion of homicides committed within the family in eastern Finland with homicide statistics for more central European countries, one notices that the excess of familial homicides among the people of Savo and Karelia consists solely of killings of persons outside the nuclear family: brothers and brothers-in-law. The eastern Finnish propensity for getting into lethal conflicts with relations was a consequence of increased population pressures, the constraints of work and a family organization that because of the growth in the size of the population offered relatively few opportunities for its members. Because of their physical and economic proximity, the relations between brothers and brothers-in-law were closer and therefore more susceptible to friction than in western countries generally.

The dissolution of an informal and loose partnership by a division of the holding was not possible especially on land owned by the nobles (frälsejord), which meant that one of the rival partners had to leave. In other systems of land tenure, again, a division of the hearth would double the taxes due to the Crown,[583] and it was therefore avoided. If the crises within the family and the partnership could not be resolved by legal or official means in a way satisfactory to the parties concerned, the unofficial system of control in extreme cases sometimes resulted in homicide.

The Effects of Depleted Forest Resources

Squabbles about land ownership and usufruct rights were the source of homicides all over Europe in the agrarian age. Usually, however, such quarrels only had fatal consequences when they were seriously prolonged. Of course, these homicides were clearly not unconnected with their sur-

---

581 E.g. Lane 1997, p. 16.
582 Rautelin 1997, p. 196.
583 Heikkinen 1988, p. 73.

roundings. The parties involved were usually members of a village or a family community who considered that they were entitled to the same disputed ownership or usufruct.[584] Ylikangas has shown that in Southern Ostrobothnia in the eighteenth century disputes about the tenure of property culminated in homicide just before the full outbreak of a wave of violence known as the Age of the Knife Fighters. The killings usually took place in the outlying regions of the province and on the fringes of the parishes, and they were an indication that the land and forest resources were giving out.[585] These crimes brought homicide into Ostrobothnian society on a large scale, but they were not themselves the actual cause of its rapid expansion.[586] According to Ylikangas, similar factors connected with the weak legal protection of real estate also explained the lawless and violent nature of society in the sixteenth and seventeenth centuries in regions of Sweden which today constitute part of Finland.[587]

For a long time there was another problem concerning the tenure of land that beset eastern Finnish peasant farmers in the area where burn-beating cultivation was practiced. The right of tenure of the land that had been taken over for cultivation was because of its temporary nature less well protected than in areas where there was established cultivation of arable land: it was more difficult to define the usufruct accurately and to register it. The court cases in which the disputes were arbitrated proceeded with excruciating slowness. Settling the actual rights of tenure was certainly not made easier by the fact that in eastern Finland many village and parish boundaries were unclear before the Land Division Statute of 1775 and in the open-field system plots might be dispersed dozens of miles away from the farmhouses. The muddle of outlying plots got even worse as the amount of forest available for burn-beating began to run out. The division of burn-beating lands also strongly contributed to the deterioration of relations among the peasant farmers. Neighbours had often cooperated in tilling the land. This cooperation involved heavy toil, but for many it was the only way of ensuring some kind of living from the land. But it was then all too easy to begin to mistrust one's co-worker.[588]

Economic development in northern Savo and northern Karelia was for a long time held up by numerous factors that were peculiar to this region. Such factors included the high and unevenly distributed taxes, the cutting-off of inland waterway communications as a result of the redrawing of the border in the peace treaties of Nystad and Åbo, the confusion about land ownership and the one-sided structure of the economy with its emphasis on burn-beating cultivation. Moreover, the ecological balance of the region began to be upset towards the turn of the century by an unforeseen

584 Cf. Lenman & Parker 1980, p. 34.
585 Ylikangas 1998a.
586 Ylikangas 1999, pp. 114–117.
587 E.g. Riissanen 1965, pp. 28–31.
588 Heikkinen 1988, p. 117; af Ugglas 1794, p. 222, Til landshöfding i Heinola, angående rätter domstol i ägotvister i Savolax, den 6 april 1781; Saloheimo 1980, pp. 321–323.

population explosion.[589] Here, the 1770s came to constitute a significant watershed in the economic and demographic history of both northern Karelia and northern Savo; after this decade demographic pressures could no longer be channelled off by just increasing in the size of the peasant class alone. The peasants of Ilomantsi had already complained to the Diet about the excessive amount of new settlers in 1775, and eleven years later the farmers of Tohmajärvi made a similar complaint.[590]

Burn-beating cultivation, which required large areas of virgin forest and sparse settlement, began to wane: the rolling landscape of conifer forests started to be taken over by deciduous trees, the rotational cycle of forest felling grew shorter, and crops decreased. The soil became impoverished as the cultivators tried to get more out of it than it could supply. The oversettlement of the land that was critical for burn-beating cultivation reached northern Karelia properly in the last years of the eighteenth century, whereas in northern Savo the first – and at this stage perhaps exaggerated – complaints about the depletion of the forests dated back to the 1750s. Even so, at the beginning of the nineteenth century, the conifer forest resources in Pieksämäki in Savo were known to be better than in the surrounding areas. Detailed information about the cycle of forest felling and burning in the parishes of northern Savo in the eighteenth century has not been gathered, but it has in northern Karelia: according to Saloheimo's calculations, the crisis in burn-beating cultivation in the province had reached Värtsilä, Rääkkylä and Kesälahti by the time of the Finnish War, and Tohmajärvi, Liperi and Kitee were all close to the critical thirty-year felling and burning cycle. In Ilomantsi, Polvijärvi, Juuka and Lieksa, on the other hand, the forest had had time to re-grow sufficiently before the next felling.[591] The crisis in burn-beating cultivation was reflected in the motivation for homicide to any great extent only in Kesälahti, but there all the more clearly. The disturbance in the ecological bearing capacity of the land also clearly began to be manifested in an increase in the number of lethal conflicts between peasant farmers in areas where settlement increased most rapidly, especially in the relatively sparsely settled northernmost parts of Savo. The phenomenon may also have been connected with a contemporaneous change in the economic base of the area, a shift to the cultivation of arable land. Where burn-beating cultivation remained the main occupation, the crisis did not explode to dramatic proportions until the 1820s, by which time the self-sufficiency of eastern Finland in grain production was a thing of the past,[592] but the problem was

589 Saloheimo 1980, pp. 66, 352–354, 358.
590 Saloheimo 1980, pp. 336, 354; Björn 1991, p. 108 (Saloheimo refers to the Diet of 1775 and Björn to that of 1778.)
591 Wirilander 1989, pp. 567–579, 586, 602–603; Saloheimo 1980, pp. 66, 352–354, 358.
592 See Soininen 1974, pp. 350–353; Kaila 1931, pp. 27–31; Jutikkala 1980, p. 209; Wirilander 1989, pp. 163, 228–241, 567–579; Saloheimo 1980, p. 354; Katajala 1997, pp. 53–54.

anticipated by numerous violent disputes over land at the end of the previous century.[593]

The Land Division Statute put the private ownership of arable land, pasture and forest on a firmer footing, and it also meant the division of the outlying tracts. It mostly benefited the farm-owners and the crofters, but for the landless population it meant a loss of privileges, including the commonage of the village forests.[594] The Land Division Statute applying to Savo and Karelia was passed in the mid-1770s, and it was linked to a new system of taxation; in northern Savo it also gave a powerful boost to the clearing of arable land, which at the same time alleviated the crisis in burn-beating cultivation there. But there were delays in applying the provisions of the statute, and in fact the land resources and conditions for gaining a livelihood had already been shared out between farms by means of a variety of arrangements ever since the mid-1760s, so that before the statute was put into effect, the forests had been depleted in an extremely irresponsible fashion.[595] In the most densely populated southern parishes of northern Karelia and northern Savo the survey work for the redistribution of land did not get under way until the 1780s, because the surveyors were still occupied in other regions of the country. The redistribution was nevertheless to a great extent completed in the 1780s and 1790s,[596] considerably earlier than in southern Savo, where it was delayed even up to the 1820s and at the same time clearly held up the process of the peasants moving over to the cultivation of arable fields.

The usufruct of forest land tended to be a source of quarrels especially prior to the expected redistribution of the land. The felling and burning of the outlying tracts and the confused dispersion of plots sowed the seeds of dissention particularly in southern Savo in the first half of the eighteenth century.[597] Homicides caused by conflicts over land in the area of this study did not generally become common until after the 1770s, when the forest available for burn-beating was already running out and the redistribution of the land in the offing.[598] An improvement in the effective use of the land was made more difficult by a problem with fodder, because moving over to the tillage of arable fields required that the number of farm animals be increased so that the land could get the manure that it needed for fertilization. This in turn led to an extensive cropping of meadowland to provide fodder.[599] The first killings resulting from the competition for land were caused by neighbours' squabbles

---

593 E.g. Riissanen 1965, pp. 28–31.

594 Sirén 1999, p. 30.

595 Saloheimo 1980, pp. 326–332; Wirilander 1989, pp. 210–216, 242–244, 582, 605–606, 613.

596 Saloheimo 1980, pp. 259–260, 328–329.

597 Wirilander 1989, pp. 168–169.

598 Saloheimo 1980, pp. 326–332; Wirilander 1989, pp. 210–216, 242–244, 582, 605–606, 613.

599 Wirilander 1989, pp. 567–579, 586, 602–603; Saloheimo 1980, pp. 66, 352–354, 358

about meadowland or by beat-burning disputes between relatives, but in the 1790s it was large-scale clashes over the cross-border usufruct of the backwoods that culminated in homicide.

Yrjö Raninen, a peasant farmer, and his son, Mikko, set on a farmer called Matti Niiranen at a wedding in Ylikylä in the parish of Tohmajärvi in 1770 and thrashed him so badly that he died within a day. In court the two men jointly denied giving the victim a beating. Their assault on Niiranen was not the first of its kind: a few weeks earlier, at another wedding, the younger Raninen had struck Niiranen, who was lying drunk on the floor, on the head with the handle of a whip and bade him "go off and clear that big meadow" (gå och röjda nu then stora ängen), the rights to which were in dispute between the two farmers. Niiranen had thus had cause to fear the Raninens from earlier treatment at their hands before the fatal encounter at the wedding.

Sworn witnesses stated that the two men had attacked Niiranen at the wedding for no apparent reason and had struck him on the forehead. When Niiranen ran to the other end of the cottage, his assailants followed him, pulling out his hair, beating him and crushing him against a bench until the other wedding guests intervened. Blood began to pour out of the nose and mouth of the victim. He became so weak that in order to avoid further beating he went to lie under a bench behind the stove. Early the following morning, the younger Raninen arrived at the cottage and hauled Niiranen by his feet over the threshold and onto a sledge, from which the almost unconscious victim managed to drag himself back to the cottage. He was unable to eat with the other guests and died on a bench in the cottage at eight o'clock that evening.

According to the autopsy report made by Barber-Surgeon Geisse, the numerous injuries found on the victim could have been caused by his state of heavy intoxication just as well as by the beating.[600] Consequently the court of appeal considered that it could show clemency and reprieve the two main defendants, commuting the death sentences given to them by the lower court on the basis of MB XXIV:1 and 6 to two full wergilds. This was legally sanctioned by MB XXXIX:2:2. Being unable to pay the fine, the sixty-year-old father, who was suffering from a hernia, was allowed to expiate his crime with imprisonment on bread and water, and the son with whipping. The reprieve was justified not only by the unclear source of the victim's injuries but also on the basis of the proof, which was questionable from the judicial point of view; the father and son had consistently denied perpetrating any kind of violence on the victim despite the contradictory testimonies of witnesses. If Juho Niiranen did not get to enjoy the yield of the contested meadow, then neither did the Raninens: The judgment register of the Åbo Court of Appeal contains an entry referring to the sentenced men escaping before the final judgment was passed on them.[601]

The confusion over the rights of tenure of individual holdings that could exist even between subjects of different realms meant that clearing and burning rights were unprotected by the law as long as there was common

---

600 The possibility of bribery in autopsies performed by Geisse must be remembered, but the essential elements of homicide required this kind of detailed analysis of the cause of death.

601 VMA: VHOA, Alistettujen asiain designaatioluettelot ja päätöstaltiot, Kymenkartanon ja Savon lääni v. 1770, Di 8, no 61.

ownership of the backwoods. That is why the nature of land disputes was for a long time quite different in Savo and Karelia from regions where arable agriculture was practised. The lack of clarity concerning the tenure of land in connection with burn-beating may partly explain why the peasant class was so strongly involved in lethal violence in eastern Finland; the parties involved in homicides arising out of usufruct quarrels were mainly farmers or pioneer crofters. However, the motivation for these crimes is not always directly reflected in the sources, for land disputes were not necessarily entered in the court records as the main motive – especially if there had been heavy drinking at the scene of the crime, or if it had been a clandestine killing.

From the 1790s, the on-going redistribution of land curbed quarrels about the use of forest land in some places in the southernmost parishes of northern Karelia and the northernmost ones of Savo. At the same time, conflicts close to the national border were exacerbated. The geographical distribution of homicides motivated by land use disputes mainly followed the border, starting from Pielisjärvi (1748), with a diversion into Liperi (1779), then back to Tohmajärvi (1770) on the border and on to Kesälahti (twice – once in 1785, and once in 1796) and Kerimäki (1801).[602] There were only two exceptions: one in Kuopio in 1763 and one in Pieksämäki in 1794. In all the former cases, the frontier played a part in either the features of the crimes or their aftermaths: either the perpetrators had come from over the border, or they escaped over it afterwards. This phenomenon substantiates in a number of ways the view that the closer the region was to the frontier, the slacker was the control of Swedish authority. This same factor inevitably created a need for various kinds of self-help.

The resources of the Swedish state to protect the usufructuary rights to the forests of the peasants who lived close to the eastern frontier were very limited because Russian subjects used their own rights, which were enshrined in ancient customary law, to practice burn-beating on the Swedish side of the border as well. The right of the peasants to use the lands for burn-beating and pasture on either side of the border had been confirmed after the Peace Treaty of Nystad (1721).[603] For example, in Suojärvi in Old Finland, local peasants established new colonies on the border regardless of previous agreements, although land use on the Swedish side remained the same.[604] The border frays between the Swedish and Russian peasants

---

602 VMA: VHOA, Alistettujen asiain päätöstaltiot, Kymenkartanon ja Savon lääni v. 1763, Di 4, no 16; Alistusaktit, Savon ja Karjalan lääni, v. 1796, no 8; Ece 36, no 8; Alistettujen asiain päätöstaltiot, Savon ja Karjalan lääni, v. 1796, Di 31, no 8. MMA, KymLKa, Saapuneet kirjeet, v. 1749, Hovioikeus maaherralle, D 11a1, no 30; VMA: VHOA, Alistettujen asiain päätöstaltiot, Savon ja Karjalan lääni, v. 1782, Di 17, no 10. MMA, KymLKa, Saapuneet kirjeet, v. 1770, Hovioikeus maaherralle, D 32 a1, no 70.1; VMA; VHOA, Alistettujen asiain designaatioluettelo, Savon ja Karjalan lääni, v. 1785, Di 20, no 62; ibid. and päätöstaltiot, v. 1803, Di 38, no 32.
603 Saloheimo 1980, p. 17. On the cultivation of outlying plots on the Swedish side of the border and the disputed territories, see ibid. pp. 109–113; also Wirilander 1989, pp. 240–241.
604 Saloheimo 1980, p. 337.

began almost immediately after the Peace of Åbo in the 1740s, but not until the end of the century did cross-border use of the land lead to discord of a dramatic kind. In the Uukuniemi area, several Swedish peasants were forcibly taken over the border and beaten. Grain sheaves were stolen by main force on both sides. This practice of resorting to violence to settle disputes went back to the seventeenth century.[605] The disagreements about land use in the vicinity of the border eventually led to disciplinary action by the community and finally to individual cases of homicide.

The long-serving Crown Bailiff of Karelia, Gabriel Wallenius, considered that the cause of the lawlessness lay in the fact that Swedish subjects often did not dare to go to law over their usufruct rights because the cases dragged on for a long time and could "turn out quite differently from the way the Swedish subject had envisaged".[606] At the same time, the uncertainty of the Crown under the threat of international disputes becomes apparent. The conflicting views of the inhabitants of the different countries led to attempts to impose the law of the strongest. Of course, the law of the strongest could not be imposed in practice because acts of lawlessness naturally led to punitive consequences, although this did not happen by any means in all cases.

In 1785 Olli Konttinen, a crofter living in Kerimäki on the Swedish side of the border, took 870 sheaves of rye that belonged to farming family called Pärnänen living on the Russian side of the parish and stored them in the barn of his master. When Matti Pärnänen came to reclaim his rye, Konttinen flew into a rage and impaled him with stave, with the result that he died from loss of blood that night. Konttinen ran away, but he was caught and brought to trial. The case was investigated in both the Swedish and the Russian lower courts. Konttinen was sentenced to death for manslaughter in the courts of all instances (MB XXIV:1 and 8) and executed in Kesälahti.[607]

In the following decade, in 1796, twenty Russian peasants from Uukuniemi in Old Finland attacked the farmstead of Matti Hirvonen in Kesälahti, killing the farmer, assaulting his son and the farmhand and stealing the farm's grain. The case was dealt with in an intermediate district court session in Uukuniemi but remained unsolved. It was not possible to ascertain the culprits by legal means.[608]

Five years later, the Kesälahti-Kerimäki area was still beset by the same kind of unrest. Assistant Judge Jakob Falk, a Swedish subject, who had taken his case against the peasants from the Russian side for practising cross-border use of land right up to the King, killed, or caused to be killed, a peasant who came to get back what belonged to him. The assistant judge managed to avoid the legal consequences thanks to his judicial expertise.

---

605   Riissanen 1965, pp. 28–31; Saloheimo 1980, pp. 342–343.
606   Riissanen, 1965, p. 29.
607   VMA: VHOA, Alistettujen asiain designaatioluettelot ja päätöstaltiot, Savon ja Karjalan lääni, v. 1785, no 62. RA: JRU, 4.10.1785, no 12.
608   Saloheimo 1980, pp. 342–343.

Assistant Judge Falk had occupied forest and meadowland in the border village of Kerimäki that the inhabitants of the Russian side of the parish of Kerimäki considered to belong to them. In the autumn of 1801, Falk removed 900 sheaves of rye that they had grown and put them in his own barns. In December, about fifty of the men from there gave up waiting for a legal settlement of the long-standing dispute and, arming themselves, angrily set off for Falk's farmyard in Mäkimajanselkä to reclaim their stolen property. Their intention was to take Falk over the border and thrash him, but he was not there. However, the following weekend, when they arrived at his farm to fight, they found the assistant judge at home. The skirmish in Falk's farmyard was a heated one; it cost the life of a peasant called Taavi Laitinen, and another of the protesters was seriously injured. The shots that killed Taavi Laitinen were fired from a window of Falk's house.

The events at Mäkimajaselkä were investigated in court for years. Neither Falk himself nor any member of his household, who had clearly been well coached by him for the hearings, confessed to the crime. The strongest piece of empirical circumstantial evidence, the results of an analysis of the gunpowder, was however strongly incriminating for Falk. However, Falk's part in this case, which upset international relations between Russia and Sweden, was left undecided by the court of appeal, and the case was adjourned *sine die*.[609]

Three homicides connected with the use of land and committed within a short period of time in a limited area first of all suggest that benefits that were unprotected by the law were obtained by criminal means; in other words, disputes were settled by means of the violent imposition of control. This happened at the same time as the region was in the grip of the crisis in burn-beating cultivation. Second, the locality of the homicides indicates that the depletion of the forest resources erupted into conflicts most dramatically in those parishes that were cut by the new border, Kerimäki and Kesälahti,[610] areas where there was only a limited amount of space for the growing population. In these regions, the local conditions for violence produced bloody deeds that were exceptional both in their motivation and in their proportions.

In addition to the plots of land that were fought over by the farmers, there were villages and even single farms in the parishes of Kerimäki, Rantasalmi, Puumala and Sulkava that were the subject of dispute between Sweden and Russia during the whole period of this research. The cameral administrations and the justice systems of the two states did not cover these so-called "disputed territories". According to Wirilander, this led to lawlessness and the rule of the strongest.[611] Particularly the disputed tracts of land around Kerimäki were affected in this way. On the other hand, those living on the manorial lands continued to be dependent on the owner of the manor, which according to Soininen prevented illegalities

---

609 VMA: VHOA, Alistusaktit, Savon ja Karjalan lääni, v. 1800, Ece 57, no 54.
610 The parish of Kesälahti was created out of the Swedish half of the divided parish of Uukuniemi.
611 Wirilander 1989, pp. 241, 301.

in the disputed areas around Rantasalmi.[612] Here, the disputed territory with its sparse population was either spared the worst cases of homicide, or they were dealt with in secret.

If it was suspected that a grave crime had been committed in the disputed territories, it was necessary to institute an exceptional judicial procedure. One homicide charge and one infanticide indictment were prosecuted in a joint court constituted by the representatives of Sweden and Russia. On the basis of a mutual agreement between the two nations, a district court was established. The board of jurors consisted half of Russian and half of Swedish subjects, and the court was jointly presided over by a Swedish and a Russian judge. The same procedure was required if the parties involved were subjects of different realms. That is why it was employed in the above-mentioned cases of Matti Pärnänen and Assistant Judge Falk.

The first case involving disputed villages was prosecuted in Kerimäki in the autumn of 1767 in order to investigate what was suspected to be the violent death of an old man called Simo Puolakka.

During the enquiry, a peasant farmer called Olavi Keinonen admitted that he had quarrelled with Puolakka over a fishing dispute two weeks before his death. He said that on that occasion he had struck the victim twice. Four bloody wounds were found on the body of the dead man. Keinonen admitted causing only two of these. The lower court considered making Keinonen take an oath of purgation in order to ascertain his involvement in causing the other wounds, but this was renounced because the defendant's knowledge of Christian doctrine turned out to be deficient. It was not possible to get a doctor to come to the locality to perform a post mortem. The lower court found on the basis of a statement made by the laymen who inspected the corpse that the wounds inflicted by Keinonen were not lethal. The old man was held to have died from some sudden attack of illness. In accordance with MB XXXV, Keinonen was sentenced to a fine of two silver *dalers* for battery.

The sentence passed by the lower court of the disputed territory was referred both to the Collegium of Justice of Old Finland and to the Åbo Court of Appeal and the King of Sweden. The Russian imperial office handled its share of the judicial process considerably more promptly than the Swedish authorities. When Collegium of Justice of Old Finland requested that its sentence be implemented, the Åbo Court of Appeal did not yet even have the documents relating to the case at its disposal. The long distances and the three-phase bureaucracy delayed the handling of the matter. The enquiry record into the Keinonen case ended up in the documents of the Chancery College of Stockholm Criminal Archives. The ruling of the Åbo Court of Appeal came by way of the Council of Justice on 15 April 1769 after the provincial governor had requested a speedy settlement of the matter. It corresponded with the judgment of the Russian Collegium of Justice given on 13 August 1768. Keinonen was sentenced to a fine of eight silver *dalers* for battery and inflicting two open wounds.[613]

---

612 Soininen 1954, p. 288.
613 VMA: VHOA, Alistettujen asiain designaatioluettelo ja päätöstaltiot, Kymenkartanon ja Savon lääni, v. 1769, Di 7, no 13.

Saloheimo's view that cases like this were sensitive with regard to foreign relations is obviously not far from the truth. As a result the penal control of the inhabitants of the disputed territory did not lead to a singe capital sentence being implemented.

The view of Ylikangas that the poor legal protection of real estate is a significant explanatory factor for the violence of mediaeval and pre-modern times finds some corroboration in the eastern Finnish research material.[614] Moreover, particularly at the local level, violence and the motives for it reflect factors connected with the natural conditions, such as the collapse of the ecological bearing capacity of the land or climatic conditions. This phenomenon was exacerbated by the institutional weakness of the Swedish state when it came to a conflict between the interests of its own citizens and those of the subjects of the Russian Empire. The beginning of the crisis in burn-beating cultivation launched a concomitant process of impoverishment, the consequences of which spread out to affect every aspect of society, including homicide. We can assume that this happened despite the fact that the phenomenon was not always simply or directly reflected in the motivation of homicides. Interests that were weakly protected or unprotected by the law included, apart from land, the physical inviolability of members of the family, and locally the rights of the tenant farmers on lands that were owned by the nobles to preserve their own means of livelihood. All of these repeatedly led to acts of homicide.

The Vengeance of the Tenant Farmers in a Truncated Parish

The parishes that were split in two by the border offered a fertile breeding ground for violence; here the factors that provided the motivation for crime were multiplied, while in some other parts of the province in practice they hardly appear at all. This was so in the part of the parish of Pälkjärvi that was left on the Swedish side of the border after the Peace of Nystad. During the period covered by this study it had only a thousand inhabitants. Kujala has estimated that even during the Finnish War it had been the most violent parish in Finland.[615] The disorder in the parish was also exacerbated by an external enemy: during the War of the Hats, Russian invaders had burnt the place to the ground, so that not a single building survived.[616]

In this truncated parish, which was then amalgamated with Tohmajärvi, there were two murders of tenant farmers on land that was owned by the nobility during the period dealt with here, and in one of them the farmer's wife was also killed. The motivation for these murders was directly linked to the socially insecure position of the tenant farmers of these lands, for

---

614 Ylikangas 2000, pp. 44–47.
615 Kujala & Malinen 2001, pp. 434, 437.
616 Saloheimo 1980, p. 29.

both deeds were committed by farmers who had been evicted from their farms. The perpetrators themselves confessed in court that vengeance had been their motive.

> Flavius Karttunen, who in 1750 had been driven off a deserted plot of land in Pälkjärvi that he had occupied, murdered his brother, a tenant farmer called Yrjänä and the latter's wife, Inkeri, on the night of Shrove Tuesday.[617] The killer said in court that he suspected that his brother had reported him to the arrendator for loose living. For the same kind of reasons, Antti Pikkarainen, had become enraged and had Juha Päivinen, the tenant farmer who replaced him, murdered in 1786.[618]

Despite their distance from each other in time these homicides were not just random acts; they reflected the widespread sense of protest that had been seething among the tenant farmers and which generally boiled over in the form of social conflicts and strike action rather than in violence against their own kind. The roots of the dispute between the tenant farmers and the arrendators went far back into history, to a time when they affected a broader spectrum of the population and the nature of the conflict was more violent than in the late eighteenth century, when the most profound reason for the disagreements between those who rented out the land that was owned by the nobles and those who cultivated it lay in the status of the land and the position of the cultivators: their rights to build permanent dwellings and to the tenure of the land were very poorly safeguarded by the law, not to mention their right to pass on the land tenure to their progeny through inheritance.

That was why the speech made by Gustav III on his accession to the throne fell on eager ears among the members of this group, and there rapidly arose among them a belief that the King had given them the same rights as the landed peasant farmers. Inspired by this obvious and perhaps intentional misunderstanding, most of the tenant farmers rose up in protest against what they felt were the unreasonable rights of the arrendators in 1773. The unrest erupted in the form of refusals to perform rent service. From Sweden itself the movement spread via Elimäki and Nastola to the villages of Ilomantsi and Pälkjärvi, the very areas where there was a strong historical tradition of peasant resistance.[619] The movement, spurred on by this tradition and encouraged by the local conditions, took on a number of features peculiar to northern Karelia: a significant cause of the protest was the heavy tax burden on the land, and the evictions carried out by the authorities also evoked violent reactions. In Elimäki in the Kymi region, some of the tenant farmers refused to cooperate with the Crown

---

617 MMA: KymLKa, Saapuneet kirjeet, v. 1750, Hovioikeus maaherralle, D 12 a1, no 23.

618 VMA: VHOA, Alistettujen asiain päätöstaltiot, Savon ja Karjalan lääni, v. 1787, Di 22, no 5; v. 1788, Di 23, no 2.

619 E.g. Katajala 2001; Katajala 1992, pp. 177–180; Jutikkala 1932, pp. 352–353; Saloheimo 1980, pp. 294–298; Ahonen 1986, p. 276.

authorities and the arrendators in any way. However, there were no longer any homicides caused by political violence directed at the gentry and the arrendators in the region studied here, unlike in the previous uprising during the Great Famine (1696—99).[620]

The protests were put down harshly everywhere. Many of the tenant farmers were evicted, those who had taken part in the movement were sentenced to harsh corporal punishment, and the rents became ever more exorbitant.[621] Moreover, in 1776 Gustav III issued a decree which departed from the general trends in political control of the times, in that it increased the punishments for certain kinds of homicide: for example, the punishment for attempting to kill one's master "on the basis of imagined injustices" was made harsher. It was to be applied to crofters, farm hands and the tenant farmers of land owned by the nobility.[622]

The spirit of protest that was aroused by the weak legal protection of the inhabitants of the villages situated on these lands in fact only very rarely erupted in homicide; the three killings mentioned above account for only 1.5 per cent of the homicide committed in the area of this study. During the Great Famine, the scale and social basis of the violence had been quite different. Even so, at the local level, two bloody deeds with three victims was a lot in the eighteenth century. Does the repetitive nature of the murders point to some common reason connected with the phenomenon dealt with in the previous chapter, the dramatic outburst of disputes over the use of land? It certainly indicates overcrowding. In the villages of Pälkjärvi, there was hardly enough land to increase the size of the holdings, let alone accommodate denser habitation. In fact, the numbers of farms in the villages increased very little during the period dealt with in this research.[623] The settlement pressures led to an increase in competitive aggression and ultimately to its eruption in the form of homicide. These killings that followed from the harder competition at the end of the era of burn-beating cultivation were a direct equivalent of the fratricides in traditional forms of society.

The national frontier was a threat to society in most of the parishes that it severed. The desperate tenant farmers of the split parish of Pälkjärvi avenged their evictions, while the border that cut straight through the middle of Kesälahti and Kerimäki meant an intensification of competition for land resulting in mass kidnappings and robberies of grain which led to fateful consequences. In the divided parish of Mäntyharju in southern Savo, again, it was bands of brigands made up of escaped criminals that exploited the administrative disunity of the locality. Rantasalmi, on the other hand, which even after its area had been truncated, was distinctly larger than the three afore-mentioned parishes, and whose new border made it into a junction of communications, avoided any significant wave

---

620 Ahonen 1986, p. 276.
621 See e.g. Katajala 2001; Katajala 1992, pp. 177–180; Jutikkala 1932, pp. 352–353.
622 Anners 1965, p. 258.
623 Saloheimo 1980, pp. 344–345.

of violence.[624] The fighting that was peculiar to Kesälahti and Kerimäki was connected in an exceptionally direct way with factors of shortage: the exhaustion of the forests and the lack of space for settlement. I believe that the latter is also the basic reason for the violent tendencies of people of the Orthodox religion in Ilomantsi and Liperi; in practical terms, the only direction in which they could move was eastwards, into Russia, because it is hardly likely that members of a faith that was discriminated against would join a settlement movement into areas peopled exclusively by Lutherans. Moreover, in Ilomantsi, the growth in the size of the population was also lower than in the rest of eastern Finland, remaining at the average level for the whole of the country.[625]

Conclusion

Among others, Janne Kivivuori and Donald Black interpret a high number of homicides as an attempt to defend interests that are not protected by the law. A lawful good can be without the protection of the law just as much as an unlawful one if it cannot in practice be successfully defended by legal means. An example of the defence of an unlawful good would be stealing stolen property from a thief,[626] while avenging a theft violently is a case of defending a lawful good by illegal means – especially if the thief has been acquitted of the charge in a court of law.[627] Homicides which are committed in answer to a problem are not so much the products of momentary impulsive aggression as a consequence of long-drawn-out conflicts or of a threat to particularly important interests. Ylikangas, too, considers that the origins of violence lie in a reaction of this kind, particularly in connection with the protection of property.[628]

The majority of crimes of various kinds can in most cultures be explained by the necessity of defending a legally unprotected benefit and the need to rely on self-help. However, this kind of reaction that is aimed at solving a problem can be exacerbated by local factors to extremes in terms of both quality and quantity. Then the attempt to find legal security results in homicide, and personal violence becomes the common way of solving disputes. However, different benefits are protected differently in different societies: that is why the pressures that impel people to commit crimes vary from one society to another.

The eruption of these pressures into personal violence is significantly curbed by control. Understood in this broad sense, control must be defined as a three-phase restraining mechanism: from personal control, which is effected by individuals themselves, via unofficial control, which is implemented by the community, to official control, which it is the responsibility

---

624 Soininen 1954, pp. 280–285.
625 Björn 1993, p. 23.
626 Cf. Black 1984a, pp. 17–18 and Kivivuori 1999, p. 75.
627 Examples of cases of this kind can be found in e.g. Heikkinen 1988, pp. 131–132.
628 Ylikangas 2000, pp. 44–97.

of society to impose. The more premeditated a crime is, the more likely it is that the perpetrator has calculated his or her chances of being punished for it. On the other hand, it is much more difficult for the criminal to predict the form of unofficial control (i.e. the reaction of the community) that the crime will encounter. In this respect, the unofficial control implemented by the immediate community is frequently more effective than official control.[629] In practice, the control of one's own actions also determines to a great extent how the conflict is settled; that is, whether it is solved violently or otherwise. The formation of self-control and the creation of moral awareness is regulated by the culture into which a person is socialized. The preventive significance of the control of psychological impulses or affects in the individual is difficult to determine in historical criminal cases, but ever since the days of Elias and Renvall the role of such moral restraints has traditionally been considered crucial.[630]

On the other hand, the need for administrative repression and legal protection may also have been a factor that drove people to commit homicide. When a killing is a way of implementing unofficial control, the perpetrator often feels that that his action is justified. Killing is a reciprocal exchange, an expression of private punitive control. The criminal solving of problems burgeoned in a wide variety of forms in eastern Finland in the eighteenth and nineteenth centuries. The defence of interests unprotected by the law was bilateral. The homicide was often a reaction to acts of lawlessness for which it was not possible to obtain legal redress. The reaction may also have been the illegal defence of an unlawful benefit.[631] There was a conflict of roles between the killer's own moral code and the point of view of the legislator; for example, the deceived husband in a *crime pasionelle* regards his victim, his wife's lover, as the aggressor. In the eyes of the law, the opposite relationship generally obtains.[632] In the area of eastern Finland dealt with here, the killer's lens transposed the roles of aggressor and victim in vengeance murders, for example, in cases where the perpetrators were incited by reports of theft made against them or evictions from their holdings. The roles were similarly reversed when criminal groups settled their internal problems, or when a villager eliminated a local robber. Seen in this light, when the settlement pressures created by the lack of available land increased, even the homicidal culmination of reactions to quarrels caused by land ownership and usufructuary rights or to family disputes becomes understandable. The need for self-help in a way also humanizes people's violent reactions to the army deserters and the border bandits. Behind these crimes there lay an attempt to restore a benefit that was unprotected by the law. They were used to patch the holes in official punitive control.

629 Cf. e.g. Spierenburg 1999, p. 113 ff.
630 Elias (1939) 1994, 452–478 and passim; also e.g.. Foucault 1977; Berkowitz 1962; Renvall 1949.
631 Kivivuori 1999, p. 116.
632 Black 1984a, pp. 8–14.

Even so, many of the homicides that were most characteristic of life in eastern Finland lacked any real retributive or punitive elements. They were rather a consequence of the need for mediatory control. Killings resulting from marital crises, land disputes or conflicts within a burn-beating partnership became in terms of their structural motivation interwoven into an unofficial extension of the peaceful legal arbitration of disputes. Thus, by illegal means, they helped to fill the vacuum of so-called therapeutic, mediatory or compensatory official control.

The justice system had proved itself to be ineffective in solving disputes connected with the usufructuary rights of forest to be felled for beat-burning cultivation. There were also restrictions on the division of farms. Quarrelling spouses, again, had in practice no satisfactory legal way of dissolving their union. Relations with parents were regulated not only by the law but also by Luther's Small Catechism, which created a biased situation for the settlement of judicial questions. The constitution and dissolution of a partnership, the ownership of chattels and personal honour were other areas where the law did not afford adequate protection. Again, in principle, the internal settlement of accounts between groups belonging to the criminal sub-culture remained outside the range of the law. The degree of premeditation in homicides committed by northern Karelians is in fact to a great extent explained by the effort to protect personal benefits by illegal means. These elements were also strongly present in the daily life of the people of northern Savo, even if its criminal aspect was less dramatic. The idealization of the harmony and concord of the traditional peasant society – be it the *Gemeinschaft* or the "Good Old Days" before the creation of the state – today usually arouses little more than historical interest.[633] Such generalizations have been shown to be without any real basis.[634] Nor does the material from eastern Finland used in this study lend itself to figures of speech that idealize the past. Nevertheless, one must remember that it would be unjustified to class the peaceful region of Savo stretching from Joroinen to Pieksämäki with the violent areas to the north and east. Here there were very few homicide trials, and they were mainly cases of lethal negligence.

Eva Österberg has described the functions of the court institution in the pre-industrial age by means of her own dichotomy, in which opposed are, on the one hand, the courts of law as a popular institution concentrating on the settlement of disputes and, on the other, their existence as a state organ oriented towards the vertical, disciplinary imposition of chastisement. Österberg considers that the forms of punishment meted out by the old district court institution conformed to a great extent to the fundamental ethical values of the collective society at the dawn of the modern age. The courts constituted a social arena for the settlement of disputes between members of the community, which was based on close

---

633 Österberg 1982, esp. pp. 46–52.
634 Cockburn 1991, p. 106; Ylikangas 1999, pp. 101–110; Aalto 1996, pp. 178–179; also Katajala 1994, p. 48 ff; Katajala 2001.

personal relationships and a micro-economy. The re-integrating nature of the punishments, that is their aim of returning the culprit to full membership of the community, is apparent, for example, in the fact that fining remained the predominant penal sanction until the seventeenth century. Capital punishment, on the other hand, was reserved in the old judicial system of the people for criminals who had transgressed the strongest taboos, and who could therefore no longer be permitted to live in the community.[635]

According to Österberg, the role of the courts assumed some ambivalent features as the state began to assert itself in the seventeenth and eighteenth centuries. In her view, the district court was gradually transformed into a theatre of power, whose rituals – cruel public spectacles of chastisement – emphasized the power of the state's authority. However, the courts never lost their significance as an institution for the arbitration of disputes, and this mediatory element began to reassert itself even more strongly in the eighteenth century; indeed in an age of land disputes, it was felt that its was the courts' primary function to settle economic disagreements.[636] The final curtain on the theatre of power began to fall at the end of the eighteenth century. As differences between groups in society grew and social mobility increased, the significance of honour and shame as defining categories in community life fell into abeyance.[637]

How can Österberg's model be employed to analyse the development that took place in punishing homicide? The setting up of the theatre of power destroyed the legislation of the popular legal tradition in two ways: the intervention of the state into local judicial life ended the arbitration of homicide, but at the same time the introduction of new rules of evidence totally prevented the punishment of the most grievous crimes. The age of the courts' mediatory role finally ended even in cases of unintentional manslaughter when the Law of 1734 came into force, because in the new criminal law code, the plaintiff lost his or her right of action in cases of both intentional homicide and violent unintentional manslaughter. The practice of arbitration survived in awarding the plaintiff's share of the *wergild* (blood money) in less serious cases of homicide, but when a death sentence passed by the lower court was commuted in the court of appeal to a wergild, the fine was, because of the indigence of the criminal, most commonly converted to corporal punishment, a cruel, public penalty that emphasized the punitive might of the state. Since the aggrieved party in practice hardly ever any more received his or her share of the blood money in amends, one can no longer speak of the arbitration of cases of homicide between individuals.

In addition to conflict settlement, the disciplinary elements associated with the practical punishments for homicide also declined. At the end of the period of Swedish power, the lower courts in eastern Finland did

---

635 Österberg 1994, p. 15; Österberg 1994a, p. 8 ff.; Österberg 1991d, pp. 163–164.
636 Ågren 1988; Furuhagen 1996, pp. 25–26, 54–55.
637 Österberg 1994, p. 15.

consistently try implement a punitive, disciplinary control on homicide, but the courts of appeal undermined this policy by their insistence on a legal proof. In examining the judicial control of aggravated homicide, it is not pertinent to try and assess the extent to which the functioning of the law was characterized by conflict between the rural population and the representatives of the Crown, in terms of an imposition of authoritarian dictates from above, and the extent to which there was cooperation between them, for the situation is almost inverted: for murders and the other gravest forms of manslaughter, the popular traditional rules of law required the imposition of a kind of authoritarian dictate in the form of compelling the culprit to pay a wergild. In this respect, the law was a kind of cement that held society together, but the new situation led to fateful consequences for the system of norms: the stipulations of the criminal law could not be implemented to anything like a satisfactory extent even when the identity of the guilty party was indisputable. The situation almost totally destroyed the moral framework of the society of Savo and Karelia. Attempts were made to solve the problem by increasing the use of confessional remand, but the deterrent effect of this institution remained low during the period dealt with in this research.

The state achieved its aim of inculcating discipline through religious indoctrination at the level of the legal culture. However, the legal culture was not monolithic; there were deviations at both the individual and communal levels – on the part of those who committed the crimes, but also on the part of those who did not report crimes to the court.

Nevertheless, it is interesting to consider the coercive imposition of the dictates of the state on homicide trials in the eighteenth century. From the point of view of eastern Finland, this imposition was represented above all by the legal theory of proof, which prevented the disciplinary implementation of the law aimed at by the lower courts in punishing those who committed serious crimes. The establishment of this testimonial practice as part of the judicial revolution meant a new kind of conflict between the authorities and the members of the local community.[638] When, in the punishment of homicide, both settlement between the parties involved and legal disciplinary action – in Black's terms, both mediatory and punitive control – are obstructed, we can justifiably speak of a crisis in official control. The statutory rules of evidence in procedural law too often prevented the implementation of the norms of criminal law, and this, harsh as it was, was thus unable to achieve its purpose, the reinforcement of public power. The effect of the law remained to a great extent illusory, and it weakened the credibility of both the district courts and the superior courts. This trend was also exacerbated in some areas of civil law by the fact that the conflict-resolving function of the lower courts was badly weakened: the district court institution failed to resolve many kinds of disputes between individuals, from marital problems to long-drawn-out disputes between peasant farmers concerning the usufruct of the forests. One reason for this was the slowness of the courts.

638 Pihlajamäki 1997, p. 94

How does the connection between factors involved in the judicial crisis and the qualitative nature of homicide at the local level correspond to the debate initiated by Arne Jarrick and Johan Söderberg about the origins of the civilizing process? On the basis of the research material from eastern Finland, it is not possible to estimate whether personal violence began to decline spontaneously or in consequence of a policy dictated from above. It is impossible to trace the origins of the civilizing process in the economic or political spheres. On the contrary, one can in fact conclude that the political sphere clearly barred to the way to its advance. Violent behaviour was sustained above all by institutional factors: the creation of a vacuum in judicial control, the regulation of people's occupations and above all their vulnerability to external threats, in other words the military operations carried out against the civilian population.

The low percentage of homicides solved in Savo and Karelia indicates a substantial weakness in the legal administration, but it would be quite unhistorical to compare it with the mediaeval or the pre-state system. The hierarchical administrative machinery was firmly in place in northern Savo and northern Karelia in the eighteenth century; local grains of sand did no more than cause friction in its gears. The former power of the kin, which offered its members protection through familial relations, had almost totally collapsed. Even when the official control did not punish crimes, the judicial sources do not point to any systematic vendettas or clan wars. They had disappeared as forms of alternative penal control even in the most violent localities, for the public criminal law had in practice already swept these institutions into history before the period dealt with in this study. On the other hand, the old idea of enforcing private control survived in the stipulations of the Criminal Law of 1734 regarding outlawry. However, we do not know whether a practical consequence of outlawry – the legal killing of an escaped criminal – was ever implemented in practice in the area dealt with here. In practice, outlawry had been reduced to mere banishment in the preceding centuries.[639] The prevalence of familial homicide also suggests that the networks of loyalty woven by kinship ties had been unravelled.

Homicides took the forms that the historical situation determined for them. The state had assumed a monopoly of punishment so as to preclude the possibility of individuals or informal collective bodies settling their own disputes and punishing offenders. In earlier centuries, the public legal system had retained an element of feudal law and left part of this penal jurisdiction in the hands of private agents of control, mainly the kin. *That was why, in the eighteenth century in particular, the increase in the number of acquittals and cases adjourned sine die was fatal for the repression of crime*; it was no longer possible to set up a parallel, private and institutionalized system of repression beside the official system of control. At the same time, some of the landless population became deracinated and remained outside the supervisory range of the clans. In this

---

639 Matikainen 2002.

sense, the qualitative deterioration in homicide was a consequence of the failure of both official and unofficial social control.[640]

Crown Bailiff Wallenius used the concepts of internal and external enemies in his analysis of the complex of problems that was peculiar to the administrative region of Karelia. In modern parlance, these terms refer to the source of threats to the state and society. Understood in this way, murderers who denied their crimes were the internal enemies of the judiciary; they destroyed the legal penal system from within and thereby demolished the values and morals of society. In addition to its other functions, criminal law is always a defence of the prevailing power system.

However, Crown Bailiff Wallenius was using the concept of an enemy within to refer rather to the internal strife and the proclivity of the Karelians for robbing and killing their own people. Therefore, "the enemy within" can be understood in this study as a metaphor for a culture of homicide in which the aggression was directed with unusual frequency at members of the perpetrator's immediate circle, in Savo and Karelia mainly at family members and kinsmen. As a psychological trope, this expression can also be used to refer to the individual, to the criminals' subjective system of beliefs and meanings and to his or her underdeveloped personal control mechanism. It was as a consequence of factors of individual psychology that the culture of homicide took the form that it did: premeditated, vengeful and brutal. Homicide was determined to an extremely high degree by the power of the external deterrent – or rather, in this case, by its debility. The basic cause of the phenomenon was the fact that the perpetrators' own personal moral code did not condemn murder; the culprits felt that they were strongly justified in committing their crimes. Therefore, there was nothing to prevent them from killing when the policy of control had failed, and the external, penal, deterrent had evaporated.

640 Kekkonen & Ylikangas 1982, p. 67

Homicide as an Instrument of Control

The origins of a crime are normally regarded as lying in individual psychological and social factors, motivation, anomy or other forms of pressure impelling the perpetrator to crime and in the forces of control that constrain these pressures. In this study I have dealt with the last in the chain of causes, control. The main aim was to ascertain the extent to which the local control of homicide affected the characteristics and the quantitative and qualitative composition of homicide. I have assumed the concept of control to be a broad tripartite mechanism for the prevention of crime: official control was implemented by society, informal control by the local community and personal control by the individual. The last-mentioned kind of control was regulated by the individual's morality and a culturally determined personal ability to restrain violent impulses. The area dealt with in the research comprised northern Savo and northern Karelia, the eastern regions of the Kingdom of Sweden, in the years 1748—1808.

****

The chronological change that took place in homicide has often been scrutinized in historical criminological research through the prism of the concept of modernization. This has revealed three central elements as the main features of the process. The first and most significant of these is the decline in this form of crime. This development took place in Europe mainly between the 1620s and the 1750s. The second element was, however, a qualitative deterioration in the quality of the acts committed, which meant that the number of murders increased at the expense of spontaneous manslaughter. This process is considered to have reached its peak at the earliest at the turn of the eighteenth and nineteenth centuries. Third, the social context of homicide became narrower; there was a increase in domestic killings from the early seventeenth century on.

The motivation for homicide has also been scrutinized in the mirror of the advent of the modern age. For example, Pieter Spierenburg, who has applied the conceptual apparatus of social psychology to the history of killing, has concluded that with the advance of history the motives for crime have become increasingly instrumental. In other words, homicidal crimes have become more and more premeditated and linked to self-interest.

In northern Savo and northern Karelia, the quantitative and qualitative fluctuations in homicide were considerable. There were many times more homicides, especially murders, in the most violent eastern parishes of Karelia than in the more peaceful regions of central Savo. However, the types of conflict that lay behind the killing did not differ between the areas with high and low homicide rates so sharply that it is possible to attribute the differences purely to motivation. The effectiveness of official control and the local efficacy of the penal system distinguished the different cultures of homicide in eastern Finland much more clearly than the motives for the deeds; killing was much rifer where the legal repression of homicide failed than in areas where it worked.

There were two main reasons for the local debility of the legal repression of homicide, a juridical one and an administrative one. *Juridically*, the concept of penal certainty was weakened by the statutory presentation of proof applied at that time, which required either a confession by the accused or the concurring testimonies of two competent eyewitnesses. The strict application of these rules meant that the proportion of unsolved homicides increased considerably. *Administratively*, the opportunities for homicidal killers to go unpunished for their crimes were increased by several local factors that existed in the early part of the period under investigation here: the open eastern frontier, the inability of the authorities to deal with acts of lawlessness, and the deplorable state of the prisons. Many of those who committed acts of homicide succeeded in fleeing from the easternmost parishes of the region over the border into Russia, although from the end of the 1770s on the number of criminals who finally escaped justice in this way began to decrease. This was a result of the reinforcement of the eastern frontier, or of a deterioration in living conditions in the region. About the same time, the amount of homicides started to wane, although their qualitative nature in terms of premeditation continued to deteriorate.

The weak repression and lack of penal certainty were not directly responsible for an increase *in all forms of homicide*. The relationship between the efficacy of the forces of law and order and homicide was qualitative rather than quantitative. The connection was clearly stronger for murder than for spontaneous manslaughter. In areas where the perpetrators of homicide regularly went unpunished for their crimes, the gravity of the deeds became increasingly more brutal and ruthless. The optimal coincidence of opportunities to commit crimes with impunity and weak control provided a spur for the most serious types of homicide in particular, i.e. those that were inspired by self-interest: contract murders, killing a prison guard or the driver of a convoy of prisoners, and murders with robbery. The crisis in juridical procedure and in obtaining a legal proof thus led to a change in the motivation for homicide, which Spierenburg mentions in connection with his modernization model. On the other hand, there may have been a more direct connection between the increase in the *quantitative* nature of homicide in certain places and other structural factors. Social factors that increased the pressures on people to commit crime included a growth in the size of the mobile population foreshadowing the incipient crisis in burn-beating cultivation, changes in the level of affluence, and the family system, which was increasingly felt to be constrictive.

The social disorganization provided a fertile soil for crime in a variety of respects. The sparse population of the region did not lend itself to strong informal control in the form of supervision by the immediate community. The number of potential eyewitnesses was less than in more densely populated areas. Informal control was also weakened by an increase in the numbers of the landless people who had become estranged from their roots, because they were no longer constrained by the traditional rules of the peasant community, such as the code of honour that prohibited theft, in the same way as were the settled populace. It was, for instance, from the vagrant population that contract murderers were recruited when this form of crime began to increase. The reinforcement of the state's monopoly of penal power had also ended the old, institutionalized intermediate form of control between official and unofficial, a form that had earlier been regarded as important: the possibilities of members of the local community to implement the repression of homicide by means of such institutions as blood vengeance.

If there is inconsistency in the implementation of capital punishment, it dissipates any preventive effect it may have. A much more significant factor of repression than execution is the fact that some punishment, whatever it is, is imposed on acts of homicide. Anyway, the penal system of criminal law normally only regulates crime when the first links in the chain of control do not function properly. This happens when individual psychological factors in the criminal have first obstructed the initiation of control over his or her personal actions, when the moral code of the perpetrator does not prohibit him or her from killing another human being, and when the informal control imposed by the immediate community subsequently fails.

The likelihood of retribution was absolutely crucial in regulating the repression of homicide among the burn-beating populace of eastern Finland in the final period of the old penal system – just as it is in modern societies. The greater was the lack of such an external deterrent and the weaker was official control, the more clearly can one speak of a crisis in personal and informal control, i.e. in private and public moral codes. The main reason for this crisis lay in the fragmented history of the frontier regions, where acts of belligerence were primarily directed against the civilian population. For example one crucial condition attached to Norbert Elias' civilizing process and the internalization of control, the removal of physical threat, was not satisfied here. Another factor that simultaneously contributed to the moral crisis was the inefficacy of the system of punishment and conflict-settlement of the age.

In fact, an analysis of the motives for the crimes reveals that the inefficiency of the justice system was a double-edged sword. Certain types of homicide are structurally characteristic of every administrative and social system. In the burn-beating community of eastern Finland, the motives for homicide included the elimination of criminals, conflicts over the tenure of the outlying lands, conjugal disputes and the eviction of a tenant farmer. The prevalence of such motives may be an indication that the authorities had problems in performing one of their primary functions: protecting the lives and property of the inhabitants. The population explosion that took place in the outlying regions simultaneously weakened the counterforce to official control: the potential security that a small community, kin or family might offer the individual. Since the justice system was unable for one reason or another to guarantee an effective machinery for the settlement of disputes, informal control proliferated, and its most extreme expression was homicide. In some cases, this also indicates that from the point of view of concrete legal security, the regulation of society was ill directed. It barred the possibilities of solving disputes through legal channels such as the division of land, or separation and divorce.

The motivation for homicide in eastern Finland was in many cases a direct consequence of the limited ability of the justice system to settle disputes and punish crimes. The need for therapeutic, conciliatory or compensatory as well as punitive control was channelled into homicide, which constituted a way of reacting to acts of lawlessness. When it erupted into violence, the nature of informal social control was purely punitive. One manifestation of the implementation of unofficial control was the internal settling of differences in the criminal subculture; killings committed within groups that lived outside organized society and murders committed against informers. In addition, the precarious state of law and order also encouraged murders committed in conjunction with robbery, which were also made easier by the remoteness of the region, as well as killings carried out by prisoners in the process of making their escape.

The deterrent effect of punishment is regarded as greatest in crimes that are motivated by self-interest. [641] Behind the murders carried out in conjunction with robbery, numerous contract murders and murders committed in conjunction with the escape of a prisoner in eastern Finland, there lurked mainly the pursuit of personal advantage. The proliferation of such crimes was a consequence of the dilution of penal certainty, a weakening in the preventive effect of punishments. In addition, the local character of homicide in eastern Finland was to a great extent a result of the simultaneous vacuum in informal control, which was furthered by the growth in population.

The succession of the crimes led to a vicious circle. The justice system was responsible for reacting to all the most serious infringements of the law, but its failure in its repressive function led to a continuing spiral of accounts being settled violently and informal control being implemented. One criminal act succeeded another and itself inspired a new repressive reaction.

The theocratic doctrine of expiation continued to exist in the minds of the people. This dogma of moral theology had, beyond its political goals, a significance for the control of crime: a transcendental agent,

---

641 Black 1984a, p. 14.

God, would inevitably avenge any crimes that the worldly justice system left unpunished. If a killer escaped punishment, blood guilt would be attached to him, a responsibility not only for the loss of the salvation of his soul in everlasting life but also for the ruination of the kingdom. The doctrine of blood guilt lay beyond the trinity of control, as a kind of outer fourth ring. In the religious beliefs of the times, this form of control was implemented by God himself. The theocratic doctrine of expiation was a type of vicarious control with which it was politically expedient to indoctrinate the people. According to Ylikangas, the doctrine of blood guilt made it possible particularly in the seventeenth century to offload the responsibility for the great burdens and sufferings imposed on the people by the constant wars from the state and society onto the shoulders of the individual wrongdoer. The doctrine also had other goals in eastern Finland: it was used to inculcate a sense of common responsibility for the apprehension of criminals in the people's minds. Thirdly, even in the eighteenth century, the doctrine of blood guilt made up for the deficiencies in the systems of official and informal control by shaping the moral ideas of the common people; it unambiguously designated the killing of another human being as a reprehensible act. The general internalization of this idea by people and its separation from its religious context later made it easier to introduce a more lenient penal system.

The proliferation of premeditated murders and the denial of guilt may also bear witness to a burgeoning secularization, a gradual demise of the concept of blood guilt and a dissociation from the ideology of the Old Testament. This is indicated by the number of homicides that were motivated by personal profit or the desire to take a new marriage partner. The perpetrators of such deeds could not have felt that their motives were fundamentally as justified as those who were driven to killing by a culturally determined code of honour. It is in fact crimes committed for personal gain that a successful penal system is most effective in preventing.

The control policy of the early years of the modern age was characterized by an attempt to create a deterrent through harsh, public – albeit, in view of the crimes that were committed, extremely inconsistent – punishments. This old-fashioned deterrent policy that was enforced at the end of Swedish rule in Finland had little effect on the most grievous crimes because it contained within itself an irreconcilable contradiction. The harshness of the punishments required a watertight method of establishing proof. The tool for creating this kind of legal security for the accused was the legal theory of proof, which in turn almost paralysed the repression of homicidal crime. Thus the old criminal justice system and the rules of procedure for prosecuting crime together created favourable conditions for the proliferation of premeditated murder that took place in the last quarter of the eighteenth century. On the other hand, the increase in the degree of premeditation involved in homicide also had its roots in the gradual collapse of the society of the estates and the incipient break-up of traditional peasant society. That is why the creation of a more comprehensive penal system in the nineteenth century was unable to prevent the number of murders from continuing to increase.

References and Bibliography

Archive Sources

Riksarkivet i Stockholm (Swedish National Archives = RA)
- Justitierevisionens utslagshandlingar (Decisions of the Council of Justice = JRU)
- Riksregistratur i Justitieärenden: Justitierevisionens registratur (Register of Legal Cases: Register of the Council of Justice = JRR) 1748-1807
- Rådsprotokoll i justitieärenden (Records of the Council of Justice), from 1789: Högsta domstolens protokoll (Records of the Supreme Court = HDP) 1748-1807
- JKÄA: Kungliga remisser (Royal Circulars)
  Fånglistor (Lists of prisoners), E III cc, 1751-1779

Kansallisarkisto (Finnish National Archives = KA)
- Karjalan tuomiokunnan tuomiokirjat (Judgment books of the Judicial District of Karelia)
- Ilomantsin ja Suojärven osan käräjät vuosilta (District Court Sessions of Ilomantsi and part of Suojärvi) 1747-1760. KOa 17-29.
- Liperin käräjät vuosilta (District Court Sessions of Liperi) 1780-82. KOa 57-59.
- Seurakuntien väkilukutaulukot (Parish population tables), Series VÄ on microfilm

Vaasan maakunta-arkisto (Provincial Archives of Vaasa = VMA)

Vaasan hovioikeuden arkisto (Archives of Vasa Court of Appeal)
- Alistusaktit (Enquiry records) 1754-1808, Series Ece
- Turun hovioikeuden alistettujen asiain designaatioluettelot, tunnustusvankiluettelot ja päätöstaltiot, Kymenkartanon ja Savon lääni (The judgment registers of cases submitted to the Åbo Court of Appeal, Province of Kymenkartano and Savo, lists of confessional remand prisoners and judgment records). Transferred from the Archives of the Åbo Court of Appeal, on microfilm in the National Archives, 1754-1775, Series Di 1-Di 10
- Vaasan hovioikeuden alistettujen asiain designaatioluettelot /nimi- ja numerohakemistot ja alistettujen asiain päätöstaltiot, Savon ja Karjalan / Kuopion lääni (The judgment registers of cases submitted to the Vasa Court of Appeal/name and number indexes and judgment records, Province of Savo and Karelia/Province of Kuopio). Up to 1804 on microfilm in the Finnish National Archives, 1776-1813, Series Di 11-Di 55

Mikkelin maakunta-arkisto (Provincial Archives of Mikkeli = MMA)

Kymenkartanon ja Savon lääninkanslia = KymLKa (Office of the Province of Kymenkartano and Savo)
- Saapuneet kirjeet (Letters received)
- 1741/1748-1775, Series D 1/1-D 37 a1/1
- Rikoskertomukset (Crime records), 1751 (1754) -1771, Series E1-E2

Library of Statistics Finland
- The Böcker Collection, population tables

Unpublished MSS

Helsingin yliopiston kirjasto (Helsinki University Library = HYK)
Matthias Calonii commenter öfver Landslagen: Matthias Calonius, Comment öfver lagboken t.o.m landslagen (=Calonii Commentar til Landslagen). I delen: Konungabalker. Del II: Tingmålabalker, Edsöresbalker, Högmålsbalker, Dråpmålabalker. s.a. I-II. s.a. HYK käsikirjoitukset; coll 432.11-12.
Calonius 1800, 1801, 1802: Matthias Calonius, Föreläsningar i Iurisprudentia Criminalis af Professoren och Riddaren Math Calonius. Åren 1800, 1801, 1802. Första delen. HYK käsikirjoitukset, Bö III.36

Calonius, Föreläsningar i processus criminalis: Matthias Calonius, Föreläsningar i processus criminalis af Matthias Calonius. Stads Råd Professor och Riddare af Keiserliga S:t Anna och Kungl. Nordenstierna Orden. HYK käsikirjoitukset, Bö III, 25.

Published Sources

1734 års lag: Sveriges rikes lag, gillad och antagen på riksdagen åhr 1734. Stockholm 1780.

Beccaria (1763) 1995: Cesare Beccaria, On Crimes and Punishments and Other Writings. (Original work Dei delitti e delle pene published in 1763.) Cambridge 1995.

Calonius (Arwidsson) 1833-36: Matthias Calonii Svenska arbeten. III-IV. Utgiven af Adolf Iwar Arwidsson, Stockholm.

Flintberg 1796-1803: Jacob Albrecht Flintberg, Lagfarenhets-bibliothek I-V. Tryckt hos And Zetterberg, Stockholm.

Jusleen 1751-87: Johan Jusleen, Samling af Kungl Maj:ts bref, vilka på inkomna förfrågningar om lagens rätta förstånd, eller eljest i sådana mål som rättegången röra, utfärdade blivit, utgifwen av Joh. Jusleen. Med Kungl. Majt:z allernådigste privilegio, Stockholm.

Lagus 1898: Ernst Lagus (ed.), Bref från Henrik Gabriel Porthan till samtida, Helsingfors.

Modée 1756-1803: R.G. Modée, Utdrag utur alla ifrån [...] års slut utkomne Publique Handlingar, Placater, Förordningar, Resolutioner och Publicationer, Som Riksens Styrsel samt inwärters Hushållning och Författningar i gemen, jemwäl ock Stockholms stad i synnerhet angå. I-XIV. Stockholm och Uppsala.

Nehrman 1751: David Nehrman, Inledning til then Swenska processum civilem, efter Sweriges Rikes lag ok stadgar författad, samt nu å nyo ökt och förbättrad, af David Nehrman, hos Gottfried Kiesewetter, Stockholm och Uppsala.

Nehrman 1756: David Nehrman, Inledning til then Swenska Jurisprudentiam Criminalem, efter Sweriges Rikes lag och stadgar, författad af David Nehrman. Stockholm och Upsala hos Gottfried Kiesewetter. tryckt hos Directeuren Carl Gustaf Berling i Lund.

Nehrman (-Ehrenstråle) 1759: David Ehrenstråle (Nehrman), Inledning til then Swenska Processum Criminalem, efter Sweriges Rikes lag och stadgar, författad af David Ehrenstråle. Stockholm ok upsala hos Gottfried Kiesewetter. tryckt hos Directeuren Carl Gustav Berling i Lund.

Norell 1800: Carl Johan Norell, Sjette samlingen af kongl maj:ts bref, rescripter och förklaringar, hwilka, uppå inkomne förfrågningar om lagens rätta förstånd elelr eljest i andre förekomne mål, blifvit sedan martii månads slut 1792, til 1798 års utgång utfärdade. Utg af Carl Johan Norell, Stockholm.

The Holy Bible (Authorized King James version)

Rudenschöld 1899 (1738): Ulrich Rudenschölds berättelse om ekonomiska o.a. förhållanden i Finland 1738-1741. Todistuskappaleita Suomen historiaan VI, Helsinki.

Schmedemann 1706: Kongl. Stadger, Förordningar och Resolutioner Ifrån Åhr 1528 in till 1701 angående Justitiae och Executions-Ährender. Utg. af Joh. Schmedeman, Stockholm.

"Sveriges Rikes Straff-lag, Gifven i Stockholms slott dem 16 februari 1864", in

Sveriges Rikes Strafflagar jämte dithörande författningar och stadganden som utkommit till den 14 oktober 1892 jämte en rättshistorisk inledning. Utgifna af Herman Antell, Lund 1892.

af Ugglas (Ugla) 1780-1798: Samuel af Ugglas (Ugla), Samling af kongl. Maj:ts bref och förklaringar, hwilka til swar på inkomna förfrågningar om lagens rätta förstånd, utfärdade blifwit. Stockholm.

Unpublished Theses and Papers

Aalto, J 1997: Jari Aalto: Tager man qvinno med våld. Naisiin kohdistunut seksuaalinen väkivalta Turun ja Vaasan hovioikeuspiireissä 1840-64. Research paper in Finnish and Scandinavian History, Department of History, Helsinki University.

Forsström 1997: Sari Forsström, Areenan akrobaatit ja teatterin sätkynuket. Käräjät ja rikollisuus Sauvossa 1685-1694. Research paper in Finnish and Scandinavian History, Department of History, Helsinki University.

Forsström 2000: Sari Forsström, Kunnia ja käräjät. Kunnian puolustaminen oikeudellisena ja yhteisöllisenä ilmiönä yksinvaltiuden ajan Sauvossa. Licenciate dissertation in Finnish and Scandinavian History, Department of History, Helsinki University.

Hirvonen 1997: Pekka Hirvonen, Kielletty hedelmä. laki ja oikeuskäytäntö salavuoteustapauksissa 1700-luvun lopun Ilmajoella. Research paper in Finnish and Scandinavian History, Department of History, Helsinki University.

Koskelainen 1995: Liisa Koskelainen, Vankeus oikeusjärjestelmän osana. Hämeen linnan vangit 1726-1776. Research paper in Finnish and Scandinavian History, Department of History, Helsinki University.

Koskelainen 2001: Liisa Koskelainen, Varkaudet ja omaisuuden suoja. Lainsäädännön muutos omaisuusrikosten tuomiokäytännössä. Research paper in Finnish and Scandinavian History, Department of History, Helsinki University.

Koskivirta 1996: Anu Koskivirta, Omankädenoikeutta itärajalla. Kymenkartanon ja Savon läänin henkirikollisuus 1748-1774. Research paper in Finnish and Scandinavian History, Department of History, Helsinki University.

Lappalainen 1998: Mirkka Lappalainen, Botved Hansson ja valta: mahtimies, paikallinen eliitti ja kruunun kontrolli 1600-luvun alussa. Master's thesis in Finnish and Scandinavian History, Department of History, Helsinki University.

Lappalainen 2000: Mirkka Lappalainen, Paikallinen mahtisuku ja suurvallan synty. Ernst Creutz ja eliittien murros Ruotsissa n. 1580-luvulta 1630-luvulle. Licenciate dissertation in Finnish and Scandinavian History, Department of History, Helsinki University.

Liliequist 1991: "Hovrätternas brottmålsresolutioner som historiskt källmaterial". Report to XXI Congress of Nordic Historians, Umeå 15-19 June 1991.

Liliequist 1992: Jonas Liliequist, Brott, synd och straff. Tidelagsbrottet i Sverige under 1600- och 1700-talet. Unpublished doctoral dissertation, Umeå.

Nurmiainen 1998: Jouko Nurmiainen, Feodalismin käsite 1900-luvun länsimaisessa historiankirjoituksessa. Research paper in Finnish and Scandinavian History, Department of History, Helsinki University.

Nyström 1994: Mari Nyström, Rikollisuus yhteiskunnallisena ilmiönä Helsingissä vuosina 1724-1741. Master's thesis in Finnish and Scandinavian History, Department of History, Helsinki University.

Paloposki 1954: Toivo. J. Paloposki, Savonlinnan ja Kyminkartanon läänin talonpoikien valtiopäiväedustus vapaudenaikana. Master's thesis in Finnish and Scandinavian History, Department of History, Helsinki University.

Piilahti 1999: Kari-Matti Piilahti, Perhe talouden lieassa? Luonnonresurssit, elinkeinot, perhe ja sosiaalinen verkosto Valkealassa 1600-luvulta isoonvihaan. Licenciate dissertation in Finnish and Scandinavian History, Department of History, Helsinki University.

Piipponen 1988: Eija Piipponen, Käyttäytymissäännöt ja niiden noudattaminen Ilomantsissa hyödyn aikana rikosten valossa. Master's thesis in Finnish History, Department of History, Joensuu University.

Rakkolainen 1999: Mari Rakkolainen, Sallittu, kielletty ja sanktioitu. Sundin kauppasveljesten oikeudellinen toiminta yhteisöllisten vuorovaikutussuhteiden kuvastajana vapaudenajan Helsingissä. Licenciate dissertation in Finnish and Scandinavian History, Department of History, Helsinki University.

Rautelin 1993: Mona Rautelin, Och Brita Matsdotter framkom: kvinnor och män på ting i Österbottens domsaga och i rådstugan i Uleåborg fredstiden 1665-1667 och krigsåren 1678-1679. Master's thesis in Finnish and Scandinavian History, Department of History, Helsinki University.

Rautelin 2001: Mona Rautelin, Den bekönade sanningen. Licentiate dissertation / manuscript. MS.

Riissanen 1965: Viktor Riissanen, Kruununvouti Gabriel Wallenius Pohjois-Karjalan rajaolojen kehittäjänä ja taloudellisena edistysmiehenä. MASTER's thesis in Finnish and Scandinavian History, Department of History, Jyväskylä University.

Siren 1993: Kirsi Sirén, Verottaja ja papisto väestökirjanpitäjinä Savon alisen kihlakunnan ja Kymin kihlakunnan väestö vuonna 1800. Research paper in Finnish and Scandinavian History, Department of History, Helsinki University.

Österberg 1994: Eva Österberg, "Fines, Shame and Death. Punishment in Sweden from the Middle Ages to the Present". Paper for the XVIIIe Congrès International des Sciences Historiques, Montreal 1994: Punishment, Penalties and Prisons in a Historical Perspective.

Published Literature

Aalto 1990: Seppo Aalto, "Rikos ja rangaistus. Sköldvikin kartanonherra Nils Rosensmittin elämä ja kuolema 1670-luvun Suomessa". Kotiseutu 3/1990.

Aalto 1996: Seppo Aalto, Kirkko ja kruunu siveellisyyden vartijoina. Seksuaalirikollisuus, esivalta ja yhteisö Porvoon kihlakunnassa 1621-1700. SHS, Bibliotheca historica 12, Helsinki.

Aalto 1997: Seppo Aalto, "Miksi rikosrakenne muuttui?" In Koskivirta 1997.

Aalto & Johansson & Sandmo 2000: Seppo Aalto, Kenneth Johansson, Erling Sandmo: "Conflicts and Court Encounters in State of Ambivalence". In Sogner & Österberg 2000.

Ahonen 1986: Markku Ahonen: "Poliittinen väkivalta Suomessa". HArk 88.

Alanen 1963. Aulis J. Alanen, Suomen historia vapaudenajalla. Suomen historia IX. Porvoo.

Alanen 1964: Aulis J. Alanen , Suomen historia kustavilaisella ajalla. Suomen historia X. Porvoo.

Andenaes 1974: Johannes Andenaes, Punishment and Deterrence. University of Michigan Press, Binghamton, NY.

Andersson 1994: Hans Andersson, "Rättssäkerhet i stormaktstidens Stockholm". In Jarrick & Söderberg 1994.

Andersson 1998: Hans Andersson, Androm till varnagel. Det tidigmoderna Stockholms folkliga rättskultur i ett komparativt perspektiv. Acta Universitatis Stockholmiensis 28, Stockholm.

Andersson, G. 1998: Gudrun Andersson, Tingets kvinnor och män genus som norm och strategi under 1600- och 1700-tal. Uppsala University, Uppsala.

Anners 1965: Erik Anners, Humanitet och rationalism. Studier i upplysningstidens strafflagsreformer - särskilt med hänsyn till Gustav III:s reformlagstiftning. Lund.

Antell 1892: Herman Antell, "Inledning". In Sveriges rikes strafflagar.

Antell 1895: Herman Antell, Om dråpsbrotten II. Mord och dråpsbrottet I. Lund.

Anttila & Törnudd 1983: Inkeri Anttila and Patrik Törnudd, Kriminologia ja kriminaalipolitiikka. Suomalaisen lakimiesyhdistyksen julkaisuja. B-sarja N:o 194. Juva.

Archer & Gartner 1985: Dane Archer and Rosemary Gartner, Violence and Crime in a Cross-National Perspective. New Haven-London.

Almquist 1926: "Tidelagsbrottet: en rättshistorisk studie". Uppsala universitets årsskrift; 1926: Juridik; 1, Uppsala.

Aronsson 1992: Peter Aronsson, Bönder gör politik. Det lokala självstyret som social arena i tre smålandssocknar 1680-1850. Bibliotheca historica Lundensis 72, Malmö.

Aunola 1967: Toini Aunola, Pohjois-Pohjanmaan kauppiaiden ja talonpoikien väliset kauppa- ja luottosuhteet 1765 -1809. Historiallisia tutkimuksia LXII, Helsinki.

Beattie 1986: J. M. Beattie, Crime and the Courts in England 1660-1800. Oxford.

Berger 2001: Kathleen Stassen Berger, The Developing Person through the Life Span. Fifth edition. United States of America.

Bergfeldt 1997: Börje Bergfeldt, Den teokratiska statens död. Sekularisering och civilisering i 1700-talets Stockholm. Acta universitatis Stockholmiensis. Stockholm Studies in Economic History 25. Stockholm.

Bergman 1996: Martin Bergman, Dödsstraffet, kyrkan och staten i Sverige från 1700-tal till 1900-tal. Skrifter utgivna av Institutet för rättshistorisk forskning grundat av Gustav och Carin Olin. Band LIII, Lund.

Berkowitz 1962: Leonard Berkowitz, Aggression. A Social Psychological Analysis. New York.

Björn 1991: Ismo Björn, Suur-Ilomantsin historia. Enon, Ilomantsin ja Tuupovaaran historia vuoteen 1860. Pieksämäki.

Björn 1993: Ismo Björn, Ryssät ruotsien keskellä. Ilomantsin ortodoksit ja luterilaiset 1700-luvun puolivälistä 1800-luvun puoliväliin. Joensuun yliopisto, Karjalan tutkimuslaitoksen julkaisuja no 106. Joensuu.

Björne 1986: Lars Björne, Oikeusjärjestelmän kehityksestä. 2. uud. painos. Helsinki.

Björne 1995: Lars Björne, Patrioter och institutionalister. Den svenska rättsvetenskapens historia. Del 1. Tiden före 1815.

Black 1984: Donald Black (ed.) Towards a Theory of Social Control. Vol 1.

Black 1984a: Donald Black, "Crime as Social Control". In Black 1984.

Black 1984b: "Social Control as a Dependent Variable". In Black 1984c.

Black 1984c: Donald Black (ed.), Towards a Theory of Social Control. Vol 2.

Blok 1998: Anton Blok, "Bandits and Boundaries. Robber Bands and Secret Societies on the Dutch Frontier 1730-1778". In Challenging Authority. The Historical Study of Contentious Politics. Minneapolis.

Blomstedt 1960: Yrjö Blomstedt, Hallinto ja oikeuslaitos, osallistuminen valtiopäiviin. In Hämeen historia II, 2. Hämeenlinna.

Blomstedt 1973: Yrjö Blomstedt, "Kuninkaallisen Majesteetin Oikeus Suomessa". In Blomstedt 1973a.

Blomstedt 1973a: Yrjö Blomstedt (ed.), Turun hovioikeus 1623-1973 II. WSOY, Porvoo.

Blomstedt 1984: Yrjö Blomstedt, "Lantadministrationen i Finland på 1700-talet". In Administrasjon i Norden på 1700-tallet. Universitetsforlaget, Karlshamn.

Bowers & Pierce 1980: William J Bowers and Glenn L Pierce, "Deterrence or Brutalization. What Is the Effect of Executions?" Crime and Deliquency 4 / 1980.

Braithwaite 1989: John Braithwaite, Crime, Shame and Reintegration. Cambridge University Press, Cambridge.

Bäckman 1996: Johan Bäckman, Venäjän organisoitu rikollisuus. Oikeuspoliittisen tutkimuslaitoksen julkaisuja 137. Helsinki.

Cederberg 1911: A.R. Cederberg, Pohjois-Karjalan kauppaolot 1721-1775. Helsinki.

Cederberg 1947: A.R. Cederberg, Suomen historia vapaudenajalla II. Porvoo.

Christie 1983: Nils Christie, Piinan rajat. Helsingin yliopisto, Oikeussosiologian julkaisuja 4. Helsinki.

Conversi 1997: Daniele Conversi, "Boundary Approaches in the Study of Nationalism". In Landgren & Häyrynen 1997.

Cockburn 1991: J.S. Cockburn, "Patterns of Violence in English Society: Homicide in Kent 1650-1985". Past & Present 130.

Cressy 1986: David Cressy, "Kinship and Kin Interaction in Early Modern England". Past & Present 113.

Daly & Wilson 1988: Martin Daly and Margo Wilson, Homicide. Aldine de Gruyter. New York 1988.

Davies 1980: Stephen J. Davies, The Courts and the Scottish Legal System 1600-1747: The Case of Stirlingshire. In Lenman & Parker 1980.

Davis 1980: Jennifer Davis, The London Garotting Panic of 1862. A Moral Panic and the Creation of a Criminal Class in Mid-Victorian England. In Lenman & Parker 1980.

Dereborg 1990: Anders Dereborg, Från legal bevisteori till fri bevisprövning i svensk straffprocess. Stockholm.

Diestelkamp, Herman Diestelkamp, Die höchste Gerichtsbarkeit in England, Frankreich und Deutschland zwischen Absolutismus und Aufklärung". In Nygren 1990.

Dollard (1939) 1947: John Dollard, Frustration and Aggression. New Haven.

Durkheim 1985: Émile Durkheim, Itsemurha: Sosiologinen tutkimus. Tammi, Helsinki.

Durkheim 1990: Émile Durkheim, Sosiaalisesta työnjaosta. Jyväskylä.

van Dülmen 1985: Richard van Dülmen, Theater des Schreckens. Gerichtspraxis und Strafrituale in der frühen Neuzeit. München 1985.

Egmond 1996: Florike Egmond, "Between Town and Countryside: Organized Crime in the Dutch Republic". In Johnson & Monkkonen 1996.

Eisenhower 1979: Milton S Eisenhower. Introduction. In Graham & Gurr 1979.

Elias 1994: Norbert Elias, The Civilizing Process. The History of Manners and State Formation and Civilization, Blackwell Publishers, Oxford.

Emsley 1999: Clive Emsley, "The Policing of Crime in the Nineteenth Century". In Lappalainen & Hirvonen 1999.

Engman 1983: Max Engman, St. Petersburg och Finland.

Evans-Pritchard 1940: Edward Evan, The Nuer. A description of the modes of livelihood and political institutions of a Nilotic people. Clarendon Press, Oxford.

Ferrer 2001: Marlen Ferrer, "Middelaldermenneskets emosjonelle atferd. Et uttrykk. for en kompleks psykologi". HTN, bind 80, no 2/2001.

Forsström 1996: Sari Forsström (ed.), Laittomuuden laitatiellä. Rikos suomessa 1500-luvulta nykypäiviin. Helsingin yliopiston historian laitoksen julkaisuja 1 / 1996. Helsinki.

Foucault 1977: Michel Foucault, Discipline and Punish. The Birth of the Prison. London 1977.

Fougstedt - Raivio 1953: G. Fougstedt and A. Raivio, Suomen väestön sääty- ja ammatiryhmitys vuosina 1751 -1805. Tilastollisia tiedonantoja 40, Helsinki.

Furuhagen 1996: Björn Furuhagen, Berusade bönder och bråkiga båtsmän. Social kontroll vid sockenstämmor och ting under 1700-talet. Kulturhistorisk bibliotek, Stockholm.

Garfinkel 1967: Harold Garfinkel, "Inter- and Intra-Racial Homicides". In Wolfgang 1967.

Garland 1990: David Garland, Punishment and Modern Society. A Study in Social Theory. Oxford.

Garland 1991: David Garland, "The Rationalization of Punishment". In Pihlajamäki 1997.

Gaskill 2000: Malcolm Gaskill, Crime and Mentalities in Early Modern England. Cambridge Studies of Early Modern History, Cambridge.

Gastil 1971: Raymond Gastil, "Homicide and a Regional Culture of Violence". American Sociological Review 36.

Gatrell 1980: V.A.C. Gatrell, "The Decline of Theft and Violence in Victorian and Edwardian England". In Lenman & Parker 1980.

Gatrell & Lenman & Parker 1980: V.A.C. Gatrell, Bruce Lenman, Geoffrey Parker, "Introduction". In Lenman & Parker 1980.

Gaunt 1983: David Gaunt, Familjeliv i Norden. Malmö.

Gaunt 1987: David Gaunt, "Rural Household Organization and Inheritance in Northern Europe". Journal of Family History Vol 12/1987.

Giddens 1985: Anthony Giddens, The National State and Violence. Volume Two of A Contemporary Critique of Historical Materialism. Oxford.

Giddens 1993: Anthony Giddens, Sociology. Cambridge.

Gillis 1996: A.R. Gillis, "As Long as They Both Shall Live: Marital Dissolution and the Decline of Domestic Homicide in France, 1852-1909". American Journal of Sociology. Vol 101.

Graham & Gurr 1979: Hugh Graham and Ted Robert Gurr (eds.), Violence in America. S.l.

Gurr 1981: "Historical Trends in Violent Crime: A Critical Review of the Evidence". Crime and Justice: An Annual Report of Research iii.

Gurr 1992: "Trends in Violent Crime: A Critical Review of the Evidence". In Monkkonen 1992.

Monkkonen 2001: Eric Monkkonen, "New standards for historical homicide research". Crime, Histoire & Sociétés 2/2001.

Gustafsson 1994: Harald Gustafsson, Political Interaction in the Old Regime. Central Power and Local Society in the Eighteenth-century Nordic States. Studentlitteratur, Lund.

Hackney 1969: Shelton Hackney, "Southern violence". American Historical Review 76, 1969.

Hagan 1985: John Hagan, Modern Criminology. Crime, Criminal Behavior and Its Control. New York 1985.

Halila 1959: Aimo Halila, "Katsaus ylimmän tuomiovallan kehitykseen ennen korkeimman oikeuden perustamista". In Mali 1959.

Hay et al. 1975: Douglas Hay, Peter Linebaugh, John G Rule, E P Thompson & Cal Winslow, Albion's Fatal Tree. Middlesex 1975.

Hay 1975: Douglas Hay, Property, Authority and the Criminal Law. In Hay et al. 1975.

Heikkinen 1969: Antero Heikkinen, Paholaisen liittolaiset. Noita- ja magiakäsityksiä ja -oikeudenkäyntejä Suomessa 1600-luvun jälkipuoliskolla (n. 1640-1712). Historiallisia tutkimuksia. Helsinki.

Heikkinen 1986: Antero Heikkinen, "Mittaammeko poikkeusyksilöillä? Tuomiokirjat mentaliteetin tutkimuksessa". Hark 88.

Heikkinen 1988: Antero Heikkinen, Kirveskansan elämää. WSOY, Juva.

Heikkinen 1996: Antero Heikkinen, Menneisyyttä rakentamassa. Yliopistopaino, Helsinki.

Heikkinen 1996a: Antero Heikkinen, "Miten tulkita noitavainoja?" In Forsström 1996.

Heikkinen 1997: Antero Heikkinen, Kirveskansan murros. Elämää Kuhmossa koettelemusten vuosina 1830-luvulla. Yliopistopaino, Helsinki.

Heikkinen 2000: Antero Heikkinen, Kirveskansa ja kansakunta. Elämän rakennusta Kuhmossa 1800-luvun jälkipuolella. Suomalaisen Kirjallisuuden Seuran Toimituksia 794, Vammala.

Hietanen & Rantatupa 1975: Lea Hietanen and Heikki Rantatupa, Maanviljelyä ja karjanhoitoa. Maataloutta ja käsityötä in Rytkönen 1975.

Hietaniemi 1986: Tuija Hietaniemi, Väkivalta ja sen selitysmallit historiallis-kriminologisessa tutkimuksessa. HArk 88.

Hood 1996: Roger Hood, The Death Penalty: A World-wide Perspective. Clarendon Press, Oxford.

Horgby: Björn Horgby, Den disciplinerade arbetaren: brottslighet och social förändring i Norrköping 1850-1910. Almqvist & Wiksell International. Stockholm.

Häkli 1997: Jouni Häkli, "Borders in the Political Geography of Knowledge". In Landgren & Häyrynen 1997.

Häyrynen 1997: Maunu Häyrynen, "The Adjustable Periphery: Borderlands in The Finnish Landscape Imaginery". In Landgren & Häyrynen 1997.

Imsen 1998: Steinar Imsen, "Kunsten å konstruere. Noen kritiske merknader til Erling Sandmos avhandling Slagsbrödre. En studie av vold i to norske regioner i tiden fram mot eneveldet". HTN, bind 77 no 4/1998, s. 481-501.

Inger 1972: Göran Inger, Svensk straffrättshistoria I. Stockholm 1972.

Inger 1976: Göran Inger, Institutet "insättande på bekännelse" i svensk processrättshistoria. Skrifter utgivna av Institutet för rättshistorisk forskning grundat av Gustav och Carin Olin, Serien I, Rättshistorisk bibliotek. Tjugofemte bandet. Lund 1976.

Inger 1980; 1983; 1986: Göran Inger, Svensk rättshistoria. Lund.

Inger 1994: Göran Inger, Erkännandet i svensk processrättshistoria II 1614-1948. Skrifter utgivna av Institutet för rättshistorisk forskning grundat av Gustav och Carin Olin, Serien I, Rättshistorisk bibliotek. Femtionde bandet, Lund.

Jaakkola: Risto Jaakkola, "Väkivaltarikosten kulttuurihistoriaa". HArk 88.

Jansson 1998: Arne Jansson, From Swords to Sorrow. Homicide and Suicide in Early Modern Stockholm. Acta universitatis Stockholmiensis, Stockholm.

Jansson, T 1997: Torkel Jansson, "Peoples and Borders - between and within States and Societies. Minorities in Balto-Scandinavia". In Landgren & Häyrynen 1997.

Jarrick & Söderberg 1994: Arne Jarrick and Johan Söderberg (eds.), Människovärdet och makten. Om civiliseringsprocessen i Stockholm 1600-1850. Uppsala.

Jarrick & Söderberg 1994a: "Inledning", in Jarrick & Söderberg 1994.

Johansson 1997: Kenneth Johansson, "Kalmarkriget och våldsbrottsligheten". In Koskivirta 1997.

Johnson & Monkkonen 1996: Eric A Johnson and Eric H Monkkonen, Violence in Town and Country since the Middle Ages. Illinois.

Johnson 1996: Eric A Johnson, "Introduction". In Johnson & Monkkonen 1996.

Jutikkala & Kaukiainen & Åström 1980: Eino Jutikkala, Yrjö Kaukiainen and Sven-Erik Åström (eds.), Suomen taloushistoria 1. Agraarinen Suomi. Tammi, Helsinki.

Jutikkala 1932: Eino Jutikkala, Läntisen Suomen kartanolaitos.

Jutikkala 1934: Eino Jutikkala, "Väestö ja asutus 1500-luvulta 1800-luvun puoliväliin". In Suolahti & Voionmaa et al. 1934.

Jutikkala 1942: Eino Jutikkala, Suomen talonpojan historia sekä katsaus talonpoikien asemaan Euroopan muissa maissa. Porvoo.

Jutikkala 1945: Eino Jutikkala, Die Bevölkerung Finnlands in den Jahren 1721-1749. Annales Academiae Scientiarum Fennicae B LV, 4. Helsinki.

Jutikkala 1978: Eino Jutikkala, Pohjoismaisen yhteiskunnan historiallisia juuria. WSOY, Porvoo.

Jutikkala 1980: Eino Jutikkala, "Maatalous". Suurten sotien ja asutusekspansion kaudet. In Jutikkala, Kaukiainen & Åström 1980.

Jutikkala 1988: Eino Jutikkala, Kuolemalla on aina syynsä. Maailman väestöhistorian ääriviivoja. WSOY, Porvoo.

Jutikkala 1997: Eino Jutikkala, Tie perinteisestä moderniin yhteisön kuolleisuuteen Pohjois-Savossa. Snellman-instituutin B-sarja 40. Kuopio.

Jägerskiöld 1964: Stig Jägerskiöld, "Hovrätten under den karolinska tiden och till 1734 års lag". In Svea hovrätt. Studie till 350-årsminnet. Stockholm.

Jägerskiöld 1984, Stig Jägerskiöld, "Kring tillkomsten av 1734 års lag". In Sveriges rikes lag. Gillad och antagen på riksdagen år 1734. Till 250-årsdagen av lagens tillkomst. Skrifter utgivna av Institutet för rättshistorisk forskning grundat av Gustav och Carin Olin. Lund.

Kaila 1931: E.E. Kaila: Pohjanmaa ja meri 1600- ja 1700-luvuilla. Talousmaantieteellis-historiallinen tutkimus. Historiallisia tutkimuksia XIV. Helsinki.

Karjalainen 1925: A. Karjalainen, Oulun kaupungin kauppa ja meriliike vuosina 1721-1765. Historiallisia tutkimuksia IX, Helsinki.

Karonen 1995: Petri Karonen, "Brottsligheten i Norden på 1500- och 1600-talen". HT (Sverige)1995/1.

Karonen 1995a: Petri Karonen, "Talonpojat oikeutta paossa. - Rikollisuudesta Keski-Suomessa 1700-luvun lopulla". In Roiko-Jokela & Pitkänen (eds.) 1995.

Karonen 1996: Petri Karonen, "Pohjolan vaarallisimmat asuinpaikat. Rikollisuus, pelko ja turvattomuus Suomen uuden ajan alun kaupungeissa (noin 1540-1660)". In Forsström (ed.) 1996.

Karonen 1998: Petri Karonen, "A Life for Life versus Christian Reconciliation. Violence and the process of civilization in the towns of the kingdom of Sweden during the years 1540-1700". In Lappalainen 1998.

Karonen 1998a: Petri Karonen, "Rättskultur och rättsskydd i stormaktstidens Stockholm. - Arviointi teoksesta Hans Andersson "Androm till varnagel ... "" HT (Sverige) 1998:3.tsek.!

Karonen 1999: Petri Karonen, Pohjoinen suurvalta. Ruotsi ja Suomi 1521-1809. WSOY, Juva.

Karonen 1999a: Petri Karonen, "In Search of Peace and Harmony? The State and Capital Crimes in Late Medieval and Early Modern Swedish Realm (ca. 1450 - 1700)". In Lappalainen & Hirvonen 1999.

Karonen 2000: Petri Karonen, ""Kunnes kuolema meidät erottaa". Yhteisö ja suunniteltu henkirikos Turussa vuonna 1643". In Matikainen 2000b.

Kaspersson 2000: Maria Kaspersson, Dödligt våld i Stockholm på 1500-, 1700- och 1900-talen. Kriminologiska institutionen, Stockholm.

Katajala 1992: "Bondeoroligheterna i Finland, lokalsamhället och statens växande ekonomiska fordringar". In Winge 1992.

Katajala 1994: Kimmo Katajala, Nälkäkapina. Veronvuokraus ja talonpoikainen vastarinta Karjalassa 1683-1697. SHS Historiallisia tutkimuksia 185, Jyväskylä.

Katajala 1997: Kimmo Katajala (ed.), Itä-Suomi ja Pietari. Kirjoituksia toimeentulosta suurkaupungin vaikutuspiirissä. Also an article of the same name by the editior. Studia Carelica humanistica 9, Kitee.

Katajala 2001: Kimmo Katajala, Suomalainen kapina. Talonpoikaislevottomuudet ja poliittisen kulttuurin muutos Ruotsin ajalla (n. 1150-1800). SKS, Historiallisia tutkimuksia 212. Vammala.

Kaukiainen 1980: Yrjö Kaukiainen, "Miksi periferia kapinoi?" HAik 1980.

Kaukiainen 1998: Yrjö Kaukiainen, "Kauppamiesten Karjala". In Nevalainen & Sihvo 1998.

Kauppinen 1997: Pekka Kauppinen, "Väkeä Pietarin vetovoimassa - Kiteeltä Venäjälle". In Katajala 1997.

Kekkonen & Ylikangas 1982: Heikki Ylikangas and Jukka Kekkonen, Vapausrangaistuksen valtakausi: nykyisen seuraamusjärjestelmän historiallinen tausta. Oikeuden yleistieteiden laitoksen julkaisuja, Helsinki.

Keltikangas-Järvinen: Liisa Keltikangas-Järvinen, Väkivalta ja itsetuho. Miten tuhokäyttäytyminen syntyy. Otava, Keuruu.

Keltikangas-Järvinen 2000: Liisa Keltikangas-Järvinen, Tunne itsesi suomalainen. WSOY, Porvoo.

Kerkkonen 1932: Martti Kerkkonen, "Maan omistusta ja käyttöoikeutta koskevia riitaisuuksia Uudenkaupungin ja Turun rauhoissa määrätyillä rajoilla Karjalassa ja Savossa". Hark 39:6.

Kivivuori 1999: Janne Kivivuori, Suomalainen henkirikos. Teonpiirteet ja olosuhteet vuosina 1988 ja 1996. Oikeuspoliittisen tutkimuslaitoksen julkaisuja 159. Helsinki 1999.

Klami 1986: Hannu Tapani Klami, Johdatus oikeusteoriaan. Finalistisen oikeusteorian perusongelmia. Lakimiesliiton kustannus. Helsinki 1986.

Kleck 1993:Gary Kleck, "The impact of gun control and gun ownership levels on violence rates".

Journal of quantitative criminology 9, 3(1993) 249-287

Koch 1984: Klaus-Friedrich Koch, "Liability and Social Structure.. In Black 1984.

Kohlberg 1984: Lawrence Kohlberg, The Psychology of Moral Development. Vol II, The Nature and Validity of Moral Stages. Harper & Row Publishers, San Francisco.

Koskelainen 1996: Liisa Koskelainen, "Vangit, vankilat ja rikollisuus". In Forsström 1996.

Koskelainen 1997: Liisa Koskelainen, "Turun hovioikeuden tuomiokäytäntö 1700-luvulla". In Koskivirta 1997.

Koskivirta 1997: Anu Koskivirta (ed.), Tie tulkintaan. Juhlakirja akatemiaprofessori Heikki Ylikankaalle 6. marraskuuta 1997. WSOY, Juva.

Kuisma 1983: Markku Kuisma, Kauppasahojen perustaminen Suomessa 1700-luvulla (1721 -1772). Tutkimus päätöksentekoprosessista. FNF 129, Helsinki.

Kuisma 1984: Markku Kuisma, "Den riksomfattande skogspolitiken, de regionala strävandena och böndernas intressen - några aspekter på det skogspolitiska beslutsfattandet (Finland 1738-ca 1770)". In Skog och brännvin.

Kuisma 1993: Markku Kuisma, Metsäteollisuuden maa. Suomi, metsät ja kansainvälinen järjestelmä 1620-1920. Helsinki.

Kujala 2001: Antti Kujala, Miekka ei laske leikkiä. Suomi suuressa pohjan sodassa 1700-1714. SKS, Historiallisia tutkimuksia 211, Hämeenlinna.

Kujala & Malinen 2001, Antti Kujala and Ismo Malinen, "Brottslighet mot liv i Finland i början av 1700-talet". HTF 4 / 2000.

Küther 1976: Karsten Küther, Räuber und Gauner in Deutschland. Die organisierte Bandenwesen im 18. u. frühen 19. Jahrhundert. Vandenhoeck und Ruprecht, Göttingen.

Laakso 1954: Kyllikki Laakso, „Kenraalikuvernööri Gr. F. von Rosénin siviilihallinto". HArk.

Lagerspetz 1998: Kirsti Lagerspetz, Naisten aggressio. Tammi, Helsinki.

Laine 1991: Matti Laine, Johdatus kriminologiaan ja poikkeavuuden sosiologiaan. Tietosanoma, Helsinki.

Laitinen & Aromaa 1993: Ahti Laitinen and Kauko Aromaa, Näkökulmia rikollisuuteen. Hanki ja jää, Helsinki.

Landgren & Häyrynen 1997: Lars-Folke Landgren and Maunu Häyrynen (eds.): The Dividing Line. Borders and National Peripheries. Renvall Institute Publications 9. University Printing House, Helsinki.

Lane 1997: Roger Lane, Murder in America. A History. Ohio State University Press 1997.

Langbein 1976: John H. Langbein, Torture and the Law of Proof. Europe and England in the Ancien Régime. Chicago and London.

Lappalainen 1998b: Mirkka Lappalainen (ed), Five Centuries of Violence in Finland and the Baltic Area. Publications of the History of Criminality Research Project, Helsinki.

Lappalainen & Hirvonen 1999: Mirkka Lappalainen and Pekka Hirvonen (eds.): Crime and Control in Europe from the Past to the Present. Publications of the History of Criminality Research Project, Helsinki.

Lappalainen, A 2001: Antti Lappalainen: Savon metsärosvojen jäljillä. SKS, Jyväskylä 2001.

Lappi-Seppälä 1982: Tapio Lappi-Seppälä, Teilipyörästä terapiaan - piirteitä rangaistusjärjestelmän historiasta. Vankeinhoidon historiaprojektin julkaisu no 9. Helsinki.

Larsson 1982: Lars-Olof Larsson, Smålandsk historia. Stormaktstiden. Norstedt, Stockholm.

Lehti 2001: Martti Lehti, Väkivallan hyökyaalto. 1900-luvun alkuvuosikymmenten henkirikollisuus Suomessa ja Luoteis-Virossa. Oikeuspoliittisen tutkimuslaitoksen julkaisuja, 178. Helsinki 2001.

Lemert 1967: Edwin M Lemert, Human Deviance, Social Problems and Social Control. New York 1967.

Lenman & Parker 1980: Bruce Lenman, Geoffrey Parker, The State, Community and the Criminal Law in Early Modern Europe. In Lenman-Parker 1980a.

Lenman & Parker 1980a: Bruce Lenman, Geoffrey Parker, Crime and the Law. The Social History of Crime in Western Europe since 1500. London.

Letto-Vanamo 1992: Pia Letto-Vanamo (ed.), Suomen oikeushistorian pääpiirteitä. Jyväskylä.

Liliequist 1999: Jonas Liliequist, "Violence, Honour and Manliness in Early Modern Northern Sweden". In Lappalainen & Hirvonen 1999.

Lindstedt Cronberg 1997: Marie Lindstedt Cronberg, Synd och skam: ogifta mödrar på svensk landsbygd 1680-1880. Lund Lunds universitet, historiska institutionen.

Lindström 1988: Dag Lindström, "Våld, förtal och förlikningar i Stockholm". In Österberg & Lindström 1988.

Linebaugh 1975: Peter Linebaugh, The Tyburn Riot Against the Surgeons. In Hay 1975.

Linebaugh 1992: Peter Linebaugh, The London Hanged. Crime and Civil Society in the Eighteenth Century. New York.

Loftin & Hill 1974: Colin Loftin & Robert H. Hill, "Regional Subculture and Homicide: an Examination of the Gastil-Hackney thesis". American sociological review 39, 1974.

MacFarlane 1981: Alan MacFarlane, The Justice and Mare's Ale. Law and Disorder in Seventeenth-century England.

Mali 1959: Matti Mali (ed.), Korkein oikeus 1809-1959. Tietoja hallituskonseljin ja senaatin oikeusosaston sekä korkeimman oikeuden historiasta, toiminnasta ja virkakunnasta. Helsinki.

Mann 1986: Michael Mann, Sources of Social Power. Vol. 1 A history of power from the beginning to A.D. Cambridge 1986.

Manninen 1917: Ilmari Manninen, Liperin seurakunnan historia Ruotsin vallan aikana. Suomen kirkkohistoriallinen seura, Helsinki

Matikainen 1995: Olli Matikainen, Iskuin ja lyönnein. Väkivalta ja käräjät Käkisalmen läänissä 1618-1651. Jyväskylän yliopisto. Historian laitos. Suomen historian julkaisuja. Jyväskylä.

Matikainen 1996: "'Miksi näkisimme vaivaa vanhan miehen veren takia?' Näkökulmia arkipäivän väkivaltaan 1600-luvun Karjalassa." In Forsström 1996.

Matikainen 2002: Olli Matikainen, Verenperijät. Väkivalta ja yhteisön murros itäisessä Suomessa 1500-1600-luvulla. SKS, Bibliotheca historica 78. Helsinki.

Merton 1957: Robert K Merton, Social Theory and Social Structure. New York 1975.

Matikainen 2000: Olli Matikainen, Rikos historiassa. Johdanto. In Matikainen 2000b.

Matikainen 2000b: Olli Matikainen (ed.) Rikos historiassa. Jyväskylän historiallinen arkisto vol 5. Jyväskylä.

Metcalf 1990: Michael Metcalf, "Det politiska spelet kring Högsta domstolens tillkomst". In Nygren 1990.

Miller 1993: William Ian Miller, Humiliation and other essays on honor, social discomfort and violence. New York 1993.

Modéer: Kjell Å Modéer, Historiska rättskällor. En introduktion till rättshistoria. Nerenius & Santérus, Stockholm.

Monkkonen 1992: Eric K Monkkonen (ed). Crime and Justice in American History 9. Part 2. S.l.

Monkkonen 2001: Eric Monkkonen, "New standards for historical homicide research". Crime, Histoire & Sociétés 2/2001.

Morris & Blom-Cooper 1967: Terence Morris and Louis Blom-Cooper, Homicide in England. In Wolfgang 1967.

Muchembled 1989: Robert Muchembled, La violence au village: sociabilité et comportements populaires en Artois du XVe au XVIIe siècle. Turnhout, Brepols.

Myhrberg 1978: Pertti Myhrberg, Rikos- ja prosessioikeuden kehitys Suomessa. Helsinki.

Mäntylä 1983: Ilkka Mäntylä, Kuopion rytyjoulu vuonna 1760. Snellman-instituutin julkaisuja I, Kustannuskiila, Kuopio.

Mäntylä 1985: Ilkka Mäntylä, Suomalaisen juoppouden juuret. Viinanpoltto vapauden aikana. SKS, Pieksämäki.

Mäntylä 1995: Ilkka Mäntylä, Suomalaisen juoppouden kasvu. Kustavilaisen kauden alkoholipolitiikka. SHS, Historiallisia tutkimuksia 192, Jyväskylä.

Mäntylä 2000: Ilkka Mäntylä, "Brottsstatistik från slutet av 1700-talet - en bortglömd rättshistorisk källa". HTF 2 / 2000.

Næss 1981: Hans Eyvind Næss, Trolldomsprosessene i Norge på 1500-1600-tallet: en rettsog sosialhistorisk undersøkelse. Universitetsforlaget, Oslo.

Næss 1994: Hans Eyvind Næss, Vold. In Sogner & Österberg (ed) 1994.

Nenonen 1992: Marko Nenonen, Noituus, taikuus ja noitavainot Pohjois-Pohjanmaan ja Viipurin karjalan maaseudulla 1620-1700. Historiallisia tutkimuksia, Jyväskylä.

Nevalainen & Sihvo 1998: Pekka Nevalainen and Hannes Sihvo (eds.), Karjala. Historia, kansa, kulttuuri. Suomalaisen kirjallisuuden seuran toimituksia 705, Pieksämäki.

Nousiainen 1993: Kevät Nousiainen, Prosessin herruus. Länsimaisen oikeudenkäytön "modernille" ominaisten piirteiden tarkastelua ja alueellista vertailua. Suomalaisen lakimiesyhdistyksen julkaisuja A-sarja No 191.

Nygren 1990: Rolf Nygren (red.), Högsta domsmakten i Sverige under 200 år. Del 1. Föreläsningar vid ett internationellt symposium 16-18 maj med anledning av Högsta domstolens 200-årsjubileum. Lund.

Odén 1991: Birgitta Odén, "Relationer mellan generationerna". In Rättsläget 1300-1900.

Odén 1994: Birgitta Odén, "Våld mot föräldrar i det gamla svenska samhället". In Ida Hydle (red) Overgrep mot eldre 2 / 1994.

Oja 1973: Aulis Oja, "Turun hovioikeuden vuotta 1827 vanhempi arkisto". In Yrjö Blomstedt (ed.), Turun hovioikeus 1623-1773. Porvoo.

Olivecrona 1981: K. Olivecrona, Om dödsstraffet. Upsala.

Orrman 1990: Eljas Orrman, Brott och mentalitet i Sverige och Finland under meteltiden och 1500-talet. HTF 4/1990.

Pajuoja 1986: Jussi Pajuoja, Matti Haapoja eli yhren onnettoman nuorukaisen elämän-vaiheet. HArk 88.

Pajuoja 1992: Jussi Pajuoja, Varhaiset rikokset ja niiden rankaiseminen. In Letto-Vanamo 1992.

Paloposki 1954: Toivo. J. Paloposki, Suomen talouden kehittäminen 1750-1760-lukujen valtiopäiväpolitiikassa. Historiallisia tutkimuksia 98. Helsinki.

Peltonen 1992: Matti Peltonen, Matala katse. Kirjoituksia mentaliteettien historiasta. Tampere.

Phillips 1988: Adam Phillips, vai d.p. Violence Marriage. In Daly & Wilson 1988.

Phillpotts 1913: Bertha Phillpotts, Kindred and Clan in the Middle Ages and After. A Study in the Sociology of the Teutonic Races. Cambridge Archaeological and Ethnological Series. London.

Pihlajamäki 1991: Heikki Pihlajamäki (ed.), Theatres of Power. Social Control and Criminality in Historical Perspective. Publications of Matthias Calonius Society 1, Jyväskylä.

Pihlajamäki 1997: Heikki Pihlajamäki, Evidence, Crime and the Legal Profession. The Emergence of the Free Evaluation of Evidence in Finnish Nineteenth-Century Criminal Procedure. Skrifter utgivna av Instituet för rättshistorisk forskning grundat av Gustav och Carin Olin. Serie I, Rättshistorisk bibliotek. Lund 1997.

Pitkänen 1976: Kari Pitkänen, Ongelmia olemattomuudesta - väestöä ja väestönmuutok-sia kuvaavien lähteiden luotettavuudesta ja käyttökelpoisuudesta lähinnä Kiteen ja Rääkkylän seurakuntien aineiston perusteella v. 1722-1877, HYHL.

Pollock-Maitland 1898, Frederick Pollock and Frederic William Maitland, The history of English law before the time of Edward I,Vol. 1. Cambridge University Press, Cambridge

Pulma 1985: Panu Pulma, Fattigvården i frihetstidens Finland. En undersökning mellan centralmakt och lokalsamhälle. Historiallisia tutkimuksia 129. Helsinki.

Pylkkänen 1990: Anu Pylkkänen, Puoli vuodetta, lukot ja avaimet. Nainen ja maalaistalous oikeuskäytännön valossa 1660-1710. Jyväskylä.

Rakkolainen 1996: Mari Rakkolainen, "Agraariajan rikollisuus ja rikollisuuden selitys-mallit Euroopassa". In Forsström 1996.

Rautelin 1996: "Kona som av olovlig beblandelse varder havande. Regionala variationer i förekomsten av barnamord i Finland på 1790-talet". In Forsström 1996.

Rautelin 1997: Mona Rautelin, "Brott mot liv i Finland på 1790-talet". HTF 2/1997.

Reinholdsson 1998: Peter Reinholdsson, Uppror eller resningar?: samhällsorganisation och konflikt i senmedeltidens Sverige. Uppsala.

Renvall 1949: Pentti Renvall, Suomalainen 1500-luvun ihminen oikeuskatsomustensa valossa. Turun yliopiston historian laitoksen julkaisuja B:33, Turku.

Renvall 1949a: Pentti Renvall, Varsinais-Suomen historia, osa 5, 1. Varsinais-Suomen historia 1500-luvulla, Valtiolliset vaiheet ja hallinnollis-oikeudellinen kehitys. Varsinais-Suomen historiantutkimusyhdistys, Turku.

Robb 1997: Robb, "Domestic Poisonings in Victorian England". Journal of Family History. April 1997.

Roiko-Jokela & Pitkänen (eds.) 1995, Heikki Roiko-Jokela and Timo Pitkänen (eds.) , Sisä-Suomen tuomiokirjat tutkimuslähteinä ja elämän kuvaajina. Jyväskylän histori-allinen arkisto. Jyväskylän yliopiston historian laitos, Jyväskylän maakunta-arkisto, Jyväskylän historiallinen yhdistys, Jyväskylä.

Rosenfeld - Messner 1991: Richard Rosenfeld and Steven F. Messner, The Social Sources of Homicide in Different Types of Societies. Sociological Forum 1991, vol 6, number 1.

Rousseaux 1997: Xavier Rousseaux, "Crime, justice and society in medieval and modern times: 30 years of crime and criminal justice". Crime, Histoire & Societes / Crime, History & Societies vol 1, 1997.

Roth 2001: Randolph Roth, "Homicide in Early Modern England, 1549-1800: the need for a quantitative synthesis". Crime, Histoire & Sociétés 2/2001.

Rusche - Kirchheimer 1939: G Rusche and O. Kirchheimer, Punishment and Social Structure, New York 1968, alkuteos 1939.

Rytkönen 1975: Antti Rytkönen (ed.), Kuopion pitäjän kirja. Kuopion kaupunki, Kuopio.

Rättsläget 1300-1900. Maktpolitik och husfrid. Studier i internationell och svensk historia tillägnade Göran Rystad. Lund.

Sahlins 1991: Peter Sahlins, "The Nation and the Village. State Building and Communal Struggles in the Catalan Borderland during the Eighteenth and Nineteenth Centuries". Journal of Modern History 60.

Saloheimo 1976: Veijo Saloheimo, Pohjois-Karjalan historia II. Joensuun korkeakoulun julkaisuja, Joensuu.

Saloheimo 1980: Veijo Saloheimo, Pohjois-Karjalan historia III. Joensuun korkeakoulun julkaisuja, Joensuu.

Sandmo 1992: Erling Sandmo, Tingets tenkemåter. Kriminalitet og rettssaker i Rendalen, 1763-1797. Oslo.

Sandmo 1999: Erling Sandmo, "Kunsten å diskutere. Svar til Steinar Imsen". 96-110. HTN, bind 78, no 1/1999.

Sandnes 1990: Jorn Sandnes, Kniven, ølet och æren. Kriminalitet och samfunn i Norge op 1500- och 1600-tallet. Oslo.

Schmidt 1951: Eberhard Schmidt, Einführung in die Geschichte der deutschen Strafrechtspflege. Göttingen.

Seth 1984: Ivar Seth, Överheten och svärdet: dödsstraffdebatten i Sverige 1809-1974. Rättshistoriskt bibliotek. Lund.

Sharpe 1980: J.A. Sharpe, "Enforcing the Law in the Seventeenth-century English Village". In Lenman - Parker 1980.

Sharpe 1981: J. A. Sharpe, „Domestic Homicide in Early Modern England". Historical Journal 24, I.

Sharpe 1984: Crime in Early Modern England 1550-1750. Singapore.

Sharpe 1985: J.A. Sharpe, "The History of Violence in England: Some Observations". Past & Present 108.

Sharpe 1990; 1994, J.A. Sharpe, Judicial Punishment in England. Faber & Faber, London.

Sharpe 1996: J.A. Sharpe, "Crime in England: Long-Term Trends and the Problem of Modernization". In Johnson & Monkkonen 1996.

Sirén 1996: Kirsi Sirén, "Korkean rikollisuuden alueet Suomessa 1700-luvun lopulla ja 1800-luvun alussa". In Forsström 1996.

Sirén 1999: Kirsi Sirén, Suuresta suvusta pieneen perheeseen. Itäsuomalainen perhe 1700-luvulla. SHS, Bibliotheca Historica 38. Helsinki.

Skog och brännvin. Studier i näringspolitiskt beslutsfattande i Norden på 1700-talet. Universitetsforlaget, Lagerblads tryckeri, Sweden 1984.

Sogner & Österberg 1994: Sölvi Sogner & EvaÖsterberg (red.), Rapport II. Normer og social kontroll i Norden ca. 1550-1850. Domstolene i samspill med lokalsamfunnet. Oslo.

Soininen 1954: Arvo M. Soininen, Rantasalmen historia. Rantasalmen kunta ja seurakunta, Pieksämäki.

Soininen 1974: Arvo M. Soininen, Vanha maataloutemme. Maatalous ja maatalousväestö Suomessa perinnäisen maatalouden loppukaudella 1720-luvulta 1870-luvulle. Historiallisia tutkimuksia 96. Helsinki.

Soininen 1980: Arvo M. Soininen, "Maatalous". In Eino Jutikkala, Yrjö Kaukiainen and Sven-Erik Åström (eds.), Suomen taloushistoria 1. Agraarinen Suomi. Helsinki.

Sopanen 1975: Paavo Sopanen, "Maalaiskunnan alueesta, rajojen muutoksista ja asutuksesta". Elinympäristö ja pitäjän asuttaminen in Rytkönen (ed.) 1975.

Spierenburg 1984: Pieter Spierenburg, The Spectacle of Suffering. Executions and the evolution of repression: from a preindustrial metropolis to the European experience. Cambridge University Press 1984.

Spierenburg 1994: Pieter Spierenburg, "Faces of Violence: Homicide Trends and Cultural Meanings: Amsterdam 1731-1816". Journal of Social History, Summer 1994.

Spierenburg 1996: Long-Term Trends in Homicide: Theoretical Reflections and Dutch Evidence, Fifteenth to Twentieth Centuries. In Johnson & Monkkonen 1996.

Spierenburg 1999: Pieter Spierenburg, "Sailors and Violence in Amsterdam, 17th - 18th Centuries". In Lappalainen & Hirvonen 1999.

Spierenburg 2001: Pieter Spierenburg, "Violence and the civilizing process: does it work? " Crime, Histoire & Sociétés 2/2001.

Stone 1983: "Interpersonal Violence in English Society 1300-1980". Past & Present 101 (1983).

Stone 1985: Lawrence Stone, "A Rejoinder". Past & Present 108.

Sundin 1992: Sundin, Jan, För Gud, staten och folket. Brott och rättskipning i Sverige 1600-1840. Rättshistoriskt bibliotek. Fyrtiosjunde bandet. Lund.

Suolahti 1925: Gunnar Suolahti, Elämää Suomessa 1700-luvulla. Porvoo.

Suolahti & Voionmaa et al. 1934:
Gunnar Suolahti, Väinö Voionmaa, Esko Aaltonen, Pentti Renvall, Lauri Kuusanmäki,
Heikki Waris and Eino Jutikkala 1934. Suomen kulttuurihistoria II.

Sykes & Matza 1957: Gresham Sykes and David Matza, "Techniques of Neutralization. A Theory of Deliquency". American Sociological Review 22 / 1957.

Söderberg 1990: Johan Söderberg, "En fråga om civilisering. Brottmål och tvister i svenska häradsrätten 1540-1669". HT (Sverige) 1990:2.

Söderberg 1992: Johan Söderberg, "Rättsväsendets utbyggnad i Sverige. Lokala konsekvenser och reaktioner 1550-1750". In Winge 1992.

Söderberg 1993: Johan Söderberg, Civilisering, marknad och våld i Sverige. En regional analys. Acta Universitatis Stockholmiensis. Stockholm Studies in Economic History 18. Edsbruk.

Sörlin 1993: Per Sörlin, Trolldoms- och vidskepelseprocesserna i Göta hovrätt 1635-1754. Acta Universitatis Umensis 114. Umeå.

Taussi Sjöberg 1990: Marja Taussi Sjöberg, "Staten och tinget under 1600-talet". HT (Sverige) 1990:2.

Taussi Sjöberg 1991: Marja Taussi Sjöberg, "Civil and Criminal Cases in Seventeenth Century Judicial Proceedings in Sweden". In Pihlajamäki 1991.

Taussi Sjöberg 1996: Marja Taussi Sjöberg, Rätten och kvinnorna: från släktmakt till statsmakt i Sverige på 1500- och 1600-talet. Atlantis, Stockholm.

Taylor & Walton & Young 1973, Ian Taylor, Paul Walton, Jock Young, The new criminology: for a social theory of deviance. International library of sociology, Routledge & Kegan Paul, London.

Teerijoki 1993: Ilkka Teerijoki, Nälkävuosien turva? Pitäjänmakasiinit Suomessa 1700-luvulla. SHS, Historiallisia tutkimuksia 175, Tampere.

Thome 2001: Helmuth Thome, "Explaining long term trends in violent crime". Crime, Histoire & Sociétés 2/2001.

Thompson 1975: E.P: Thompson, "Whigs and Hunters. The Origins of Black Act". In Hay et al. 1975. Harmondsworth.

Thunander 1993: Rudolf Thunander, Hovrätt i funktion. Göta hovrätt och brottmålen 1635-1699. Skrifter utgivna av institutet för rättshistorisk forskning grundat av Gustav och Carin Olin. Rättshistoriskt bibliotek. Fyrtionionde bandet. Lund 1993.

Tilly 1990: Charles Tilly, Coercion, Capital and European States AD 990-1990. Cambridge, Massachusetts 1990.

Tönnies 1963: Ferdinand Tönnies, Community and Society. New York 1963.
Törnudd 1969: Patrik Törnudd, "Syytutkimus - kriminologian umpikuja". Sosiologia 3 / 1969.
Utriainen 1985: Terttu Utriainen, Rikosoikeudellisen vastuun alkujuurilla. Rikosoikeudellisen vastuun kehitysvaiheista primitiivisistä yhteisöistä 1700-luvun luonnonoikeudelliseen koulukuntaan. Lakimiesliiton kustannus Oy, Helsinki.
Vampilova 1997: Ludmila Vampilova, "The Northern Ladoga Region and Karelian Isthmus as a Route of Migration for Nations". In Landgren & Häyrynen 1997.
Verkko 1949: Lähimmäisen ja oma henki. Suomalaisen lakimiesyhdistyksen julkaisuja B: 33, Helsinki.
Verkko 1967: Veli Verkko, "Static and Dynamic 'Laws' of Sex and Homicide". In Wolfgang 1967.
Viitala 1997: Heikki Mikko Viitala, "Alkusanat". In Jutikkala 1997.
Virrankoski 1966: Pentti Virrankoski, "Etelä-Pohjanmaan puukkojunkkarikauden esiintymisen syyt". Alkoholipolitiikka 1966.
Virrankoski 1970: Pentti Virrankoski, "Tuomiokirjojen käyttö historiantutkimuksessa". Turun Historiallinen Arkisto XXIII. Turku.
Virrankoski 1975: Pentti Virrankoski, Suomen taloushistoria kaskitaloudesta atomiaikaan. Keuruu.
Voionmaa 1969 (1915): Väinö Voionmaa, Suomen karjalaisen heimon historia. Porvoo.
Vold & Snipes Bernard 1998: Thomas J. Vold, George B. Snipes, Jeffrey B.Bernard, Theoretical Criminology. Oxford University Press, New York.
Waris 1999: Elina Waris, Yksissä leivissä. Ruokolahtelainen perhelaitos ja yhteisöllinen toiminta 1750-1850. SHS. Bibliotheca historica 48. Helsinki.
Warpula 2002: Kirsi Warpula, "Honour Thy Father and Thy Mother" The formation of authority in seventeenth-century Sweden. In Manslaughter, Fornication, Sectarianism. Norm-breaking in Finland and the Baltic Area from Mediaeval to Modern Times.
Weber 1956: Max Weber, Wirtschaft und Gesellschaft, I. Tübingen.
Weisser 1979: Michael R. Weisser, Crime and Punishment in Early Modern Europe. Bristol.
Williams 1996: James Williams, (ed.), The Girard Reader. Cambridge.
Winberg 1985, Christer Winberg, Grenverket. Studier rörande jord, släktskapssystem och ståndsprivilegier. Skrifter utgivna av Instituet för rättshistorisk forskning grundat av Gustav och Carin Olin. Serie I, Rättshistorisk bibliotek. Trettioåttonde delen, Lund.
Winge 1992: Harald Winge, Lokalsamfunn och ovrighet i Norden ca 1550 - 1750. Universitetsforlaget, Oslo.
Winslow 1975: Cal Winslow, "Sussex Smugglers". In Hay 1975.
Wirilander 1946: Kaarlo Wirilander, "Itä-Suomen avioalueet 1700-luvulla". Suomen sukututkimusseuran vuosikirja XXX.
Wirilander 1964: Kaarlo Wirilander, ´Savon väestöoloja 1721-1870". Hark 59.
Wirilander 1989 (1960): Kaarlo Wirilander, Savo kaskisavujen aikakautena 1721-1809. Savon säätiö, Kuopio.
Wolfgang 1967: Marvin Wolfgang (ed.), Studies in Homicide. Harper & Row Publishers, New York, Evanston and London.
Wolfgang 1967b: Marvin Wolfgang, "Criminal Homicide and the Subculture of Violence". In Wolfgang 1967.
Wolfgang & Ferracuti 1967: Marvin Wolfgang, Franco Ferracuti," Subculture of Violence - A Socio-Psychological Theory". In Wolfgang 1967.
Ylikangas 1967: Heikki Ylikangas, Suomalaisen Sven Leijonmarckin osuus vuoden 1734 lain naimiskaaren laadinnassa: kaaren tärkeimpien säännöstöjen muokkautuminen, 1689-1694. SHS, Helsinki.
Ylikangas 1971: Heikki Ylikangas, "Väkivaltarikosten motivaatiopohja 1500-luvulla Suomessa". Hark 65.
Ylikangas 1973: Heikki Ylikangas Väkivallanaallon synty. Puukkojunkkarikauden alku Etelä-Pohjanmaalla. Helsingin yliopiston historian laitoksen julkaisuja 3/1973. Helsinki.

Ylikangas 1976a: Heikki Ylikangas, "Major Fluctuations in Crimes of Violence in Finland. A Historical Analysis". Scandinavian Journal of History 1976.

Ylikangas 1976b: Heikki Ylikangas, Henkirikos keskiajan lopun ja uuden ajan alun Suomessa. Oikeustiede VIII/1976.

Ylikangas 1982: Olaus Petrin tuomarinohjeet. Olaus Petrin tuomarinohjeet. Markkinointi-instituutti, Helsinki.

Ylikangas 1983: Miksi oikeus muuttuu. Laki ja oikeus historiallisen kehityksen osana. WSOY, Porvoo.

Ylikangas 1984: Heikki Ylikangas, Murtuva säätyvalta. WSOY, Porvoo.

Ylikangas 1985: Heikki Ylikangas, Knivjunkarna. Våldskriminaliteten i Österbotten, Borgå.

Ylikangas 1988: Heikki Ylikangas, Valta ja väkivalta keski- ja uudenajan taitteen Suomessa. WSOY, Juva.

Ylikangas 1990: Heikki Ylikangas, Mennyt meissä. Suomalaisen kansanvallan historiallinen analyysi. Porvoo.

Ylikangas 1991: Heikki Ylikangas, "Kommentar till Eva Österberg". HTN 1/1991.

Ylikangas 1993: Heikki Ylikangas, Käännekohdat Suomen historiassa. Pohdiskeluja kehityslinjoista ja niiden muutoksista uudella ajalla. Juva.

Ylikangas 1994: Heikki Ylikangas, "Ätten och våldet. Våldsbrottsligheten i Norden vid övergången till nya tiden". HTF1/1994.

Ylikangas 1996: Heikki Ylikangas, Nuijasota. Kolmas ajanmukaistettu painos. Otava, Keuruu 1996. (Neljäs painos 1997)

Ylikangas 1998: "What happened to violence? An analysis of the development of violence from mediaeval times to the early modern era based on Finnish source material". In Lappalainen 1998b (Julkaistu myös Ohio State University Pressin sarjassa vuonna 2000).

Ylikangas 1998a: The Knife Fighters. Violent Crime in Southern Ostrobothnia 1790-1825. The Finnish Academy of Science and Letters, Humaniora 293. Helsinki.

Ylikangas 1999: Väkivallasta sanan valtaan. Suomalaista menneisyyttä keskiajalta nykypäiviin. WSOY, Juva.

Ylikangas 2000: Heikki Ylikangas, Aikansa rikos historiallisen kehityksen valaisijana. WSOY, Juva.

Zehr 1976: Howard Zehr, Crime and the Development of Modern Society. Croom Helm, London.

Zemon Davis 1987: Natalie Zemon Davis, Fiction in the Archives: Pardon Tales and Their Tellers in Sixteenth-century France. Stanford University Press, Stanford, CA:

Ågren 1988: Maria Ågren, "Att lösa ekonomiska tvister - domstolarnas främsta sysselsättning på 1700-talet?" HT (Sverige) 4 / 1988.

Ågren, H 1998: Henrik Ågren, Tidigmodern tid. Den sociala tidens roll i fyra lokalsamhällen 1650- 1730. Studia historica Upsaliensia 185. Stockholm.

Åström 1980: Sven-Erik Åström, "Itä-Suomen uusi vientitavara. Artikkeli Raimo Rannan artikkelissa Ulkomaan- ja kotimaankauppa". In Jutikkala & Kaukiainen & Åström 1980.

Österberg & Lindström 1988: Eva Österberg and Dag Lindström, Crime and Social Control in Medieval and Early Modern Swedish Towns. Acta Universitatis Upsaliensis, Uppsala.

Österberg & Sogner 2000. Eva Österberg and Sölvi Sogner (eds.), People Meet the Law - control and conflict-handling in the courts. The Nordic countries in the post-reformation and pre-industrial period. Universitetsforlaget, Oslo.

Österberg 1982: Eva Österberg, "'Den gamla goda tiden'. Bilder och motbilder i ett modernt forskningsläge om det äldre agrarsamhället" Scandia 1 / 1982.

Österberg 1983: Eva Österberg, "Våld och våldsmentalitet bland bönder: jämförande perspektiv på 1500- och 1600-talens Sverige". Scandia 1983 (49).

Österberg 1987: Eva Österberg, "Svenska lokalsamhällen i förändring ca 1550-1850: participation, representation och politisk kultur i den svenska självstyrelsen: ett angeläget forskningsområde"HT(Sverige) 1987:3.

Österberg 1989: Eva Österberg, "Bönder och centralmakt i det tidigmoderna Sverige: konflikt - kompromiss - politisk kultur". Scandia 1989(55).

Österberg 1991a: Eva Österberg, "Violence among Peasants. Comparative Perspectives on Sixteenth- and Seventeenth-century Sweden".In Österberg, Eva, Mentalities and Other Realities. Essays in Medieval and Early Modern Scandinavian History. Lund.

Österberg 1991b: Eva Österberg, "Social Arena or Theatre of Power? The Courts, Crime and the Early Modern State in Sweden". In Pihlajamäki (ed.) 1991.

Österberg 1991c: Eva Österberg, "Kontroll och kriminalitet i Sverige från medeltid till nutid. Tendenser och tolkningar". Scandia 1:1991.

Österberg 1991d, Eva Österberg, "Brott och kontroll i Sverige från medeltid till stormaktstid. Goctycke och grymhet - eller sunt förnuft och statskontroll?" HT 2 / 1991.

Österberg 1993: Eva Österberg, "Brott och rättspraxis i det förindustriella samhället. Tendenser och tolkningar i skandinavisk forskning". HT (Sverige) 1993:2.

Österberg 1994: Eva Österberg, "Normbrott och rättspraxis i Norden under förindustriell tid. Problem och positioner". In Sogner & Österberg 1994.

Österberg 1996: Eva Österberg, "Criminality, Social Control and the Early Modern State: Evidence and Interpretations in Scandinavian Historiography". In Johnson & Monkkonen 1996.

Abbreviations

FNF Bidrag till kännedom av Finland natur och folk
HAik Historiallinen aikakauskirja (Finnish Historical Review)
HArk Historiallinen arkisto (Historical Archives)
HDP Högsta domstolens protokoll (Records of the Supreme Court)
HT (Sverige) Historisk tidskrift, Sverige
HTF Historisk tidskrift för Finland
HTN Historisk tidsskrift, Norge
HYHL Helsingin yliopisto, historian laitos (Department of History, Helsinki University)
JKÄA Justitiekanslernsämbetets arkiv (Archive of the Office of the Counsellor of Justice)
JRR Justitierevisionens registratur (Registry of the Council of Justice)
JRU Justitierevisionens utslagshandlingar (Judgment records of the Council of Justice)
KA Kansallisarkisto (Finnish National Archives)
KM Kuninkaallinen majesteetti (His Royal Majesty)
KymLKa Kymenkartanon ja Savon läänin lääninkanslia (Office of the Province of Kymenkartano and Savo)
KrLL Kristofers landslag (King Christopher's Law of the Land)
MMA Mikkelin maakunta-arkisto (Mikkeli Provincial Archives)
MB 1734 års lag, Missgärnings balken (Criminal Code, Law of 1734)
RA Riksarkivet i Stockholm (Swedish National Archives)
RB 1734 års lag, Rättegångs balken (Procedural Code, Law of 1734)
SHS Suomen historiallinen seura (Finnish Historical Society)
SKS Suomalaisen kirjallisuuden seura (Finnish Literary Society)
Str.B 1734 års lag, Straff balken (Penal Code, Law of 1734)
VHO Vaasan hovioikeus (Vasa Court of Appeal)
VHOA Vaasan hovioikeuden arkisto (Vasa Court of Appeal Archives)
VMA Vaasan maakunta-arkisto (Vasa Provincial Archives)
ff. and the following pages
ffol. and the following folios
s.a. year of publication unknown
s.l. place of publication unknown
tk talvikäräjät (Winter court sessions)
sk syyskäräjät (Autumn court sessions)

Index

www.ingramcontent.com/pod-product-compliance
Lightning Source LLC
Chambersburg PA
CBHW081738270326
41932CB00020B/3324